TOWARDS A NE
FRAMEWORK FOR A LEGAL PROFESSION IN TRANSITION?

TOWARDS A NEW ETHICAL FRAMEWORK FOR A LEGAL PROFESSION IN TRANSITION?

Proceedings of the European conference on ethics and the legal profession, held at the Ghent University (Belgium) on 25 and 26 October 2001

Koen Raes and Bart Claessens

editors

Intersentia
Antwerp - Oxford - New York

Distribution for the UK:
Hart Publishing
Salter's Boat Yard
Folly Bridge
Abingdon Road
Oxford OX1 4LB
UK
Tel: + 44 1865 24 55 33
Fax: + 44 1865 79 48 82

Distribution for North America:
Transnational Publishers
410 Saw Mill River Road
Ardsley
New York 10502-2615
USA
Tel: + 1 914 693 5100
Fax: + 1 914 693 4430

Distribution for Switzerland and Germany:
Schulthess Verlag
Zwingliplatz 2
CH-8022 Zürich
Switzerland
Tel: + 41 1 251 93 36
Fax: + 41 1 261 63 94

Distribution for other countries:
Intersentia Publishers
Churchilllaan 108
2900 Schoten
Belgium
Tel: + 32 3 680 15 50
Fax: + 32 3 658 71 21

Towards a new ethical framework for a legal profession in transition?
Koen Raes and Bart Claessens

Antwerp - Oxford - New York
http://www.intersentia.com

ISBN 90-5095-231-3
D/2002/7849/22
NUR 820

CONTENTS

ACKNOWLEDGMENTS

The organisation of the conference entitled "Towards a new ethical framework for a legal profession in transition" at the Ghent University on 25 and 26 October 2001 and the publication of these conference proceedings would not have been possible without the financial support of the Flemish Minister of Education and Formation. This support was part of a specific action to promote research in Flanders.

Special thanks must also go to the Council of the Bars and Law Societies of the European Union (CCBE), the Union Internationale des Avocats (UIA), Ghent University and the City of Ghent for facilitating the organisation of this conference.

The organizers would also like to thank the chairpersons of the consecutive sessions during this conference:

- Prof. em. dr. Jean Van Houtte, Former Rector of UFSIA and Emeritus Professor of Law and Sociology,
- Mrs. Valérie Bauer, Secretary-general of the CCBE,
- Mr. Jacques Leroy, First Vice-President of UIA,
- Prof. dr. Koen Raes, Professor of Applied Ethics, Ghent University.

PREFACE

Kim Economides, Professor of Legal Ethics and Head of School of Law, University of Exeter

It is a great pleasure and honour to have been asked to introduce these proceedings which record many of the discussions and papers presented at a European conference, held in the historic city of Ghent last October, investigating the theme *Towards a New Ethical Framework for a Legal Profession in Transition?* The organisers, as well as their sponsors, are to be congratulated for their vision and imagination in tackling a difficult but fascinating question for the future of our European legal professions and for bringing together academic lawyers and practitioners who typically inhabit quite different and distinctive worlds. A real synergy emerges from this collection and it is encouraging to witness the historic gulf separating legal practitioners and academics being bridged and with such positive results. This volume not only records new ideas to inform and guide future developments in the field of professional regulation but evidences a new relationship transcending disciplinary, jurisdictional and professional boundaries out of which a whole new understanding of professional ethics can be built. It is very fitting that Ghent was the location for this historic conference and that it was here that so many barriers - linguistic, cultural and professional - fell down.

The central conference theme investigated the speed and nature of the many changes and challenges now confronting the legal professions in Europe. The participants focused, however, not just on describing the minutiae of ephemeral change at the national level (which so often characterises contemporary legal journalism) but rather they sought to understand latent forces which shape and circumscribe professional regulation, and behind that, ideology. National regulators invariably seem preoccupied with the rules or technology necessary to police effectively the conduct of individual lawyers and thereby overlook "entity regulation" at the intermediate level of the firm or, more significantly, those essential macro-perspectives of a more educational or inspirational, rather than regulatory, nature in which one may glimpse those fundamental values touching upon the responsibilities of lawyers wherever they may choose to practice law. In short, the conference participants rose above subjective and disciplinary parochialism and successfully collaborated to identify a set of emergent frameworks - ideological, educational as well as regulatory and economic - within which the future identity of European lawyers will be constructed.

I believe that each of the many different groups represented at the Ghent conference - which included national, European and international professional bar associations, law firms of different size, style and orientation, individual lawyers working in both the public and private sectors, as well as academic lawyers from both the common and civil law worlds - should now have a much clearer understanding of their respective - and collective - roles in constructing and transmitting a system of values to inform and enrich the future practice of law in Europe and beyond.

I commend this book warmly and without reservation to anyone interested in understanding the future agendas for European lawyers and the new ethics that undoubtedly will determine the nature and scope of the services we can expect to see offered their clients.

INTRODUCTION

Koen Raes, Professor of Applied Ethics, Ghent University and Bart Claessens, Research Assistant of the Fund for Scientific Research – Flanders

During the seventies, the legal profession was in most European countries confronted with, on the one hand, a spectacular growth in the quantity of legal claims brought before the courts and, on the other with a variety of new legal actors such as neighbourhood law centres, law shops or offices for legal aid. The challenge to the legal profession was local and took the form of various initiatives to democratise the access to justice or to develop alternatives to "formal" legal dispute resolution such as mediation. From the observation that only a small part of the population found its "way to the law" and inspired by an egalitarian ethics of "equality of opportunity", most countries took initiatives to fill "the gap in legal aid provisions". The last quarter of the 20th century initiated both a boom in lawsuits brought before the courts and a boom in law students and in legal professionals.

In these years, the relation between "law" and "society" was mainly perceived in terms of a "democratic deficit" that came from within the local domestic society and that could be solved by the establishment of institutions which would enhance the interactions between citizens and the courts. Law was meant to be used by the activist - or "responsive" - welfare state in its pursuit of social justice. Legal markets expanded and fragmented as new legal actors appeared, competition for legal work augmented and the legal profession's monopoly diluted.

At the beginning of the 21st century, the legal professions are confronted with radically different challenges arising from the globalization of the world economy, the process of financial, economic, social, political and cultural interconnection that is accelerated by the cheapening of transport costs and the incorporation of a variety of new information and communication technologies in institutions, from companies to law firms, and families.

Globalization has produced a proliferation of new international legal norms, regimes and processes whilst human rights, the environment, business transactions and all the new information and communication technologies know no national borders. It has forced states to amend existing domestic laws to conform to international treaties, to submit new regulatory initiatives to the arbitration of trade tribunals and to acquiesce in the creation by large transnational corporations of private legal regimes which are often immune from state regulation. This new economy has reshaped the legal profession's work, organisation, self-image and ethos which gradually modified its institutional structures and notions of professionalism.

The emergence of international law firms in the service of global enterprises and the incursion of international legal regimes into formerly more or less self-contained domestic jurisdictions is one of the most visible consequences of these developments. And exactly these international law firms, some of which take the form of multidisciplinary teams, have inspired the conference organisers to focus during a two-day conference held at the Ghent University, 25 and 26 October 2001, on the need for "a new ethical framework for a legal profession in transition". This book contains (most of) the proceedings of this conference.

If the legal market is more and more dominated by large international law firms, is fair access to justice not threatened - once again - because of the obvious inequality between "one shooters" and "repeat players" in the courtroom or between "local" and "global" actors? And what about the relation between a domestic judge or court and such large scale firms?

As this is also the case with the medical profession, a collectivisation and specialisation is taking place of practices at the bar. The independent, individual solicitor or barrister is replaced by a team, often with a legal identity of its own which is different from its constituent members and sometimes managed by a person who is not even a barrister at all. No doubt, such collectivisation and specialisation serves the goals of efficiency. But on the other hand, the division of responsibilities may become vague.

Globalization has not only transformed law and the legal profession. It has - or will have - a significant impact on existing systems of legal education too. Europe became, by means of the famous Bologna- and Sorbonne-declarations interested in the higher education systems in order to advance social and economic policies. As other faculties, the law faculties will be held to more exacting performance standards and quality labels and will be forced into greater inter- and intra-faculty competition for scarce resources and students. As the manager becomes a central figure in a law firm or a chamber of barristers, so the dean of a law faculty is expected to manage his faculty in terms of efficiency norms. Law faculties which are highly rated on indices of research and teaching productivity will get more means than those that are not. Pressures also mount from within the universities themselves for greater devotion by the law faculties to the project of scholarship. Does it, in a globalizing world, make sense to focus the legal curriculum mainly on domestic law or should the curriculum itself not be the expression of a globalizing legal community? However, law faculties are also being pulled in the opposite direction, away from scholarship and toward specific kinds of very practical training programs with a fast output in terms of application. Here, they are responding to the needs of the legal profession, favouring thus a less "academic" or scholarly emphasis and a greater "professional" focus on directly useful legal information and legal skills.

Such processes, however are not "natural" ones. The market may put pressures on law faculties in order to become mere "training schools" as it may inspire international law firms to a greater division of tasks and specialisation. But that does not mean that there is no more room for human decision-making and, more precisely, for human decisions based on ethical values.

However, what is clear is that the old ethical frameworks, meant to guide the individual and independent legal professional are not adapted to the new large-scale law firms and their institutional responsibilities within a new division of tasks. Rules and professional values concerning confidentiality, trust and independency will have rather different meanings and implications when applied to institutions. There is a need for new ethical rules of good practice and of frameworks of thought for the new environment wherein the legal profession is functioning. It thus is not surprisingly that the ethics of the legal profession or legal ethics has been one of the most widely debated issues over the last years. This volume is no exception to this.

In his contribution, Hugo Lamon argues that as other liberal professions, lawyers constitute undertakings for the purpose of the competition law. They are thus bound by the same rules concerning (the prohibition of) collective price fixing as other undertakings on the market. Restrictions to competition, due to professional codes are justified in light of their aims to act with dignity, honesty, competence, independence, discretion and loyalty, as far as they are not disproportionate to these aims, taking into account the economic and legal context. Piet A. Wackie Eysten and John M. Bosnak argue that alternative dispute resolution can be an attractive alternative to a legal proceeding in court when international commercial relations and different legal systems and cultures are at stake; here the informality of ADR may be one of its advantages. According to Willy Van Eeckhoutte, law firms have to accept the consequences of the way in which they are organized in terms of their employment relations. Although Belgium and Italy do not yet recognize the salaried lawyer, there is for Jean-François Gerard, no doubt that the salaried lawyer will become a reality in all the European countries. Dirk Van Gerven, for his part, develops the (Belgian) legal framework in which the law firm as a fully integrated exercise of the legal profession will be able to meet the high quality standards that are imposed by clients. John Pickup argues in favour of the introduction of management standards in legal practice and gives a presentation of Lexcel, the Law Society of England and Wales Practice Management Certification Scheme which awards quality marks to practices and legal departments that have been independently assessed as having achieved the Law Society's Practice Management Standards. In his contribution, Mark Ford looks at the effects of "e-lawyering" and argues that there is a need for guidance and rules of good practice on the use of these new technologies by the bar associations.

The next three contributions all discuss different aspects of multidisciplinary practices or partnerships (MDPs) wherein lawyers and non-lawyers (most notably the accountancy profession) cooperate. John G. Fish argues that there are important ethical issues arising from such MDPs, particularly concerning personal liability in the decision-making process, the very fundamental role which lawyers play in the course of the administration of justice and the values of confidentiality, fidelity and independence. Although these ethical issues are not insurmountable, it is of fundamental importance that a strict division between services provided by lawyers and those provided by non-lawyers remains intact. Jo Stevens, for his part, develops the reasons of the Belgian bar association's decision of 1990 to prohibit multidisciplinary partnerships in Belgium. Marc Vandemeulebroeke, on the contrary, argues in favour of such MDPs as they will improve the quality of services which are available to clients, will increase competition in the professional services sector and will increase consumer choice.

Avrom Sherr looks at recent research work in Scotland, England and Wales about clients' views of their lawyers and about what we know of how clients view advice agency services providing similar services whilst Daan De Snoo presents information about the pilot project in the Netherlands with respect to the handling of complaints and disputes regarding legal services.

In his contribution, Peter Kunzlik analyses extensively the social and ideological processes which were responsible for the Bar in England and Wales surrendering to modernisation. Many of the principles that have hitherto provided the ideological foundation of the "cathedral" of the Bar have crumbled and if the structure is to be re-built and to have a future beyond the present generation, it will need to be based upon a more solid foundation than that provided by the "sole practitioners" principle which is, according to this author, amongst the last, outmoded vestiges of a disintegrated professionalism.

Koen Geens analyses the implications of scaling-up, specialisation, interdisciplinarity and increasing competitiveness for the legal profession together with the internationalisation of its service provision. The legal profession will have to contend with these new challenges if it wants to safeguard its own future and that of the principles onto which the free choice of profession is grafted. A professional is an entrepreneur, so he concludes, but he is an entrepreneur able to say "No" to a client who asks him to do the impossible, the unreasonable or the unethical, as well as to the government authority that wants to force him to choose the easiest or the cheapest route: that should always remain the case.

Carl Bevernage focuses on the practice of law in the framework of a regulated profession in Europe and in the USA, where the globalization of commerce and industry has prompted the creation of cross boundary forms of co-operation and mergers between law firms, leading to self-styled global players. But notwithstanding the enormous diversity and differences in economic and financial underpinning of the practice of law, all lawyers concerned spontaneously refer to themselves as members of a liberal regulated profession, bound by particular deontological rules, which may differ from one legal culture to another. Exactly the absence of regulations governing the cross-border legal practice should give rise to cross-border rules of good practice that can guarantee that ethics remains the cornerstone of the legal profession.

John Flood looks at the impact of elite law firms on the globalization of legal practices. Local law is more and more in the process of becoming subsumed under highly competitive systems of law that market themselves aggressively. As a result, local law declines in importance whilst the Anglo-American axis is too powerful to defeat in the capital markets field, as it dominates most transnational institutions. Local bar associations are simply powerless, but what we are beginning to see is the emergence of a transnational bar association, which has a direct interest in pursuing these matters, either as a matter of ethical concern or because the elites who populate these bar associations wish to consummate their paramount position.

In a final contribution to this volume, Julian Webb identifies some of the issues regarding teaching legal ethics in the context of the fundamental changes, the legal profession is confronted with. We have, so he argues, still to do much more work to develop a conceptually or philosophically grounded understanding of the values of the legal profession and of individual lawyers, who are often "managing uncertainty". Thinking about one's own values and the values of the legal system goes to the hearth of any meaningful notion of professionalism.

Before we can develop a new ethical framework for a legal profession in transition, it is of the utmost importance to have a clear view what these processes of transition exactly imply. The editors hope that this book will contribute to a clearer understanding of what is going on in a legal profession that is now working on a world scale. Perhaps this could inspire readers to develop professional rules which are adapted to such a scale, which has been for quite a long time the ethical perspective by excellence of moral thinking.

LAWYERS, BAR ASSOCIATIONS AND COMPETITION LAW: LIMITS OF REGULATIONS

Hugo Lamon, Member of the Board of Directors of the Vereniging van Vlaamse Balies[1] and Director of the Department Study and Advice

1. It has recently ceased to be seriously disputed that lawyers[2] constitute undertakings for the purpose of competition law. Although the competition laws were already incorporated in the Treaty of Rome of 1957, it took until the early 90's before the European Commission identified liberal professionals as enterprises. This development led to important changes in the practice of professions and the consequence was that many deontological rules have come under review again.

Anyway, this provides us with a good opportunity to reflect in detail on the essential characteristics of the profession of the lawyer and on the most efficient way to safeguard these fundamental principles. Many bar associations are obliged to redefine the identity of the lawyer at the dawn of the 21st century.

1 THE APPLICABILITY OF COMPETITION LAW

2. The European Community is based on an open market economy with free competition, to ensure the promotion of the effective allocation of resources (article 98 and article 105(1) of the EC Treaty).

A system of this type of unadulterated competition can only be guaranteed if equal opportunity is given to all the various participants in the market.[3]

The concept of "workable competition" is central, which is competition that is required to offer new entrants to the market the opportunity to become as active as any other participant in the market in question. By intervening in the structure of the economy, it is desired to make markets flexible in order to release the drive to exert initiative and innovative abilities.

3. The EC Treaty contains several types of rules concerning competition. The first series of rules is oriented toward undertakings (article 81 and 82) and can be divided into three categories:

---

1 Association of Flemish Bars (after the recent legal change to become the Order of the Flemish Bars). The views expressed in this paper are personal to the author.

2 The term "laywer" is the professional who is entitled to pursue his activities in accordance with Directive 77/249/EEC (lawyer, avocat, advocaat, advokat, aboado, avvocato, advogado, Rechtanwalt, lögmanns, henkilöslisyystrodistus).

3 Court of Justice, 13 December 1991, RTT/GB INNO, C-18/88, *Jur.* 1991, I-5941.

- The prohibition of agreements and concerted practices that restrict competition[4] (article 81). These rules prescribe the limits within which undertakings may collaborate.
- The prohibition on abuse of a dominant position (article 82). This lays down the rules that undertakings with a strong economic position must abide by.
- The Regulation 4064/89 of 21 December 1989, on the control of concentrations between undertakings added a new dimension to the competition rules.[5] Concentrations of undertaking shall be subject to prior notification and control.

As regards the applicability of article 82 EC, it may be stated that if a bar authority introduces an economic limitation under the standard of a deontological obligation, this will amount to a collective abuse of a dominant position in the market for legal services. Such decisions should then also be included in the scope of application of article 81(1) EC, so that we may safely leave this hypothetical situation out of our discussion.

4. For the legal profession, article 81 of the EC Treaty is of principal importance. This provision contains a directly operative prohibition that shall be enforced not only by the European Commission (empowered at European level to enforce competition laws), but also by the national courts. The EC Treaty requires the European Commission and the duly authorised national authorities to supervise conformance to the competition laws.

The "agreement" may take several forms:

- agreements between undertakings;
- decisions by associations of undertakings;
- concerted practices

1.1 Agreements between undertakings

5. The concept of undertaking under the European competition law is far wider in scope than the concept of dealer or goods supplier. The following can be viewed as undertakings: dealers, partnerships, companies, foun-

4 Art. 81 says: "may effect trade between the Member States and which have as their object or effect the prevention, restriction or distortion of competition within the common market". This ban applies to both the horizontal agreements (at the same stage of production, processing of marketing) and to vertical agreements (the firms concerned operating at different stages of the economic and commercial process and not being in competition with one another).

5 The regulation stipulates that "a concentration with a Community dimension which creates or strengthens a position as result of which effective competition in the common market or in a substantial part of it is significantly impeded is to be declared incompatible with the common market."

dations and associations, the majority shareholders of a company, the holder of a patent, independent professionals, artists who pursue the practice of their art for economic gain, etc...[6] What is decisive for the interpretation of the concept of an undertaking is not the legal constitution but the question of whether an economic activity is being carried on within the meaning of every activity, including activity not directed at achieving a profit, whereby contact is made with the traffic of economic transactions.[7] The cartel authorities shall, of course, ultimately be guided by the actual economic reality, with the result that there are no forms of organisation that are, by definition, excluded from the scope of the competition laws. In order to be able to speak of an agreement within the meaning of article 81(1), it shall be sufficient that the parties express the wish to each other to conduct themselves in a particular way in the market. Whether and how this relationship is actually formalized is of little relevance. The competitive system is more interested in the economic consequences of agreements rather than the legal form that these might take.

It is by no means necessary that the agreement or understanding between the entrepreneurs is legally binding, since this is already the case as soon as the parties agree to something that limits or can limit commercial freedom or by which they determine the specific line of action or a simultaneous abstinence from action on the market. A contractual sanction is also not required and there is also no need for the agreement to be set down in writing.[8]

1.2 Decisions by associations of undertakings

6. An association of undertakings is an association, in most cases, a legal entity, to protect the economic interests of the members attached to it. The fact that the association in question is a trade association to which government has assigned certain tasks and responsibilities that place it in a position to regulate a profession, and that its legal form is that of a public-law corporation under the laws of that country, shall not keep it from it being regarded as an association of undertakings.

In a decision of 18 June 1998, the Court of Justice did not determine that the fact that the National Council of Customs Agents was constituted as a public-law entity as per the law of Italy was relevant. The Court also determined

---

6 R. VAN DEN BERGH, E. DIRIX and H. VANHEES, *Handels-en economisch recht in hoofdlijnen*, Antwerp, Intersentia, 1997, p. 209 (see also Commission decision of 26 May 1978 relating to a proceeding under article 85 of the EC Treaty, *O.J. L.*, 15 June 1978, 127/39.)

7 Court of Justice, 20 March 1985, Italy/Commission, 41/83, *Jur.* 1985, 873. See also Court of Justice, 16 November 1995, FFSA, C-244/95, *Jur.* I-4013, par. 14 en 21.

8 Commission Decision of 7 December 1988, Vlakglas, *O.J. L.*, 33/34, par. 623. See also Court of Justice, 20 June 1978, Tepea, 28/77, *Jur.* 1978, 1391.

that the judicial framework within which such agreements (meaning decisions between association of undertakings) were entered into and or within which such decisions were taken, and the legal nomenclature that is used to describe this framework under the various national legal systems, did not have any effect whatsoever on the applicability of EC competition law and especially of article 81 of the Treaty.[9]

A protection of interest of this type can take several forms, such as, for example, the collection and dissemination amongst the members of such an association of all the information about matters of common interest, the formulation of the most suitable mode of conduct and sending recommendations concerning the same to the members, the representation and protection of the interests of the concerned industry in all matters before all the authorities in which common action was deemed desirable.

Article 81(1) speaks of decisions by such associations of undertakings. Even here, there is no strict formalism. What is involved is a recommendation, irrespective of how exactly it may be characterised in legal terms, a decision of an association of undertakings within the meaning of article 81(1), if it accurately represents the will of the association and has the objective of co-ordinating the conduct of the members of the association in the market in question and in accordance with such a recommendation.

1.3 Concerted practices

7. The last category of prohibited practices has to do with concerted practices that may be defined as "a form of co-ordination between undertakings that without an actual agreement coming into existence, consciously replaces the risks of mutual competition with a collaboration that leads to competitive conditions that, taking into account the nature of the products in question, the size and the number of the undertakings, and the comprehensive nature of the market in question does not correspond to what may be regarded as normal market conditions."[10]

The concerted practices thus not only include, by their very nature, all the components of an agreement, but may be the result of, among other things, a co-ordination which manifests itself on the market, and which does not flow from the market situation but instead from a mutual contract between the concerned parties. If, for example, from the circumstances it already appears

---

9 Court of Justice, 18 June 1998, Commission/Italy, C-35/96, *Jur.* 1998, I-3851, par. 40. See also Court of Justice, 30 January 1985, Clair, 123/83, *Jur.* 1985, 391, par. 17.

10 A.M. VAN DEN BOSSCHE, Artikelsgewijze commentaar handels- en economisch recht – commentaar met overzicht van rechtspraak en rechtsleer, Antwerp, Kluwer, s.d., comment (ex) art. 85, p. 80, nr. 28.

that simultaneous price increases are the consequence of a concerted practice, there is no need to look further into whether the price increases stem from an agreement. To qualify as such practices, it shall be sufficient if independent undertakings knowingly modify their conduct to the wishes of another undertaking.

From the decision practices of the European Commission and the judgements of the Court of Justice and the Court of First Instance, it appears that the agreement mostly relates to target prices, price initiatives, rates, discount scales, quota systems with a view to sharing the market or, more generally, the exchange of commercially sensitive information that would normally be regarded as being business/trade secrets. A concrete consequence is elaborate quota systems, the complete demarcation of markets, whether or not on the basis of the home market principle, uniform price or identical sales conditions such as discounts.

2 THE APPLICATION OF ARTICLE 81(1) EC TO LIBERAL PROFESSIONALS

8. It was only since the beginning of the 90's that the European Commission focussed its attention on the application of article 81 EC to independent and liberal professionals.

The decision of the Commission of 30 June 1993, concerning the Italian customs agents represents the first application of the competition law to liberal professions by the European Commission. It was, at that time, expressly confirmed that the profession of customs forwarding agent is regarded as an independent profession in Italy, notwithstanding the fact that customs forwarding agents are undertakings that carry on economic activities.[11]

The Court of Justice later confirmed the stand taken by the Commission and also ruled that a customs agent is an undertaking within the meaning of article 81(1) EC.[12] The fact that the activity of customs agent is an intellectual profession that depends on an authorisation was not enough for the Court to decide that a non-economic activity was being carried on. An independent professional therefore carries on an economic activity since he provides services on payment of a fee.

9. In a decision of 12 September 2000, the Court determined that "the medical specialists provide, in their capacity as self-employed economic operators, services on a market, namely the market in specialist medical services. They are paid by their patients for the services they provide and

---

11 Decision of the Commission, recital 40.

12 Court of Justice, 18 June 1998, Commission/Italy, C-35/96, *Jur.* 1998, I-3851, par. 36-38.

assume the financial risks attached to the pursuit of their activity".[13] This brought the Court of Justice to the determination that independent medical specialists carry on an economic activity and are therefore undertakings within the meaning of article 81 (1) EC.

Legal theory also provides, in general terms, that all independent professionals who supply specific services to interested parties on payment of compensation, must be regarded as supplying economic services within the meaning of the decision of the Court of Justice, and must therefore be regarded as an undertaking within the meaning of article 81(1) EC.[14]

Professor Lenaerts, himself a Judge at the Court of the First Instance, also shares this opinion and also observed that law firms must be regarded as undertakings since they act as economic entities on the market.

10. Although at the present moment, neither the Court of Justice nor the Court of the First Instance have made observations about whether a lawyer should be regarded as an undertaking within the meaning of article 81(1) EC, there is no longer any doubt in legal theory about the fact that this is, in fact, so, since a lawyer can exercise his profession as a independent professional in all the countries of the European Community.

Incidentally, this position was also confirmed by the Advocate General in the cases of Wouters[15] and Arduino.[16] In his opinion, he stated, in the case of Wouters:

> *"Where lawyers practise as independent agents, they offer services on a particular market, namely the market for legal services. They demand and receive from their clients remuneration in return for the services performed. In addition, they carry the financial risks attaching to the performance of their activity since, if there should be an imbalance between their expenses and their receipts, they must bear the losses themselves. In accordance with the criteria laid down in the Court's case-law, lawyers must be classified as undertakings for the purpose of Community competition law."*[17]

---

13 Court of Justice, 12 September 2000, Pavlov, C-180/98 and C-184/98, par. 76, not yet published in *Jur.* For a comment, see E. LOOZEN, "Pavlov en Van der Woude: meer dan een Pavlov-reactie?", *Nederlands Tijdschrift voor Europees Recht* 2000, 301-307.

14 K. LENAERTS, "L'application du droit communautaire de la concurrence et la convention européenne des droits de l'homme à la profession d'avocat", X. (ed.), *L'avocat et son nouvel environnement concurrentiel,* Liège, *Ed. du* Jeune Barreau de Liège, 2001.

15 Opinion of Advocate-general Léger in the case C-309/99, Wouters, 10 July 2001.

16 Opinion of Advocate-general Léger in the case C-35/99, Arduino, 10 July 2001.

17 Opinion of Advocate-general Léger in the case C-309/99, Wouters, 10 July 2001, par. 51. In the Arduino case he stated: "(...) it appears from the file that lawyers practising in Italy, as independent operators, offer services of legal advice and representation of their clients before the courts. Italian lawyers therefore offer services on a market, namely the market of legal services. Furthermore, it is clear from the file that Italian lawyers prac-

The Advocate General stresses that lawyers occupy a central position in the administration of justice as intermediaries between the public and the courts. The opinion emphasises that lawyers perform activities that are essential in a state governed by the rule of law. They make it possible for individuals to have a better understanding of the rights granted to them and to enforce those rights more efficiently.

3 IS THE BAR AN ASSOCIATION OF UNDERTAKINGS WITHIN THE MEANING OF ARTICLE 81(1) EC?

11. As already indicated above, the competition laws are not exclusively directed toward agreements and arrangements between individual market participants. The cartel prohibition contained in Article 81 (1) EC shall also apply if competition is limited, obstructed or distorted as a consequence of *"decisions of associations of undertakings"*. In many cases, cartel practices are not always the result of agreements between two or more entrepreneurs, but the result of the - in many cases mandatory - consequences of decisions of the associations of undertakings to which they owe allegiance.

Associations of undertakings protect the economic interests of the members of such associations. The fact that mention is made of the protection of "economic" interests of the members does not preclude the possibility of organisations of independent professionals - that obviously also perform other duties - from being regarded as associations of undertakings within the meaning of article 81 (1) EC.

The associations of liberal professionals mostly have the objective of promoting the public interest, namely they are there to ensure that their members conduct themselves in accordance with the requirements peculiar to the work assigned to them in the course of the practice of their profession. The functional extension of the concept of the undertaking does not allow an interpretation in the context of the specific instructions of the association of independent professionals whereby members would fall outside (or be otherwise excluded from) the scope of competition law. In particular, the circumstance that a task assigned under or by dint of the law satisfies the condition that "it places them in a position to regulate the profession" is essentially irrelevant, just as the circumstance that its legal constitution is that of a public law co-operation under national law.[18] When an association of under-

---

tise with a view to making a profit. The referring court has stated that Italian lawyers demand and receive form their clients remuneration in consideration for the services provided. In these circumstances, the supply of legal services by Italian lawyers must be regarded as an economic activity within the meaning of the Court's case-law", par. 47-48.

18 Commission Decision, 30 January 1985, COAPI, O.J. L., 122/37, par. 33. See also Court

takings of this type takes decisions with the objective or consequence of limiting, hindering or distorting competition to a marked degree, this may be said to be in conflict with competition law. In concrete terms, what is involved are regulations laid down by the governing bodies of the association exercising the power delegated to them, the characteristic of these regulations being such that they are binding on all the members, either due to their content, as such regulations may be couched in terms that have mandatory force, or on the basis of the bye-laws or internal rules of the association.

The decisions of these associations of undertakings are mostly based on the specificity, the characteristic properties and the finality of the independent profession. In practice, it will also be necessary to examine whether the decisions of associations of undertakings (such as, for example, the Bar associations) have the objective or the effect of limiting or misusing competition or have the potential to do so.

12. In the decision of the European Commission of 7 April 1999 concerning the EPI code of conduct[19] (Code of conduct of the representatives before the European Patent Office), a very clear differentiation was made between (permissible) rules that are closely linked to deontology, on the one hand, and rules that limit the economic freedom of the independent professionals, on the other. With regard to the latter rules, the disciplinary authority (the associations of undertakings) must show that such rules are necessary to ensure the observance of deontological rules (which cannot be economic or competition-limiting rules). In this connection, considerations of public interest may be taken into account.

13. In the EPI case[20], the European Commission determined that the following deontological regulations do *not* limit competition:[21]

---

of Justice, 18 June 1998, Commission/Italy, C-35/96, *Jur.* 1998, I-3851, par. 40. For a comment, see A.M. VAN DEN BOSSCHE, "Voor economische vrijheid en mededingingsrecht: hoe vrij is de plichtenleer in het beperken van de economische keuzevrijheid van vrije beroepers ?", *T.P.R.* 2000, 18-22.

19 Commission Decision, 7 April 1999, EPI, O.J. L., 106/14.

20 The Court of First Instance annulated the decision of the Commission on two specific points:
- The provision that seeks to ensure that a professional representative does not rely unduly on professional relationships is not a restriction of competition.
- The provision that prevents a representative, when offering services to a client, form discrediting a fellow professional by questioning his conduct of a case which has been terminated is not a restriction of competition.
Court of First Instance, 28 March 2001, Institute of Professional representatives before the European Patent Office/European Commission, T-144/99, par. 70-72 and 97-100, not yet published in *Jur.*

21 See L. NEELS, "Vrije en intellectuele en dienstverlenende beroepen: deontologie, concurrentie en publiciteit. Een complexe driehoeksverhouding", paper for FIVB (Belgian Fe-

- The principle that members shall be regarded as having knowledge of the code and cannot claim that they are not familiar with its contents.
- The principle that a violation of the code cannot be justified by reference to the instructions given by the client.
- The determination of professional requirements concerning impartiality, expertise and responsibility.
- Rules concerning the relations between the members of the institute.
- The forbidding of persons who are not a member from carrying out professional actions in its name.
- The liability of the member for the actions of its employees who are themselves not members of the association.
- The obligation to take care of and pay attention at all times to all the work entrusted to the member by the client, and to apply the required expertise in the performance of such work.
- The obligation to keep clients informed of the status of their file.
- The forbidding of making the identity of a client known except with the express permission of the person in question.
- The right to ask the client for advances.
- The obligation to demonstrate collegiality toward other members of the association.
- The forbidding of discriminating between members particularly on the grounds of language or nationality.
- The rules in connection with the transfer of case papers, if the client gives instructions to pass a case over to another member.
- The principle that advertising is allowed in general, so long as it is in keeping with the facts and objective and is in conformity with the basic principles of honesty and respect for professional secrecy.
- The forbidding of offering unrequested services to clients in matters that are being handled by another authorised person.

14. The scope of deontological actions by associations of undertakings (professional associations) must also be pruned down to the bare minimum, in particular the rules of conduct that are *in no way connected to* or have anything to do with the economic freedoms of the practitioners in question of the profession, and the rules limited to those that are *necessary* to achieve these non-economic objectives. These are, therefore, the rules that are "necessary" to ensure the impartiality, the expertise, the integrity and the responsibility of the "person practising the profession", to prevent conflicts of interest and misleading advertisements (and) to protect professional se-

---

deration of intellectual and liberal professions), 24 February 2000, FIVB Rondetafel: vrije beroepen ontmoeten elkaar, p. 98-102 (nr. 45-46).

crecy".[22] Such a description shall be sufficient to exclude competition law from the essential core tasks of the independent profession.

With regard to the Bar, it can be seen from various decisions issued by the Court of Justice[23] that rules to protect the *professional secrecy*, the *independence* and the *impartiality* of the profession of lawyer are seen as being in the public interest, and the fact that such rules may simultaneously limit competition is justified on that ground. On the other hand, is must be clear that it cannot be accepted that rules which regulate the exercising of a profession fall as a matter of principle outside the scope of article 81 (1) EC merely because they are classified as *"rules of professional conduct"* by the competent bodies.[24]

In the decision in the AM & S case, the Court of Justice observed that the requirement concerning the position and capacity of independent lawyer (...) rests on an image of the role of the lawyer as a servant of the system of the administration of justice who must provide, totally independently and in the main interests of this administration of justice, the legal assistance his client requires. The other side of this protection is the system of professional disciplinary action, that has been set up in the public interest by and under the supervision of institutions duly authorised for the purpose.[25]

In the decision in the Gebhard case, the Court observed that the rules concerning organisation, technical competence, professional ethics, supervision and liability justify legal and administrative measures on the grounds that they further the public interest.[26]

In the decision in the Van Binsbergen case, the Court of law observed that professional regulations concerning organisation, technical competence, professional ethics, supervision and liability serve the cause of the public interest.[27]

In the decision in the Reisbüro Broede case[28], the Court observed that the application of professional regulations, in particular, concerning organisation, technical competence, code of conduct, supervision and liability, provide end-users of judicial services with the required guarantee of integrity

---

22 Commission Decision EPI, par. 38.

23 The decisions referred to matters relating to free movement but are also interesting with regard to competition law.

24 Court of First Instance, 28 March 2001, Institute of Professional representatives before the European Patent Office/European Commission, T-144/99, par. 64, not yet published in *Jur.*

25 Court of Justice, 18 May 1982, AM & S Europe, 155/79, *Jur.* 1982, 1575.

26 Court of Justice, 30 November 1995, Gebhard, C-55/94, *Jur.* 1995, 4186, par. 35.

27 Court of Justice, 3 December 1974, 33/74, *Jur.* 1974, 1299.

28 Court of Justice, 12 December 1996, C-3/95, *Jur.* 1996, I-6511.

and experience, and also ensure the proper administration of justice, as enshrined in the concept of public interest.

15. The specific function of a lawyer was also debated in the discussions about the draft Directive to prevent the use of the financial system for money laundering. On 14 July 1999, the European Commission tabled a proposal to update the 1991 Directive (91/308/EEC) on the prevention of the use of the financial system for money laundering. On 17 October 2001, the Ecofin Ministers of the EC accepted a compromise. The crucial part of the deal is that lawyers will have to inform the authorities if they know that their client is seeking advice for money-laundering purposes. But when representing clients in legal proceedings, or giving legal advice where they do not suspect money laundering, lawyers may retain their professional secrecy, which is accepted as an essential part of the profession.[29]

16. In a recent paper, the Office of Fair Trading[30] of the United Kingdom concluded:

> *"Clearly there are fundamental arguments for protecting the exchanges between clients and their legal advisers. However, where the subject of these exchanges is advice that could equally be provided by a member of another profession, there is a case on efficiency and competition grounds for either a reduction in the scope of the privilege of legal advisers or a limited extension of privilege to others in order to remove the distortion of competition that favours the lawyer."*[31]

17. Professor Neels rightly observes the following:

> *"It is therefore necessary for the independent professions to understand that competition-limiting regulations are no longer practicable and that the insane arguments of old belong in the history books.*

---

29 The approved text on October 17, 2001 considers: "However, where independent members of professions providing legal advice which are legally recognised and controlled, such as lawyers, are ascertaining the legal position of a client or representing a client in legal proceedings, it would not appropriate under the directive to put these legal professionals in respect of their activities under an obligation to report suspicions of money laundering. There must be exemptions from any obligation to report information obtained either before, during or after judicial proceedings, or in the course of ascertaining the legal position for a client. Thus, legal advice remains subject to the obligation of *professional secrecy* unless the legal counsellor is taking part in money laundering activities, the legal advice is provided for money-laundering purposes, or the lawyer knows that the client is seeking legal advice for money-laundering purposes." (recital 16).

30 The OFT is a non-ministerial government department divided into (i) the Competition Policy Division and (ii) the Consumer Affairs Division. Both divisions are supported by a legal division.

31 OFFICE OF FAIR TRADING, *Report on competition in professions* (a report by the Director General of Fair Trading), March 2001, nr. 47.

The question must also be asked whether we are really seriously considering the introduction or enforcement of a regulation that is closely linked to deontology or regulations that limit the economic freedom of the practitioners of an independent profession. This simply cannot be tolerated any longer. Professional bodies who enforce such regulations not only run the risk of penalties but shall also not be competent to impose sanctions in the event of violation of such regulations, since an objection based on competition law shall be sufficient to lead to the nullification of the deontological Order, and in some cases, the nullification of the very rule or regulations themselves".[32]

18. The code of conduct for lawyers of the European Union of the Council of the Bars and Law Societies of the European Union (CCBE) is a good example of a restricted code of conduct in accordance with competition law.[33] The code declares that the many obligations to which a lawyer is subject, require his absolute independence, free from all other influence, especially that as may arise from his personal interests or external pressure.

"Such an independence is as necessary to trust the process of justice as the impartiality of the judge. Therefore, the lawyer must avoid any impairment of his independence and be careful not to compromise his professional standards in order to please the client, the court or third parties."[34 35]

---

32 L. NEELS, *o.c.*, p. 103, nr. 50 (translation of the Dutch text).

33 Ex. Art. 2.1: The many obligations to which a lawyer is subject require his absolute independence, free from all other influence, especially such as may arise from his personnel interests or external pressure. Such independence is as necessary to trust in the process of justice as the impartiality of the judge. A lawyer must therefore avoid any impairment of his independence and be careful not to compromise his professional standards in order to please his client, the court or third parties.
This independence is necessary in non-contentious matters as well as in litigation. Advice given by a lawyer to his client has no value if it is given only to ingratiate himself, to serve his personal interests or in response to outside pressure.
Art. 2.3: It is the essence of a lawyer's function that he should be told by his client things which the client would not tell to others, and that he should be the recipient of other information on a basis of confidence. Without the certainty of confidentiality there cannot be trust. Confidentiality is therefore a primary and fundamental right and duty of the lawyer. The lawyer's obligation of confidentiality serves the interests of the administration of justice as well as the interests of the client. It is therefore entitled to special protection by the State.

34 R. MULLERAT, "A new step in the MDPs conflict", *The European lawyer*, September 2001, p. 7.

35 The CCBE published on 22 February 2001 a statement of position on lawyers' confidentiality, which mentioned: "We have watched with increasing anxiety developments in (...) countries regarding lawyers' obligation of professional secrecy and confidentiality. It is hardly an exaggeration to say that proposals for limiting the scope of the lawyers' obligation are submitted almost daily. (...) We consider it beyond doubt that the citizens of our countries must have one point of communication, which is fully protected from exposure. This has become all the more important given that, in modern society, a citizen's communication with other persons such as doctors, priests and social workers

4 LIBERAL PROFESSIONS IN THE LIGHT OF NATIONAL COMPETITION LAW

19. We have not, within the framework of the present debate, gone into the plans to redraft European competition law, which is supposed to bring about further decentralisation, whereby the national cartel authorities will be assigned a higher level of authority. In addition, national competition law will remain in force in all the Member States.[36]

4.1 Belgium

20. In Belgium, the applicability of competition rules to independent professions was primarily brought into focus by the decision of 31 October 1995[37], whereby the President of the Competition Council takes up an application for temporary measures.

The facts that give rise to the dispute were quite simple. An architect was penalised by the Architects Association since he did not adhere to the deontological rules concerning the mandatory fee rate to be applied. During the disciplinary proceedings, the architect started proceedings before the Competition Council in which he stated that the provisions of the deontological regulations containing the schedule of architects' fees constituted a violation of Article 2 (1) of Belgian Competition law.[38]

The President of the Competition Council took up the application (in a procedure concerning temporary measures), but in its decision of 14 November 1996, the Court of Appeal at Brussels revised the decision.[39] The Court of Appeal emphasised that the decision of the (President of the) Competition

---

does not always enjoy full protection. Given the high standards of professional conduct which are imposed upon members of the legal profession, and their long experience of working in accordance with obligations of professional secrecy and confidentiality, they remain best suited to being the protected point of communication."

36 Proposal for a Council Regulation on the implementation of the rules on competition laid down in articles 81 and 82 of the Treaty and amending Regulations (EEC) nr. 1017/68, (EEC) nr. 2988/74, (EEC) nr. 3975/87, COM (2000), 582 final (version 27.09.2000).

The national competition authorities will be obliged to apply art. 81 of the Treaty. The national jurisdictions will also apply this article 81 (concurrent application).

37 Decision of The President of the "Conseil de la concurrence / Raad voor de Mededinging" (Belgian competition authority), 31 October 1995, *J.T.* 1996, 346 and *J.L.M.B.* 1996, 263.

38 Law of 5 August 1991, last amended by the laws of 26 April 1999. The coordinated text is published in the official Statute Book of Belgium (Belgisch Staatsblad/Moniteur Belge) of 1 September 1999. Article 2 of the law is inspired by art. 81 E.U. treaty.

39 Court of Appeal Brussels, 14 November 1996, *Jaarboek Handelspraktijken en Mededinging*, 1996, 816.

Council constituted interference in the authority of disciplinary tribunals that were duly constituted under the law.

The Court of Appeal was of the opinion that the incompatibility of the prescribed schedule of fees with competition law should have been placed before the authorities that are charged with the enforcement of disciplinary procedure and exercise their powers under the supervision of the Cassation Court (highest court of Belgium). The decision reads as follows (free translation):

> *"That it is the legal responsibility of the bodies of the Architect's Association who are assigned with the task of enforcing the disciplinary regulations under the supervision of the Cassation Court, to examine, if the same is claimed by way of objection, whether there is a conflict between article 12 of the regulations of the professional obligations and the deontological provisions norm no. 2, and article 2 § 1, of Belgian competition law".*

The Court of Appeal ultimately did not touch on the grounds of the case but, meanwhile attention was focused on the problematic nature of some so-called "deontological" rules.

21. In connection with the decision of 19 March 1996, the Competition Council raised a preliminary ruling before the Belgian Arbitration Court[40] concerning the authority of the Council *vis-à-vis* the independent professions. The case involved the procedure instituted by Mr. Tambue before the Competition Council. Mr. Tambue had failed professional competence examination conducted by the bar (the so-called "Buba" or "CAPA" exam[41]), as a consequence of which the Council of the local Arlon Bar Association instituted a proceeding to strike the name of the said apprentice from the list of "stagiaires" (trainees). Mr. Tambue took the position that the regulations concerning the competence test and the limitation on the number of "stagiaires" assigned to each "lawyer/trainer", issued by the National Bar Association and the local Arlon Bar Association, were corporatist and in conflict with Belgian competition law. The National Bar Association and the Arlon Bar Association took the stand that in the light of the separation of powers, the administrative courts were not competent to sit in judgement on the regulations.

In its decision, the Court of Arbitration held that the legislature (in articles 506 and 611 of the Belgian Legal Code) has brought about a differential treatment in favour of the Bar authorities and this differential treatment is justified, since the lawyers profession is dedicated to public service, namely the administration of justice.

---

40 Arbitragehof/Cour d'Arbitrage, a kind of constitutional court.

41 BUBA = professional competence exam for practising the profession of lawyer.

This does not mean that the Bar authorities are not subject to competition law and cannot be punished in connection with the same. It does mean that the Competition Council does not have authority in individual instances of disciplinary action but, however, recourse to the intervention of civil law Courts and judicial authorities is, of course, open to the aggrieved party. Even civil Courts can enforce competition law although they do not have at their disposal the same means to investigate competition-limiting practices.

The question of whether regulations as such (and thus in distinction to actual cases involving disciplinary action) can be subjected to sanctions by the Competition Council is and remains the subject of much discussion and debate.[42]

22. The Cassation Court also recently expressed an opinion about the applicability of Competition law to independent professions and this in connection with the so-called "pharmacists' decision".[43] The terms of the decision are particularly lucid:

> *"Taking into consideration that the Pharmacist's Association is an association of undertakings to which all practitioners of the profession are bound by law to be affiliated;*
>
> *And that the government has delegated certain duties and responsibilities to the Association, especially to supervise the fulfilment of the deontology and the enforcement of honourable conduct, modesty, honesty and worthy conduct on the part of its members; and that the Association is not hereby seeking to achieve any economic objective, but is discharging a legal obligation in connection with which it has also been given regulatory authority by the government;*
>
> *And that this does not alter the fact that it is an association of undertakings within the meaning of article 2§1 of Competition law, the extent to which its decisions contrive to or cause prejudice to competition must be examined by disciplinary authorities of the Association for compatibility with the requirements of competition law;*
>
> *And that a decision of an authority under the Association that imposes competitive limitations in connection with one or more of its members, and such limitations are not required to enforce the fundamental rules of the profession, and instead, actually promote certain material interests of pharmacists, or contrive to install or maintain in force an economic system, may well be a decision of an association of undertakings, the nullification of which can be decided on by the Appeals Council by means of legal action".*

---

42 The case of Mr. Tambue is actually dealt with by the Belgian Competition Council.

43 Cass. 7 May 1999, *T.B.H.* 1999, 499 and *Jaarboek Handelspraktijken en Mededinging* 1999, 856.

Judge Verougstraete also correctly states that after this judgement it is clear that the professional associations are obliged, when they issue decisions in connection with disciplinary action, to take advice about the effect of their decisions on free competition, and states (free translation):

> *"It is often difficult to define the line between what is directly related to the hard core of deontology and patent corporatism – in other words, not required for the enforcement of the reliability of the practitioners of the profession, which of course, does not alter the fact that the line must be drawn."*[44]

23. It is also interesting to note that the commission "for finances and economic affairs" of the Belgian senate is discussing the draft of a new law "to amend the law of 5 August 1991 to protect economic competition"[45] introduced by Mr. Monfils. According to the explanatory memo, the draft law is intended to bring about judicial clarity after the above-mentioned appeals decision. The proposal for the law made the following comment (free translation):

> *"If one analyses the tasks that the national legislator has delegated to professional associations, one will quickly realise that the description is very vague, so that the professional associations in Belgium that are already engaged in dealing with problems which are inseparable from questions of public interest, cannot satisfy the stringent conditions that are imposed, so that the involvement of the European or national competition regulations seems almost inevitable (...)*
>
> *As soon as an action that is in conflict with competition law is placed before them (the Associations) via a national law (...), competition laws are not applicable to them (...)*
>
> *The compulsion, if any, that is imposed by the law makes it possible to propose a temporary solution, mainly if one bears in mind that it can never be disputed that competition laws cannot be applied to actions of professional associations if they are attempting to realise unmistakably legitimate objectives in order to achieve what is in the public interest (...)*
>
> *The draft is intended to put an end to the uncertainty that hangs over the role and powers of professional associations under competition law. It is necessary to define what exactly "public interest" entails, so that these professional associations can no longer add to it in an arbitrary manner. The decisions or orders issued by professional associations that satisfy the legal and proper definition of public interest will therefore escape the application of competition law."*

---

44 I. VEROUGSTRAETE, "Institutionele wijzigingen", in J. STUYCK and P. WUYTINCK (eds.), *De hervormde Belgische Mededingingswet*, Antwerp, Kluwer, 2000, p. 33, nr. 27, with reference to the Annual report of the court of Cassation of 1999, p. 175.

45 Wetsvoorstel tot wijziging van de wet van 5 augustus 1991 tot bescherming van de economische mededinging, *Parl. St.*, Senaat, 1999-2000, 2-126/1.

On the 14 February 2001, the concerned Senate Committee held a hearing attended by representatives of all legally recognised liberal professions. The majority of professional associations demand, even now, a very broad (and in the light of the evolution of competition law, archaic) description of "public interest" as a result of which their entire code of conduct will fall outside the scope of the competition law, often with a misinterpretation of the decisions of the Court of Justice. Other professional associations still try to maintain that their Association should not be regarded as an association of undertakings.

The Belgian Bar (both the Association of Flemish Bars as well as the Conference of French and German Bars) has pointed out that, given the current condition of the law (and taking into account European and Belgian judicial precedents), it is now clear that deontological rules fall outside the scope of competition law and other regulations (that are directly related to the carrying out of professions on an economic basis and are therefore competition rules that are limiting in nature) must be assessed under the economic regulations concerning competition law.

The draft of the new law also addresses legislative objections, taking into account the serious misgivings as to whether it can be brought into conformity with European law, which, incidentally, takes precedence over Belgian law and which Member States are required to apply loyally (including the legislative power). It seems that this draft bill will give rise to further in-depth discussions and will certainly not be included in the Belgian Statute Book in its present form.

4.2 Other countries[46]

24. In *Germany*, the law of concerted practices[47] is applicable to liberal professions.

In *Italy*, the competition authorities decided on 26 August 1991 that a regulation fixing a tariff and establishing a disciplinary code adopted by the Assiveri (National association of auditors and accountants) was violating competition law and that it could not benefit from an exemption.

In *the Netherlands*, the liberal professions have been subject to competition law since 1997 (although legal exceptions are provided).

In *France*, various professional associations and even some professionals themselves were condemned on various grounds, including the fixing of

---

46 See C. MATRAY, Lawyers and competition law, paper for the regional Terralex meeting, September 2000.

47 Gesetz gegen Wettbewerbesränkungen (GWB)

tariffs. Fines were often imposed. The professions targeted by the competition authorities include pharmacists, lawyers[48], architects, surveyors, biologists and doctors.

In *the United Kingdom,* the liberal professions come under the authority of the "MCC" (the Mergers and Monopolies Commission[49]) and since 1999 the Competition Commission. Various of these professions, including solicitors, chartered accountants, opticians, veterinary surgeons... modified some of their practices[50] following the MCC's observations.

5 CONCLUSIONS

25. Briefly, the effects on the application of competition law include the following.

5.1 Prohibition of collective price fixing

26. The collective fixing of prices is traditionally regarded as a serious violation of competition laws (it constitutes a violation of community law and in most cases of national competition law). Price-fixing agreements are "especially" serious. *"The Court of Justice considers that, by its very nature, an agreement fixing the price of goods or services has as its* object *the restriction of competition on the market."*[51]

It is not necessary to examine whether the collective fixing is the result of an agreement between professional themselves or if it is originates in a decision by a professional organisation (*e.g.* a Bar association).

In the Arduino case the Advocate General Léger set out that he does not think that these principles apply to the decision of a bar association adopting a "draft scale of fees", when it is a preparatory act in the legislative procedure laid down by the legal system of a country. The Italian "Consiglio Nazionale Forense" (CNF) is a body composed of lawyers elected by their peers. The CNF is required, every two years, to set the criteria for determining the fees and emoluments payable to lawyers. The draft scale is then submitted to the Minister for Justice. Without approval by the Minister, the members of the profession and third parties are legally bound to apply the

---

48 Decisions of the Competition Council, nr. 96D.78 and 96.D79 of 3 December 1996, B.O.C.C.R.F., 11 February 1997.

49 Now the "Competition Commission". The Competition Commission is an independent public body. It replaced the Monopolies and Mergers Commission on 1 April 1999.

50 C. EHLERMAN, "Concurrence et professions libérales, antagonismes ou compatibilité", *Revue du Marché Commun* 1993, p. 140-141.

51 Opinion of Advocate-general Léger in case C-35/99, Arduino, 10 July 2001, par. 64.

scale contained in the preceding ministerial decree. Advocate General Léger considers:

> *"The decision therefore does not have the effect of restricting competition on the (...) market in legal services. Any restriction in competition is only the consequence of a subsequent act of the (Italian) authorities when they adopt the ministerial decree approving the decision of the CNF. Consequently, I consider that (...) the Treaty does not preclude a professional association of lawyers, such as CNF, from adopting a draft scale setting the minimum and maximum fees for services provided by members of the profession, when this draft scale is intended* exclusively *for submission to the public authorities (...)".*[52]

5.2 Professional codes of conduct

27. Public authorities grant a monopoly with respect to the carrying out of some activities. But, as a countermeasure, they require the representatives of the profession carrying out these activities to fulfil various conditions in order to qualify. They also require these representatives to act with dignity, honesty, competence, independence, discretion, loyalty.

Usually, the rules contained in deontological codes applicable to lawyers fall into three categories:

- Rules relating to courtesy and politeness between lawyers.
- Rules aimed at protecting the interests of the profession
- Rules aimed to ensuring the dignity, honesty and virtue of the profession.

Competition law is aimed at ensuring three freedoms: the freedom of access to markets for undertakings; their freedom of action on these markets and the freedom of choice for consumers. The restrictions to competition as the result of professional codes are justified in light of their aims and if they are not disproportionate to these aims, taking into account the economic and legal context. As a consequence professional rules are admissible which aim to ensure independence, partiality, integrity and responsibility of the lawyers, or rules aimed at preventing conflicts of interests or misleading advertising. Other rules may be judged as restraints on competition.

28. Liberal professions will only maintain their competitive position as a result of the quality of their qualifications, their services and the appropriateness of the fees they charge. Rules that restrain competition are not likely to maintain one's competitive situation if the quality of the services provided is inadequate. Competition does not threaten this quality but generates it. Lawyers will only be able to retain clients or acquire new ones if they admit

52 *Ibidem*, par. 71-72.

the necessity of continuing qualification and openness to legal evolution in the area of competition law.[53]

[53] C. MATRAY, Lawyers and competition law, paper for the regional Terralex meeting, September 2000, p. 8.

ADR: A NEW FIELD OF LEGAL PRACTICE

Piet A. Wackie Eysten, Partner De Brauw Blackstone Westbroek, The Hague, and Council Member of the Dutch Mediation Institute and of the ADR-centre for Industry and Commerce and John M. Bosnak, Partner CMS Derks Star Busmann, Arnhem, and Mediator affiliated with the Dutch Mediation Institute

1 ADR. GENERAL REMARKS

Alternative methods of conflict resolution aim at reaching an optimal solution for all parties concerned, rather than "winning the battle" at the other party's cost.

The origins of ADR are to be found in the USA. In common law jurisdictions ADR has developed very rapidly. In the US ADR is offered by various organisations, such as the American Arbitration Association (AAA) and the Institute for Dispute Resolution, which was established in 1979 by the Centre for Public Resources (CPR). The CPR-institute has established a registry of some 900 major companies who have undertaken to explore the possibilities of settling disputes through ADR before litigating.

In the UK the Centre for Dispute Resolution (CEDR) has successfully launched mediation and other forms of ADR. The new Civil Procedure Rules (CPR), in force as of 26 April 1999, based on Lord Woolf's report "Access to Justice", enable the courts to stay proceedings to encourage alternative dispute resolution. At case management conferences the parties are required to state whether the question of ADR has been discussed. The judge is entitled to suspend the proceedings at any time to give the parties a chance to try and settle their dispute through ADR.

During the last few years the concept of ADR has further developed on the continent of Europe as well. Legislation has been enacted in France, Germany, Belgium and some other countries. The European Commission too recognises the importance of alternative dispute resolution. In April 2001 the Commission issued a Recommendation "on the principles for out-of-court bodies involved in the consensual resolution of consumer disputes" along with a Communication on "widening consumer access to alternative dispute resolution". It identifies four principles that should be guaranteed: (a) impartiality of those responsible for the procedure, (b) transparency, (c) effectiveness, and (d) fairness of the procedure.

Although the scope of this Recommendation is limited to consumer disputes the basic principles of the ADR procedure set out therein are of great value for ADR in general and may well be instrumental in bringing about a common European concept of alternative dispute resolution methods and procedures.

2 RECENT DEVELOPMENTS IN THE NETHERLANDS

The *Stichting Netherlands Mediation Institute* (NMI) became operational in the course of 1995. NMI is an independent organisation which aims at stimulating the broadest possible use of ADR. It has played an important role in creating awareness for new types of ADR, especially mediation. NMI has developed criteria for training and educational programmes for mediators and quality standards. It has initiated a set of professional rules and a system of disciplinary proceedings for mediators, certified with the NMI.

ACB Conflict management Centre for Industry and Commerce was established in 1998. Many Dutch organisations felt the need for an independent mediation organisation that focuses entirely on the needs of the business environment and assures high quality standards. ACB was established under the auspices of the Confederation of Netherlands Industry and Employers (VNO-NCW). The active involvement of VNO-NCW clearly illustrates the interest businessmen take in this new development. ACB is a joint initiative of some large companies and representatives from the legal professions. It is a not-for-profit organisation that stimulates businesses to use mediation as a management tool.

In 1995 the *Netherlands Arbitration Institute* published its "Minitrage" Rules, a Dutch form of minitrial, whereby disputes are dealt with by the parties in front of a committee of three, consisting of executive officers at a high level in each of the companies that are parties in the dispute, presided over by a neutral chairman.

In 1996 an Advisory Committee was installed by the Minister of Justice. The task of this "ADR Platform" was to advise the Ministry of Justice with regard to "strategic policy decisions" to be taken concerning new forms of dispute resolution both on their own merits and with a view to reducing the growing demand for judicial remedies.

The Dutch government takes a great interest in the development of ADR. One of the recommendations in the final report of the ADR Platform was that experiments be undertaken with court-annexed mediation. This was followed up by the Government in a Policy Statement which identified four principal objectives:

- deformalising dispute resolution,
- ensuring efficient dispute resolution,
- creating multiform access to the law with a greater degree of responsibility for the parties themselves,

- decreasing the caseload for the judiciary.

On the basis of this government policy a court-annexed mediation pilot project was launched. At the end of 2003 the project will be evaluated. Depending on the results further initiatives will be taken.

3 THE ACTUAL MEDIATION PROCESS

The process is non-binding, informal and conducted under strict confidentiality. Either party can opt out at any stage of the proceedings. Once a settlement is reached that settlement is a binding agreement, but before that stage the mediation takes place on a purely voluntary basis. There is no coercion whatever to proceed with mediation. There may be an obligation to enter into mediation by virtue of a mediation clause in a contract. Some contracts provide that mediation or conciliation should be attempted before arbitration or litigation may be initiated.

ADR is characteristically informal. The most striking informality is the possibility that the mediator speaks with each of the parties separately: the "caucus". This is an enervating concept to seasoned traditional litigants, who unconditionally believe in the principle of "audite et alteram partem". And admittedly, it is important that the mediator maintains a perfect balance between the parties. If he talks to the claimant in private, he should also talk with the defendant. The "caucus" is perhaps the clearest sign that mediation is essentially different from court proceedings.

A mediation process typically consists of four stages:

I. Introduction mediator and parties
Presentation of case by parties
Summary by mediator
Calendar for further sessions

II. Collecting facts and data
Experts, witnesses

III. Explore and develop alternative solutions
Analyse options

IV. Select best solution
Write down and execute settlement agreement.

4 PERSONAL QUALITIES OF THE MEDIATOR, EDUCATION AND TRAINING

A frequently asked question is what talents are needed to be an effective mediator and whether or not one can be taught to be a mediator. Since the whole idea of ADR is based on an interest-based form of negotiating (as opposed to position-based) it is the primary task of the mediator to uncover the real interests of the parties. The mediator therefore needs to be a good listener.

Further, the mediator must have a good sense of fairness and equity. He must be able to weigh the justified and less justified interests and desires of both parties, taking into account their personal, social and legal situations.

These qualities can be enhanced by training. Even for the most talented mediator it will be useful if he is made aware of what he is doing, in terms of communication, negotiating techniques etc. The best way to develop one's abilities as a mediator is the actual practice of it. All the best educational programmes devote a lot of time to play-acting in mock mediations. Another way to gain experience is co-mediating, i.e. doing a real mediation side by side with an experienced mediator.

5 THE ROLE OF THE LAWYER IN MEDIATION

5.1 The lawyer as counsel in mediation

Although it is of the very essence of mediation that disputes are not solved by legal argument, the law is inevitably relevant and important. Most cases are bargained in the shadow of the law. The law and legal positions and arguments influence negotiations. Predictions are made about what would happen in court should the parties opt to litigate. The law allows them to assess the opportunities and risks involved.

What role lawyers have in mediation depends to a large extent on the style of negotiations. Lawyers play a leading role in negotiations based on expectations of the opportunities and risks of litigation, but much less in negotiations that focus on the parties' underlying interests. It is therefore a logical consequence that the lawyer's role becomes less important as the mediation proceeds successfully. In the beginning it will be perceived as important that the positions of both parties are clearly defined. But as the mediation proceeds the parties themselves will play a larger role, they want to come out of the process with a done deal. This is a major difference with traditional litigation where the litigation lawyer remains in charge until the end. Nevertheless, counsel can play an important role as coach and trusted advisor to his client.

Legal skills are appropriate in any case when it comes to laying down the settlement in writing. Needless to say that this document must be drawn up in a legally correct way for, if all is well, it will form the basis for what is hoped to be a longstanding relationship between the parties.

5.2 The lawyer as mediator

This is not the place to enter into the question of whether a lawyer is better equipped to become a mediator than other professionals. For the purpose of this article it is sufficient to state that it is advantageous, if in complex cases at least one of the mediators has a legal background.

6 CONCLUSIONS

Can we do without courts and without arbitrators henceforth? Of course not. There will always be commercial and other disputes that cannot be dealt with in a satisfactory way through ADR or where the advantages that can theoretically be achieved are not relevant, for instance where there is no future relationship. Neither does ADR seem to be an appropriate alternative where a principal point of law must be decided. But this does not alter the fact that in many cases ADR can be beneficial. This can particularly be the case in international commercial relations, where differences in legal systems and cultures may form a handicap in legal proceedings, be it in an international court of law or in arbitration. In the international context the informality of the ADR-process is one of its many advantages. In any case, it is certainly a development which presents lawyers with interesting new challenges.

RECENT CASE-LAW IN BELGIUM REGARDING LAWYERS-EMPLOYEES

Willy Van Eeckhoutte, Professor of Labour and Social Security Law (Ghent University), Supreme Court Attorney

The purpose of this paper is to give a personal opinion of the legal position of lawyers, of solicitors under the Belgian labour and social security law in force at present. The immediate cause is a recent and rather unusual judgement by the Brussels Labour law tribunal of 8 December 2000, which identifies a lawyer working under specific conditions as an employee.

1 EMPLOYEES AND THE SELF-EMPLOYED

As in many countries, Belgian social law (labour and social security law) makes a distinction between wage earners and subordinate workers or employees on the one hand and independent or self-employed workers on the other hand. The criterion for this distinction is subordination or - seen from the other side - authority: an employee is subordinated to or works under the authority of his employer, a self-employed worker does not.

As a rule, the so-called liberal professions are carried out by people who are self-employed: the doctor, the dentist, the architect, the accountant has his or her patients or clients and provides them with services completely independently, without having to obey their orders. Of course, a patient or a client can ask for what he wants but it is the professional who decides if he will do what is asked for and how he will do it.

In the legal professions, the situation is no different. The notary public, in Belgium a cross between a civil servant and a practitioner of a profession, and the lawyer work for their clients with intellectual and moral independence. Also, the multitude of clients prevents a subordinate link with the legal professional.

A problem can arise when a legal practitioner has but a single client - a hypothesis I will leave aside here - or when he works with or, more precisely, *for* other people, at least if this occurs on a more or less regular basis: in general, occasional freelance work will hardly ever be considered as subordinate work.

Roughly speaking, there are two situations in which there is a chance (or shall we say: a risk) that a lawyer is considered as working under the authority of someone else: traineeship and collaboration between lawyers.

2 TRAINEESHIP

First of all, there is the situation of traineeship or apprenticeship. In Belgium, candidates who want to become a notary public, bailiff or process-server or lawyer have to undergo a period of training or apprenticeship which lasts several years. An experienced notary public, bailiff or lawyer will act as their patron. There is no doubt that an apprentice works under the authority of his patron. Not without reason "patron" (in Dutch "patroon") also means "protector", "supporter" as well as "chief" or "boss". (Coincidentally the Latin idiom "patronus" from which "patron" is derived, also means, in addition to protector and supporter, defender in court or lawyer). The essential purpose of an apprenticeship is to learn a skilled practical trade. This cannot be done without guidelines, instructions, orders, admonitions, control, discipline and so on, all of which are characteristic of subordination or authority. The *Oxford English Dictionary* even says that an apprentice learns his skills from "an employer" and is "employed" as an apprentice.

Does this mean a legal apprentice is the employee of the notary public, the bailiff or the lawyer who is his patron? Certainly not.

Under Belgian law - but the same is also the case in other legal systems- there is quite a difference between an apprenticeship contract and a labour contract, a contract of employment. Although both labour relationships are characterised by subordination, their outcome is different. The purpose of an apprenticeship is, as already mentioned, to learn the practical aspects of a skilled profession. The reason for the existence of a labour contract, on the other hand, is to earn a wage, in order to be able to support or keep oneself and one's family. Therefore, the trainee, the apprentice is not a wage earner and is therefore not an employee.

The practical consequences of this are that the legal trainee does not fall under employment contract law nor under most other parts of labour law. Thus, for example, he is not entitled to the minimum wage which is due to employees, the patron does not have to respect the terms of notice applicable to employees, and so on. On the other hand, a trainee does not come under the social security protection for wage earners: his patron does not have to pay social security contributions on top of and deducted from the trainee's pay as he does on top of and deducted from the wages of his employees. The trainee's fee is not essential in his labour relationship and is not to be considered as a wage, as remuneration for the performance of the apprentice. Performance is not exactly what is expected from a trainee. What his patron is entitled to expect, is that the trainee works together with the patron to the best of his ability, in order to learn the professional skills as soon and as well as possible.

For the same reason a trainee *as such* is not to be considered as an independent or self-employed worker, in the social security sense of this term. Under Belgian law a person is only compulsorily insured in the social security system for the self-employed if that person has a professional activity, which means a regular activity aimed at making a profit. As stated above, this is not the aim of a traineeship or apprenticeship.

As far as Belgian social security law is concerned, trainees are *as such* to be regarded as neutral: they are neither employees nor self-employed workers. If, in spite of this, trainee lawyers are treated as "independent workers" in the social security law sense of the term, this is due to the fact that, in addition to their training, they are entitled to practice the profession of a lawyer throughout their entire traineeship. Because this activity *can* yield a profit, it is a professional activity. This profession is practised without any subordination toward the clients or the patron.

And this brings us to a very delicate point in the relationship between the legal trainee and his patron. As experience proves, the first few months (according to some even the first few years) of a legal traineeship are generally characterised by a pure investment of time, of attention to training by the patron, almost without any useful contribution by the trainee or, to be more precise, any contribution which is worth the time the patron spends on the trainee and the compensation he pays him. This may be the case for a certain period of time but it cannot be denied that after a number of months or years, the ratio between the patron's investment and the trainee's contribution is reversed: the patron has to guide the activities of his trainee less and less and the trainee performs more and more.

At this stage the risk emerges of the trainee *becoming* an employee. When the emphasis is placed on his output and no longer his training and the authority of the patron continues, which is often but not always the case, it can be said that the nature of his labour relationship with his patron has gradually changed from a traineeship, an apprenticeship agreement into a labour contract. This means the trainee will be entitled to all legal protection and benefits given to employees: minimum wages, holiday pay, terms of notice, etc.

Of course, in practice it is very difficult if not impossible to determinate the exact moment at which the scales are tipped and it becomes a labour contract. Therefore, it is my opinion that the legally or deontologically determined period of traineeship or apprenticeship should be accepted as the normal period during which learning exceeds achievements, performance. Only if there is a clear imbalance between the two in favour of performance, should a trainee be considered as an employee of his patron. This clear imbalance has to be proved by the trainee or the social security administration, which, as a rule, is not an easy thing to do.

3 COLLABORATION BETWEEN LAWYERS

If, following a successful training period, a lawyer continues to work for his patron, he may become the employee of the latter if the subordination which characterizes his traineeship continues in the new labour relationship which then came into being between both parties. Whether or not this is the case will depend upon the actual circumstances under which the former apprentice continues to work: is it his former patron (or another lawyer) who determines what the ex-trainee has to do, does the latter have to report to the other, is he tied by a strict time schedule, does he have to account for his absences, does he have to ask permission to take a holiday, does he work in a material context (in an office, with the infrastructure and the personnel) not determined or agreed by himself, but by the other party or the firm, does he have the opportunity to develop a clientele of his own and so on?

For far too long it has been said and accepted that it is impossible for a lawyer to act as a lawyer under the authority of another person. The independence, the autonomy, the professional responsibility of a lawyer would be an impediment to entering into a contract of employment. It goes without saying that this reasoning is incorrect. Of course a lawyer is independent, autonomous and professionally responsible when practising law. But this has nothing to do with the notion of subordination which characterises a labour contract. In the liberal legal professions, many people act with a comparable independency and autonomy, even in the field of law, *e.g.* the lawyers working in the legal department of a company. It does not prevent them from being employees. The same arguments (intellectual independence, moral autonomy, professional responsibility) have been put forward in the past in order to deny employee status to teachers, university professors, architects, pharmacists and medical doctors. Today nobody denies that all these professions can be practised under the authority of a school, a university, a firm of architects or a clinic. The Belgian Court of Cassation has repeatedly made clear that freedom and personal responsibility when carrying out activities do not necessarily exclude subordination. As the idea of the protection of workers progresses, labour law no longer has any key personal limits: all professional activities can be exercised by an employee (although the reverse is not the case).

Therefore, the fight to keep lawyers from being covered by employment contract law has to be considered as a rearguard action. To exempt the legal profession on principle from the normal rules of labour law, would be discriminative, perpetuate the existing hypocrisy and set up a certain kind of unacceptable immunity.

Of course this need not and does not mean that all lawyers working for a law firm are employees. In the first place, the partners are not, neither are lawyers working with the firm, who can do their job without being subordinated to a partner or to the firm. The fact that the latter to a certain extent guides and supervises the activities of these lawyers does not automatically mean that the man or woman is an employee.

On the other hand, even a trainee can be an employee, not - as explained before - because of the authority exercised by his patron during his apprenticeship but because of his activities in addition to his traineeship.

This was the case with the situation of a young lawyer as dealt with in a recent judgement by the Brussels labour law tribunal.[1]

The person in question was a part-time (half-time) assistant of a professor in procedural law at one of the Belgian law faculties. At the same time he was a trainee with a lawyer who apparently did not care very much about training his apprentice, since in addition to the three days a week this young man spent at the university, he also worked 32 hours for a law firm other than that of his patron.

The Labour law tribunal of Brussels decided the lawyer was an employee, not of his rather dubious patron, but of the law firm he also used to work for. The criteria on which the court based its opinion, are the following:

- the co-worker received a fixed monthly wage,
- he was obliged to work mainly and full-time on the cases of one partner of the law firm,
- painstaking control was exercised by this partner on his use of his time,
- the firm placed an office and its infrastructure at his disposal,
- there was a holiday arrangement which gave the co-worker twenty paid days holiday,
- the co-worker was partly responsible for carrying out translating work for the English-speaking partner he worked for,
- he was obliged to account for absences,
- all documents containing information for clients had to be submitted to the partner for correction and approval.

It is striking that none of those who commentated on this judgement fundamentally disapproved of it, although certain authors rightly draw attention to the "neutrality" of certain elements considered by the court. But as far as

1 Brussels labour law tribunal 8 December 2000, *Journ. proc.* 2001, afl. 408, 20, comment P. DE KEYZER, *Journ. Jur.* 2001 (A. FALJAOUI), afl. 1, 2, *Soc. Kron.* 2001, 159, comment, *A.J.T.* 2000-01, 646, comment by S. RENETTE, *J.T.T.* 2001, 137, comment C. WANTIEZ, *R.W.* 2000-01, 1208, comment and *T.B.B.R.* 2001, 210.

the principle is concerned, all commentators underline the need for a more reality-based approach to the legal situation of co-workers in law firms.[2]

4 CONCLUSION

Until recently the bar has been regarded as a sacred institution, to a certain extent escaping the normal rules of everyday life. However, the twenty-first century is an age of desacralization, at least it is in Western countries. The European Court of Justice has already made clear that the particularities of the profession of lawyer, *e.g.* his professional deontology, do not prevent the application of competition law. Each individual lawyer and each law firm is an undertaking and the bar association is to be considered as an association of undertakings.

The Brussels Labour law tribunal made it clear that the same applies in the field of labour relationships: employment relationships within law firms do not differ substantially from those in other companies. Whether a lawyer is self-employed or an employee entirely depends upon the real and actual circumstances of his activities. Like any other undertaking, a law firm must accept the consequences of the way it is organised.

2 P. DE KEYZER. "[L'avocat-employé]. Révolution ou fin d'une hypocrisie?", *Journ. proc.* 2001, afl. 408, 26-27 en 30-31; S. RENETTE, "Heeft de advocatuur zijn Bosman-arrest?", *A.J.T.* 2000-01, 653-661; C. WANTIEZ, "Avocat et contrat d'emploi", *J.T.T.* 2001, 140-141. The same opinion is held by C. VERCAMMEN, "Na de geneesheer nu ook de advocaat in ondergeschikt verband", *R.W.* 1992-93, 1353-1365.

LAWYERS IN MULTINATIONAL PRACTICES

Jean-François Gerard, Lawyer, General Secretary of Ius Laboris, International Employment Law, Pensions and Employee Benefits Alliance

1 INTRODUCTION

One of the many questions that managing partners in multinational firms have to confront is the individual status of lawyers whom they hire. Throughout Europe one continues to encounter diverse situations that could become a source of difficulty and could act as a break against attempts to harmonise the status and work conditions of lawyers within the same multinational firm.

The purpose of this report is to have a look at the various situations as they exist in different European countries, *i.a.* France - where for the last 10 years there has been a law that allows lawyers to be employees of a law firm - and in Belgium, where a recent sentence of a Labour law tribunal (December 2000, appeal still pending) characterises a lawyer as an employee, while it is still generally accepted by the profession that a lawyer may only be a self-employee in this country.

We will further attempt to identify the needs of the multinational law firms as regards the legal description of their working relationship with their lawyers. We will observe if changes and/or harmonisation are sought by these firms (and if these are (or would be) possible according to the national or international regulations), taking into account the evolution of the profession.

2 SITUATION IN EUROPEAN COUNTRIES

2.1 Group A: all or most of the lawyers are employees

The majority of lawyers/attorneys working as legal counsel in structured national or multinational law firms are salaried in the countries outlined below. This applies to trainees, associates and even for partners (as it is only the fixed share/equity partners or the shareholder who are designated as self-employed workers). Below are some examples:

2.1.1 *United Kingdom*

The legal profession in the United Kingdom is split between solicitors (who are regulated by the Law Society) and barristers (who are regulated by the Bar Council).

As a general rule, solicitors work in private practice (that is to say, for a firm of solicitors) or in-house (that is to say, as part of a legal team providing advice to their employer's group) or as part of an organisation providing advice to its members, such as a trade association. In these circumstances the solicitors will almost always be employees.

Barristers, on the other hand, tend to work in "Chambers" (that is to say, as part of a grouping of barristers working together). They are self-employed whether they are junior barristers or Queens Counsel. There is however nothing to stop a barrister being employed by a solicitor's firm as a barrister. In that event they would become employees of the solicitor's firm, although they would still be regulated by the Bar Council.

Solicitors will also have para-legal and trainee solicitors and they will once again invariably be employees.

The position of the partners depends on whether they are an equity partner, a fixed share partner or a salaried partner. Only the last category are employees. The other two are self-employed though, unlike barristers, they work in partnership.

There is at present no debate in this country on these distinctions.

Solicitors are regulated by codes of conduct which are issued by the Law Society. Solicitors are also officers of the court and as such have certain responsibilities over their conduct. There is no conflict between their responsibilities as officers of the court and their responsibilities as employees. If, for example, they were asked to do something improper by a client, then they must decline to do so; otherwise they could lose their licence to practice as well as their job.

2.1.2 Denmark

Associates and trainees are generally employees, partners are generally self-employed.

2.1.3 Germany

Trainees are employed as government officials for the duration of their 24 months traineeship. They are paid by the state. If they succeed in passing their second exam they are able to become a judge or a lawyer. Training in a private law firm is only one small part of the whole traineeship. (Sometimes - but it is not compulsory - trainees get additional payment if they are working as part of a trainee program within a private law firm, without having the status of an employee.)

The status of the associates is generally open. Following the change of government in 1998 there is a new law placing "apparently self-employed" people (who are not, in reality, self-employed) inside the employees social security system which is causing high financial contributions to be paid out in social insurance for both parties – the law firm and the associate. The new rule aims to provide social protection to "apparently self-employed" people as well as filling the system's cash boxes.

Since that new law nearly all of the medium and big law firms in Germany have put associates under the status of employees (as many of them had already done before anyway). Only a few very small units dare to argue with the officials (to keep the self-employed status) whereas medium and big law firms do not want to run that risk.

The debate was vociferous in 1999 and 2000 but is presently calming down.

Partners who are shareholders of the law firm are self-employed and are not employees. (Even so, it remains possible for lawyers to become salaried partners.)

2.1.4 *The Netherlands*

Associates and trainees are employees within the law firms. Partners are self-employed. This is a simple application of the rules governing the employment contract (the "line of subordination").

2.2 Group B: all or most of the lawyers are self-employed

2.2.1 *Belgium and Italy*

Lawyers are only self-employed in countries such as Belgium and Italy. Apart from a recent case in Belgium, there are no significant discussions on this issue. The reason for this self-employed scenario is the same in all the countries concerned: it is a heritage from the time when lawyers used to work alone, in their own practice and it is linked to the high degree of independence requested (by law, by ethical rules etc.) from these people.

In Italy all the lawyers are considered self-employed even if they work in an international law firm, and there is currently no debate on this matter.

2.2.2 *Luxembourg*

The lawyers generally work as self-employed persons, even within law firms. However lawyers can have the status of employees according to the "rules of the Luxembourg Bar". There the question of lawyer "independence" concerns the relationship with other professions or functions and not the relationship among lawyers. There is no current debate on this issue.

2.2.3 *Spain*

In Spain most of the lawyers are self-employed, however there are some international law firms where all the lawyers are salaried (trainees, associates, etc). Nowadays, there is no debate on this issue. The independence requested from a lawyer is compatible with the fact that he or she is an employee.

2.2.4 *France*

In France, until the start of the 1990's, two professions coexisted: judicial adviser and lawyer. The former could be salaried while the latter was self-employed. There were a number of cases in the 70's and 80's where the judges re-qualified the relationship between an independent associate and his firm in an employment contract. In 1977 a law was passed to reinforce the idea that a lawyer may not be salaried. But this law did not stop the growing movement that was emanating from both the court and some legal authors who thought that there was no incompatibility between an employment contract and the exercise of a liberal profession.

The fusion of the two professions enacted by the law of 31 December 1990 brought with it the introduction of the "salaried lawyer".

This law and the subsequent decree of 27 November 1991 leaves the choice open for lawyers to have either employee or self-employed status.

Indeed, it was written in the law that the "line of subordination", the base element of any employment contract, is solely restricted to the work conditions. This was the means used by parliament to protect the independence of the lawyer, even if he or she was working as salaried lawyer. This restriction means in effect that the lawyer benefits, in the exercise of his entrusted assignments, from the independence contained in his oath.

However, the question of knowing which points are actually covered by the idea of work conditions remains a delicate one because time and time again one is having to go against the common law of contracts in order to respect the independence of the profession. In other words, labour law is often considered to be in conflict with the professional code of practice. For some this means that a new reform is needed to institute a special contract (neither an employment contract, nor self- employment) for the associate lawyers.

The law of 1990 further specifies that the conflicts arising from a lawyer's employment contract be subject to the arbitration of the President of the Bar with possible recourse to the Appeal Court.

This subordination is, in law, underlined by the fact that it is forbidden for the salaried lawyer to have private clients. The presence or absence of private clientele has already become the discerning factor in the mind of many for determining if there is an employment contract or a contract of collaboration. But it is necessary to remember that this is not the sole criterion. The court decisions after 1991 confirm this to be the case (the judges having of course preserved their power to re-qualify a work relationship).

The number of salaried staff has not exploded after the reform of 1990, far from it in fact.

In practice there are only about 4.000 salaried lawyers in France (out of a total of 30.000 lawyers - figures from 1999), who are to be found, for the most part, in the former judicial advice companies that, due to their origin, have become law firms while preserving the salaried status. This is indeed what happened for example at an important employment law firm, which began as a firm of advisers wherein each jurist was salaried, and which is now an important law firm employing more than 160 salaried lawyers. It is important to underline that here even the partners are salaried, a position which they hold together with that of being shareholders (the concept of the "salaried manager"). This particular firm, for reasons essentially linked to the business culture, wanted to preserve a single status for all lawyers, including partners. None of them have "private clients" (as it is taken for granted that you must have one, in order to be a self-employed lawyer).

In France we find a similar line of departure as in the UK: the salaried staff adapt better to the role of giving advice, the salaried lawyers are found in the big consulting firms. The continuation of an independent contract of collaboration is often to be found among those who plead in the courts.

(Sources: R. MARTIN, "Avocats: De collaboration en Salariat", *JCP-semaine juridique Entreprises et Affaires,* 21 January 1999, p. 119; J. BARTHELEMY, obs. under Cass. 8 March 2000, *Droit Social,* May 2000, p. 548)

3 THE CHALLENGES

The question of qualification is, of course, important for the lawyer who considers himself employed: The proven existence of a work contract will allow he or she to benefit from the agreed protection for employees in areas such as breach of contract, remuneration etc. (although in multinational firms, lawyers are under the shelter of financial need).

Certain lawyers may have other objectives in view, such as, for example, the question of their civil responsibility. Even the partners of very large firms could wish for protection at this level, not being invited to participate in the strategic choices and decisions taken by the management of the firm or by certain colleagues and therefore not wishing to be co-responsible.

On the firm's side, having the possibility to employ salaried lawyers may be a way to harmonise the individual statuses of their lawyers across the world and allow them not only to organise but also to really manage their work.

3.1 Evolution

3.1.1. The question of an international harmonisation (towards a generalised salaried status) does not raise passionate debates. This is probably because, in practice, all the players are globally satisfied with the existing national situations. Any attempt to develop the regimes is normally the result of individuals acting within a particular context, as was the case in Belgium which led to the decision of 8 December 2000.

Thus the Anglo-Saxon firms, however used they may be to having salaried lawyers, may have a purely financial interest in preserving the status quo in countries where lawyers are still independent, as in Belgium or Italy. They thus reduce the overhead costs by avoiding the social charges and the heavier taxes levied on those salaried.

In all probability, the question will only be raised in multinational firms that are looking to implement an equal and uniform application of internal rules (notably linked to work methods or to systems of compensation) before any financial considerations.

From the lawyers' point of view, reactions remain isolated. There are no collective claims arising in the countries of group B. Those who work in multinational firms are certainly happy with their lot and appear to find themselves in a financial situation which is not pushing them to react. And yet without doubt, there is a tendency to remain discreet in order to facilitate a possible transfer to another firm. The careers of lawyers remain (and the incessant to-ings and fro-ings of transfers among the large Anglo-Saxon firms prove it) very individualistic.

3.1.2. The difference in status from country to country is clearly not without risk for the larger firms who by means of their quasi-exclusive Anglo-Saxon origin, are used to having salaried lawyers and naturally behave themselves as employers even in countries such as Belgium. All their acts, documents, memos and customs, could the case arising, turn against them in the context of a judicial procedure initiated by a local lawyer. This is true since, generally, the line of subordination can readily be revealed by the facts and the daily working out of the work relationship (whatever the possibly signed contract terms). It is perhaps the accrued presence of these large firms in the countries of the second group who are going to agitate for development, either consciously, or simply as a result of their employer's behaviour (and the increase of judicial procedures aimed at obtaining the requalification).

This being so, every development towards the generalisation of the salaried status is delicate and certainly not without risk. There will always be a plurality of statuses: it is quite impossible to ensure by law that all the lawyers are to be independent (there is always a possible re-qualification) in the same way that it is impossible to decree that all are to be salaried (no profession is integrally subjected to a single status). The best way forward is perhaps to be satisfied with organising the profession, even if it means splitting it into two categories as in the UK. This will assure the lawyers who plead in court that they have a greater independence and that those who only advise, that they are allowed to be salaried.

3.2 Incidence of international regulation

The directive 98/5/EC of the European Parliament and of the Council dated 16 February 1998, which voted to facilitate, on a permanent basis, the practice of the profession of lawyer within a Member State other than that in which the qualification was obtained, refers to the coexistence of the two statuses across Europe.

Article 8, named "Salaried practice" states too that: "A lawyer registered in a host Member State under his national professional title may practise as a salaried lawyer in the employment of another lawyer, or an association or firm of lawyers, or a public or private enterprise to the extent that the host Member State so permits it for lawyers registered under the professional title used in that State".

In other words, this means that lawyers covered by the Directive, whether salaried or self-employed in their home Member State, may practise as salaried lawyers in the host Member State, where that Member State offers that possibility to its own lawyers.

This is recognition of a possible co-existence between both statuses. And perhaps it goes even further. Indeed, what good is it to strongly defend the independent status in Belgium if the same person can exercise the same profession simultaneously in France or in the Netherlands under the status of a local employee?

The Lawyers' Directive is not a regulation, and therefore relies on the national legislatures of Member States to create and implement laws. There are still some difficulties in the implementation in some countries (The Commission decided earlier this year to make a case against France, Ireland and Spain)

3.3 MDPs

Here, perhaps, lies the real question, as up until now, in talking of multinational firms, we have been dealing with homogenous groups of lawyers: a group of employees in the Netherlands and a group of independents in Belgium, for example. With the possible integration of other traditionally salaried professions (such as consultants) at the heart of the same legal structure in the same country, the situation will be different and certainly more delicate.

4 CONCLUSION

A status quo will certainly remain in most of the countries concerned within the short/mid term period. There are no significant current moves from either the firms or the lawyers in the direction of a general harmonisation and an exclusive use of the salaried status. The EU directive could help make things more uniform, but it is too recently implemented to allow us to say this. The debate on the MDPs could be another "angle of attack" for a generalisation of the salaried lawyer. There is still the possibility of having a political decision on this, with a change being initiated by the government of one of the countries concerned.

But one day the salaried lawyer will certainly be a reality in all the European countries. It is just a matter of time, like many other evolutions of the profession (on ethics, marketing and promotion, management...) where the continental countries were influenced by the model of the Anglo-Saxon firms. We have seen that only a very few countries continue not to recognise the salaried lawyer. (In our study, only Belgium and Italy.)

THE LAW FIRM: A CHOICE FOR A FULL INTEGRATED EXERCISE OF THE LEGAL PROFESSION IN ORDER TO MEET THE HIGH QUALITY STANDARDS IMPOSED BY CLIENTS

Dirk Van Gerven, Partner NautaDutilh, Member of the Brussels and New York Bars, Director of the Institute for Formation of Lawyers of the Brussels Dutch-speaking Bar, Former member of the Council of the Brussels Dutch-speaking Bar, Research Fellow Jan Ronse Institute Law Faculty of the University of Louvain

1 PURPOSE OF THIS REPORT

1. This report discusses the legal framework available to Belgian law firms, and discusses the advantages and disadvantages of opting for a partnership.

It will also touch on the types of internal organisation available to law firms under Belgian law.

2 INTRODUCTION

2. Belgium, like other Latin speaking or influenced countries, has traditionally been adverse to large law firms. The legal profession was long exercised by individual lawyers who are not supposed to work together.

Initially, partnerships were prohibited because contrary to the personal relation that prevails in the contact with the client.[1] In the 1930's legal authors started to argue that lawyers should be entitled to work together in a partnership. This resulted in the creation of the first law firms in the beginning of the 1950's. Opposition continued to exist against international law firms with partners of foreign Bars. But the 1960's were also the start of changing of mentality in this respect, and slowly it was generally accepted that Belgian lawyers could be part of partnerships with lawyers of other countries.[2]

3. The Belgian landscape of law firms has been in turmoil for several years. Large foreign and especially U.K. law firms are looking to expand into continental Europe.

This trend is not new. Back in the 1960's, U.S. and other European firms came to Brussels in order to be close to the European Commission with a view to practising European law. However the particularity of the current

---

1 PANDECTES BELGES, "Règles et usages de l'Ordre des Avocats en Belgique", 1940, nr. 1837; J. STEVENS, *Regels en gebruiken van de advocatuur te Antwerpen*, Antwerp, Kluwer, 1997, 495.

2 See W. VAN GERVEN, "Pleidooi voor multilaterale Europese advocatenkantoren", *R.W.* 1969-1970, 1953.

trend is that the expansion is not solely been organised through setting up branches in Belgium, but has taken the form of taking over entire departments of larger Belgian firms and even in some cases taking over an entire Belgian firm. In this latter case, the take-overs have been accompanied with dismissing Belgian lawyers or encouraging Belgian partners to leave the Belgian firm which the foreign firm intends to take over in order to keep only the most profitable partners.

This trend is only starting and will continue for several years. It will result in a complete reorganisation of the Belgian legal market. Examining the reasons, the methods and the implications of these "take-overs", however tempting it may be, is not the object of this contribution. Nevertheless, it may be worth looking at the near future, as this may be important for the type of legal structure Belgian firms may wish to choose.

4. The current trend of take-overs has been focused mainly on larger Belgian firms. Indeed for several years Belgian firms have been looking for forms of close co-operation with foreign firms in order to better serve international clients, which have activities in several countries, and to be able to compete with large U.S. firms with branches throughout the world. As a result larger Belgian firms have merged with European continental firms from The Netherlands and France and have established forms of co-operation with other European firms, including U.K. firms.

Recently, U.K. firms have decided to set up branches in other European countries in order to offer international groups and credit institutions an international service in the fields they practice. Where in the beginning they limited themselves to creating branches and attracting Belgian lawyers (or other European lawyers) in order to be able to offer advice on national law, they quickly started to examine the possibility of attracting high profile partners from local firms, and take over entire departments of larger local firms. In order to do so they offered high remunerations, which inevitably resulted in higher fees being charged to Belgian based clients.

This expansion policy of U.K. firms has already changed the Belgian market for larger law firms. We are growing to two types of larger firms. The first type is the international U.K. firm which focuses on specific fields of the law which are highly profitable (*e.g.*, mergers and acquisition; corporate and finance). The second type is the local or continental firm which offers a larger range of services at lower hourly rates.[3] Typical for the continental firms is that they are the result of a merger of Belgian firms with Dutch or Luxem-

3 Mr R. Nieuwdorp has, in a press interview, qualified these firms "relatiekantoren", *i.e.*, firms which offer an overall service in order to assist companies in all stages of their development (*De Standaard* of 12 September 2001, p. 19).

bourg firms. The larger local and continental firms seek to service international clients by using a network of best friends, which are local firms of high quality in other countries. The future will show whether a third type of larger firms can exist in Belgium, *i.e.* the international integrated group of European firms which to a certain extent keep their independence with respect to culture and remuneration of the partners; in such cases the integration relates to the quality of the work, the integrated offer of services and work.

In the field of larger firms, the U.S. firms still have to react to the new foreign policy of the larger U.K. firms. It may be expected that in the further integration of the European market, U.S. firms may seek to co-operate more closely with or take over local firms or merge with U.K. firms.

5. Besides the larger firms, which in reality constitute a minority of the law firms in Belgium, a large number of smaller or mid-sized firms exists. They can be divided into several categories:

a) The fully integrated law firm (see below) which tends to offer an overall service to clients, through specialised partners, *i.e.* by attributing cases to the partner considered the specialist for the type of matter. This type of firm tends to grow to become a larger firm. A fully integrated firm is defined - for the purposes of this report - as a firm in which fees are invoiced by the firm, and distributed to the partners, after payment of costs (including associate remuneration), in a manner which does not solely depend on the turnover of each partner. It will be explained hereafter that in my opinion, a not fully integrated firm cannot in practice develop as a larger firm in which cases are allocated to relevant specialised lawyers.

b) The specialised firm which works in a clearly defined niche.

c) The integrated firm in which several lawyers work together in order to practice the legal profession, and in which they seek to assist each other in their legal practice. The partners of this firm do not attribute cases on basis of their speciality.

d) The non-integrated firm in which several lawyers work together to share costs.

e) The individual lawyer. The individual lawyer works of course for his own account, and does not need to set up a legal entity. However, he may choose to create a company, such as the single person company. One of the reasons to set up a company, is taxation: a company benefits from the lower corporate tax rate. As regards the type of company, he has no choice. He will have to choose for the *société privée à responsabilité limitée*, which can be set up by a single person.[4]

3 DEFINITION OF THE LAW FIRM

6. A law firm is generally defined as a partnership of lawyers who decide to exercise the legal profession through a partnership. This implies that the lawyers who work in the partnership, as partners or associates, exercise the legal profession on behalf and for the account of the partnership.

Under Belgian law, the partnership of lawyers is considered a profit sharing organisation governed by the Companies Code. It is a contract between two or more lawyers with the intention to exercise the legal profession together in order to make profits to be distributed among the partners.[5] The lawyers who founded the partnership, and those who join the partnership afterwards and receive profits upon distribution, are partners. Other lawyers who work for the partnership and are paid a fee or remuneration, are considered associates.

Associates are considered self-employed under Belgian law. However, recently the Brussels labour law tribunal held that associates in a larger firm, who work fixed hours and under continuous supervision of the partners, should be qualified employees.[6] As a consequence, the termination of their contract is governed by the Act of 3 July 1978 on employment contracts. An appeal has been filed against this court decision. It is too early to asset the implications of this decision, which goes against the traditional independence of the legal profession. Article 437 of the Judicial Code, which provides that the legal profession is not compatible with employment under authority unless it does not prejudice the independence of the lawyer nor the reputation of the bar, applies only to employment outside the legal profession.[7]

7. The partnership has no legal personality. It is considered a contract governed by the rules applicable to the contract of partnership, *i.e.*, Articles 18 to 22 of the Companies Code.

Although the rules differ from Bar to Bar, it is generally accepted that partners can incorporate the partnership in a company with legal personality. The Belgian National Bar[8] has limited the choice to the *société en nom collectif*

---

4 Art. 211 of the Belgian Code on Companies.

5 See Article 1 of the Code on Companies.

6 Labour law tribunal Brussels, 8 December 2000.

7 A. BRAUN and F. MOREAU, *La profession d'avocat*, Brussel, Bruylant, 1985, 37-38.

8 The National Bar will be replaced by the Bar of Flemish Bars and the Bar of French-speaking and Germanspeaking Bars, in accordance with the law of 4 July 2001 (Belgian Official Gazette of 25 July 2001). See F. GLANSDORFF, "La loi de réforme des structures

(SNC) or *vennootschap onder firma (VOF)*, the *société coopérative* (*SC*) or *coop-eratieve vennootschap (CV)*, and the *société privée à responsabilité limitée* (*SPRL*) or *besloten vennootschap met beperkte aansprakelijkheid* (*BVBA*).[9] This will be examined hereafter.

8. When lawyers set up a partnership to exercise their profession in common, the profession is, exercised by the partnership for its own account. The partners do not exercise the legal profession; it is the partnership that does, and should therefore be considered as the lawyer. The regulations of the Brussels Bars qualify this partnership as an integrated firm, as opposed to a grouping of lawyers.[10]

The incorporation of an integrated law firm has several legal implications. First, when a client does not pay its fees, only the partnership is entitled to sue the client for payment. A claim initiated by one of the partners is inadmissible.[11]

Second, any contract relating to the business of the law firm has to be entered into by the partnership, and therefore by its legal representatives, in accordance with the Articles of association of the partnership. This will depend on the legal form that the partnership has chosen.

Third, partners who exercise a part of their legal profession outside of the partnership, without the authorisation of the partnership, could be sued for unfair competition. Indeed the partners will actively manage the partnership and exercise their profession through the partnership. They will be managing partners, or managers of the partnership. Any competition against the partnership would constitute a breach of the duties of trust towards the partnership.[12]

The Belgian Bars do not recognise the fact that the partnership exercises the legal profession. They do not list the partnerships as lawyers besides the individual lawyers. In this they differ from the Institute of Certified Auditors, which lists audit firms as recognised auditors.

---

du barreau", *J.T.* 2001, 625. The existing regulations of the National Bar will remain in effect until they are replaced by regulations of the new regional bars (Art. 507 of the Judicial Code, as modified by the law of 4 July 2001).

9 Art. 1 of the National Regulation of 25 May 1972 of the National Bar of Belgium. See also J. STEVENS, *Regels en gebruiken van de advocatuur te Antwerpen*, Antwerp, Kluwer, 1997, 510.

10 Art. 283 and 284 of the Deontologische regels en huishoudelijk reglement of the Dutch-speaking Brussels Bar; Art. 85 and 86 of the Nouveau règlement d'ordre intérieur of the French-speaking Brussels Bar.

11 Justice of the Peace of Brugge, 27 April 1992, *T.B.R.* 1992/1, 45.

12 Comp. J. RONSE, *Algemeen deel van het vennootschapsrecht*, Leuven, Acco, 1975, 451; D. VAN GERVEN, "Gezamenlijke vennootschappen: vennootschapsrechtelijke aspecten van joint ventures", *R.D.C.* 1995, 123.

9. Integrated partnerships should be distinguished from cost sharing partnerships.[13] The cost sharing partnership does not exercise the legal profession. It is set up in order to share costs related to the exercise of the legal profession, or to manage a common infrastructure.

Lawyers may wish to set up a cost sharing partnership to acquire a common building, or to rent premises together in order to organise their offices, or to acquire a common library, and in general to manage the offices together: a common reception, secretary, telephone connection, etc.

A cost sharing partnership is not a law firm, as the lawyers exercise their profession as individuals in their own name and for their own account. They remain independent of each other, and represent as many law offices as there are lawyers.

Cost sharing partnerships may be set up as a company with legal personality. These can be set up under the form of any type of company, including an economic interest grouping (EIG). As a cost sharing partnership is not a law firm, it will not be further examined in this report.

However, it should be noted that the partners of a cost sharing partnership should be careful not to create the impression with third parties, such as their clients or creditors, that they practice the legal profession in common. If this is the case, the third parties may consider that a "professional" partnership has been created among the partners. This could be interesting in the event of professional liability, *e.g.* if the lawyer who has been negligent is insolvent. In such event the prejudiced client may sue the other lawyers also in respect of an equal share. In general, the partners of a partnership bare an equal share of liability towards third parties which have a claim resulting form working with the partnership.[14]

10. Besides integrated law firms, and cost sharing partnerships, lawyers can also set up networks of preferential referral, also qualified as *organieke correspondentie* or *correspondance organique*.[15] The members of the network undertake to refer clients under certain conditions (*e.g.*, they have too much work, or do not have the know-how to handle the case) to the other mem-

---

[13] See with respect to the Dutch-speaking Brussels Bar: E. BOYDENS, "Associaties en groeperingen: wat is het verschil?", *Informatieblad of the Dutch-speaking Brussels Bar* 2001-2002, 329.

[14] Art. 52 of the Code on Companies. As a law firm is not a commercial business under the Code of Commerce, the law does not provide for a joint liability which applies to commercial partnerships (Art. 52 of the Code on Companies).

[15] Art. 285 of the Deontologische regels en huishoudelijk reglement of the Dutch-speaking Brussels Bar; Art. 96 of the Nouveau règlement d'ordre intérieur of the French-speaking Brussels Bar.

bers of the network, instead of refusing the work or referring to another law firm.

The network is not a partnership as the members neither exercise the profession in common nor share the costs of their practices.

The names of the lawyers forming part of the network may be mentioned on the letter heading of the members of the network. The network may also have its own name.[16]

4 DEFINITION OF THE INTEGRATED FIRM

11. The integrated firm implies that the partners have decided to exercise the legal profession through the firm (see nr 8).

The firm is fully integrated if the partners integrate their entire legal profession in the law firm, and the profits are distributed in accordance with the rules laid down in the Articles of association. It is only partly integrated if (i) only a part of the legal profession of the partners is exercised through the law firm, or if only certain defined fields of law are exercised in the firm, and (ii) only part of the total revenues is distributed in accordance with the rules laid down in the Articles of association.[17] How the profits are distributed is not decisive for the degree of integration; the only requirement is that the distribution of the profits resulting from the common legal practice is effected within the firm in accordance with the rules laid down in the Articles of association of the firm. This requirement is embedded in the qualification of the firm as partnership.[18]

The ethical rules applicable to fully and partly integrated law firms are identical. Indeed in both cases the firms are integrated, but in the latter case, the integration is limited to part of the legal profession. An example of the latter is a group of lawyers who decide to join forces for the practice of employment law as they all have individual clients looking for a team of employment law specialists. They set up a law firm in which they together exercise employment law and engage associates to assist them. Services in other fields of the law are provided outside the law firm. This type of firm is rather exceptional.

Finally, lawyers authorised to plead in civil cases before the Belgian Supreme Court (the *Hof van Cassatie* or *Cour de cassation*) exercise a ministry

---

16 Art. 302 of the Deontologische regels en huishoudelijk reglement of the Dutch-speaking Brussels Bar; Art. 102 of the Nouveau règlement d'ordre intérieur of the French-speaking Brussels Bar.

17 Art. 283 of the Deontologische regels en huishoudelijk reglement of the Dutch-speaking Brussels Bar.

18 And follows from Art. 1 of the Code on Companies.

which is granted by Royal Decree. This grant is personal, and therefore not to the integrated partnership. It must be kept outside the partnership.[19] This rule, which follows from the personal character of the function of lawyer admitted to the Belgian Supreme Court, does not prevent the pooling of fees resulting from the cases handled by such lawyer, and the contribution of such fees in accordance with the rules laid down in the Articles of association of the partnership.

12. Integration can also be defined on basis of the manner in which the profits are distributed among the partners. Profit distribution in law firms is generally effected in two ways: payment of fees to the partners in their capacity as working partner, or payment of net profits (dividends) to the partners in their capacity of partner. In law firms all partners are also working partners, as they are involved in the business of the firm. The payment of fees is tax deductible in hands of the partnership. The distribution of dividends is made after taxation, and comes out of the net profits.

Partners are in general free to determine the manner in which the profits resulting from the common exercise of the legal profession are distributed. However, as the profits are profits of the law firm, the distribution of the profits should be effected by the firm in accordance with the rules agreed among the partners. This distribution is laid down in the Articles of association or in an internal regulation. In the same manner associates and employees of the firm are paid by the firm, as they are employed by the firm.

As regards the manner in which profits are distributed, a firm is fully integrated if the fees invoiced by the firm are distributed to the partners, after payment of costs (including the remuneration of associates), in a manner which does not solely depend on the turnover of each partner. From this definition it results that a firm is not fully integrated if (i) the remuneration of associates is paid by each partner depending on whether such partner works with such associate, and/or (ii) the fees, after deduction of costs, are completely or mainly distributed in accordance with the turnover.

When a firm is not fully integrated (within the latter meaning), it will be difficult if not impossible to develop a full service firm in which cases are allocated to the specialised partner. As the turnover of each partner will determine his part in the distribution of the profits, each partner will tend to keep cases which generate important fees for himself even if one of his partners is better placed to serve the client in this case.

The obligation for partners to pay the associates he uses from his personal share, will encourage him not to use associates, or to create a group of asso-

---

19 Art. 293(1) of the Deontologische regels en huishoudelijk reglement of the Dutch-speaking Brussels Bar.

ciates around him with whom he enters into an agreement as regards the remuneration of the associates (which results in creating a firm within the firm).

The situation is of course different for a "niche" firm, which consists of partners with the same practice or speciality. In such event the cases are handled by the partners contacted or, alternatively, requested by the client.

13. An example of a fully integrated firm is the firm in which partners are paid an equal share in the profits, combined with a lock-step system for younger partners. This system is based on 100 points, in which 100-point partners earn an equal part of the profits. Beginning partners start at a lower number of points, and receive additional points for each year of partnership until they have 100 points and thus receive the same share of profits as the other 100-point partners.

This system supposes that all partners achieve a similar turnover, or that partners who do not, contribute other assets to the firm, such as management skills or clients.

14. The incorporation of the law firm as a legal entity may be helpful in creating an integrated firm. A legal entity will facilitate the creation of an institution which is intended to survive its founding partners. Many firms do not survive the founding partners because the latter do not invest in the creation of an integrated firm which will continue to operate after their departure.

However, the incorporation of a partnership with legal personality is certainly not decisive, as the integration will in reality depend on the rules agreed among the partners, and laid down in the articles of association or the internal regulations.

Nevertheless, the choice of the most appropriate corporate form may be helpful in creating an integrated firm, in which partners and associates feel that the firm operates as a business of people, and not as a firm around a few partners.

5 LEGAL CORPORATE FORMS AVAILABLE TO BELGIAN LAW FIRMS

15. It is generally accepted that a Belgian law firm can be incorporated in the corporate form of a société en nom collectif (SNC) or vennootschap onder firma (VOF), a société coopérative (SC) or coöperatieve vennootschap (CV), and a société privée à responsabilité limitée (SPRL) or besloten vennootschap met beperkte aansprakelijkheid (BVBA). The shares can only be held by lawyers.

The above corporate forms are allowed by the National Regulation of 8 March 1990 on the exercise of the legal profession in co-operation.[20] This Regulation does not permit the creation of legal entities of another corporate form, such a *naamloze vennootschap* or *société anonyme*. However, this National Regulation only applies to partnerships with lawyers who are member of at least two Bars.[21] It does not apply to a partnership between lawyers of the same Bar. This follows from Article 1 of this Regulation which explicitly refers to co-operation between lawyers admitted to several Bars.[22] This is in accordance with the limited tasks of the National Bar, which was charged with establishing unified rules for relations between lawyers admitted to several Bars.[23]

It is of course possible not to create one of the above companies, and exercise the legal profession in a partnership without legal personality. Lawyers who work together in their legal practice will by law form a partnership governed by the rules applicable to partnerships.[24] In a partnership, each partner bears unlimited liability for the obligations of the partnership.[25] However, as the law firm is not a commercial business, the liability is not joint. Each partner is therefore liable for an equal part. In consequence if an unpaid creditor wishes to sue the partnership[26], he will have to sue all the partners in order to obtain full payment. If he sues only half of the partners, he will only recover half of his claim. In the event that some of the partners are insolvent, the creditor is not entitled to recover their part on the other partners liable to pay the creditor's claim. However, the partners can agree with the creditor otherwise, and for example contractually stipulate joint liability for the payment of the obligation.[27]

16. Traditionally the legal profession cannot be exercised in a *naamloze vennootschap* or *société anonyme* ("NV"). The reason is the capitalist nature of such a company, *i.e.* in a NV the intention to gather capital takes precedence over the identity of the shareholders. This capitalist nature results in the

---

20 Art. 1 of the National Regulation of 8 March 1990 of the National Bar of Belgium.

21 See the preliminary statements of the National Regulation of 8 March 1990, which indicate clearly that the Regulation only seeks to regulate partnerships between lawyers of different bars; L. VANHEESWIJCK, "Enkele vragen over advocatenvennootschappen en een poging tot antwoord", *Informatieblad of the Dutch-speaking Brussels Bar* 1999-2000, 45; See also D. VAN GERVEN, "Kan een stagiair vennoot zijn in een advocatenvennootschap?", to be published in one of the following issues of *Poelaertplein*.

22 The other Articles of this Regulation refer also to the intervention of the Council or the Stafhouder or Bâtonnier of several Bars, for approval and solution of litigation.

23 See Art. 494 of the Belgian Judicial Code.

24 Artt. 18 through 55 of the Code on Companies.

25 Art. 52 of the Code on Companies.

26 He cannot sue the partnership as it does not exist as a legal entity.

27 Brussels 8 November 1999, *R.P.S.* 2000, nr. 6805, p. 155.

freedom to transfer shares to third parties, and the anonymous character of the shareholding. In consequence it is also possible to issue bearer shares, which makes control over the identity of the shareholders impossible or at least more difficult. Thus, there is no certainty as to whether all shares are held by lawyers. For these reasons the National Bar has opposed the use of the NV as corporate form for a law firm. This is unlikely to change in the near future. Most local Bars also prohibit the use of the NV.[28]

However, a NV can be closely held, if the Articles of association require that the shares be in registered form, and cannot be changed into bearer shares. Furthermore, the Articles of association may contain transfer restrictions, which render the uncontrolled transfer of shares impossible. Sure, rendering the transfer of shares impossible is contrary to the nature of the NV; any clause to such effect is null and void.[29] But this rule only seeks to ensure that a shareholder can leave the company by selling his shares. It is therefore valid to provide that if a shareholder wishes to leave the company, the other shareholders are required to purchase, or propose a third party to purchase, the shares of such shareholder.

The Dutch-speaking Brussels Bar has therefore explicitly stated that lawyers can form a NV provided the shares are in registered form.[30] But the choice of an NV is limited to partnerships consisting of exclusively lawyers admitted to the Dutch-speaking Brussels Bar.

17. In any event, even if a NV is created, only lawyers can be a partner in the NV. Non-lawyers are not allowed to become a partner.

It is unclear why law firms should not be able to attract capital by investment in shares. To the extent that the third party investors do not manage the company, and do not intervene in the exercise of the legal profession by the company, there is no reason to prevent third parties which are not lawyers from investing by underwriting share capital. Guarantees against the third party investor intervening in management of the firm can be created by prohibitions to that effect in the Articles of association. Furthermore, the necessary guarantees should be made to safeguard professional secrecy. The third party investor should of course be able to veto certain decisions relating to investment by the firm in certain types of assets if this were to affect his investment. This situation, however, does not differ from the case where

---

28 Art. 85 of the Nouveau réglement d'ordre intérieur of the French-speaking Brussels Bar; Chapter 4 of the Codex of the Antwerp Bar; Art. 3.7.3. of the Deontologische Code of the Bar of Ghent.

29 Art. 510 of the Code on Companies.

30 Art. 286 of the the Deontologische regels en huishoudelijk reglement is drafted in such manner that it does no longer prohibit the use of a NV.

a bank granting a credit to a law firm requires that its prior approval is requested for certain important investments.

18. The choice between one of the available corporate forms with legal personality should be made after careful examination of the advantages and disadvantages of each corporate form. It is therefore useful to summarise briefly the differences between these types of companies.

19. The VOF (*société en nom collectif* or *vennootschap onder firma*)[31] is characterised by the joint and several liability of the partners for all obligations of the company. This includes any professional liability for negligence committed by one of the partners in the exercise of the profession on behalf of the VOF. Clients which suffer damages, sue in tort to obtain reimbursement of these damages from the VOF and from each of the partners, regardless which partner acted negligently. The non-negligent partners will afterwards have to recover their payment from the negligent partner.

The management of the VOF is very flexible. The partners have a large freedom in the organisation of the management.

20. The BVBA (*société privée à responsabilité limitée* or *besloten vennootschap met beperkte aansprakelijkheid*)[32] is a company with limited liability of its partners. It can be incorporated by one founder. Upon incorporation the partners should contribute a minimum capital of 18,600 euros, which should be paid up for 6,200 euros. Shares are in registered form, and entitle the holder to one vote, and an equal share in the profits.[33] This equal distribution of profits in accordance with the number of shares applies of course only to the payment of dividends, and not to the payment of fees to the managing partners (see nr. 12 above). The deed of incorporation must be signed before a notary.

In general, the BVBA is incorporated with the minimum capital required by law. However, the law provides that in the event of bankruptcy within three years from incorporation, the court may hold the founders liable for the debts towards the creditors, if the capital upon incorporation was insufficient, to continue the normal business during two years taking into account all financing and expenses which could have foreseen at that time.[34] To this effect the founders should establish a financial plan to justify the capital.[35] However, as a BVBA which exercises the legal profession does not operate a

---

31 Governed by Artt. 201 through 209 of the Code on Companies.

32 Artt. 210 through 349 of the Code on Companies.

33 Artt. 232 and 239 of the Code on Companies.

34 Art. 229, 5° of the Code on Companies.

35 Art. 215 of the Code on Companies.

commercial business, it cannot be declared bankrupt. In consequence this founders' liability does not apply.

Unless the Articles of association provide otherwise, third party creditors cannot sue the partners for the obligations of the BVBA. This rule also applies to professional negligence.

The management of the BVBA is delegated to a manager or several individually acting managers, or a board of managers which decides by majority unless otherwise provided in the Articles of association. If there is a board of managers, the Articles of association may provide that the BVBA can be represented towards third parties by one or a defined number of managers (the single, double or multiple signature clause).

21. The CV (*société coopérative* or *cooperatieve vennootschap*)[36] must have at least three partners. The CV has a capital which consists of a fixed and a variable part. The fixed part of the capital can only be changed by a modification of the Articles of association; the variable part changes in function of the admission and departure of partners. The shares are in registered form.[37] Each share entitles the holder to the rights as defined in the Articles of association. If the rights are not defined, each share entitles its holder to an equal share in the profits.[38]

It can be incorporated with limited liability or with unlimited liability. If the CV has unlimited liability, the partners bear unlimited and joint liability for the obligations of the company. This may have important consequences as regards professional liability (see nr 19 above with respect to the VOF).

If the CV is incorporated with limited liability, the partners are not liable for the obligations of the CV unless otherwise provided. In this event, the founders must contribute a capital of at least 18,600 euros, which should be paid up for 6,200 euros. The same obligation of sufficient capital provided for the BVBA applies to the CV with limited liability.[39] The deed of incorporation must be signed before a notary.

The partners can organise management in the Articles of association as they wish. If nothing has been provided, the CV is managed by one director, to be appointed by the Partners' meeting.[40]

---

36 Artt. 350 through 436 of the Code on Companies.

37 Art. 356 of the Code on Companies.

38 *I.e.*, an equal part in the dividends. The distribution of profits in the form of fees to the managing partners, is not a distribution of dividends sensu stricto (see nr. 12 above).

39 See nr. 20; the regulation applicable to the CV is laid down in art. 405, 5° of the Code on Companies. The obligation of a financial plan is laid down in art. 391 of the Code on Companies.

40 Art. 378 of the Code on Companies.

22. At the Dutch-speaking Brussels Bar, lawyers can incorporate a law firm in an NV, provided that all shares are in registered form, and all shares are held by lawyers of the Dutch-speaking Brussels Bar. Title to shares in registered form is established by registration in the share register of the NV, held at the offices of the NV.

The minimum capital of the NV is 62,000 euros, fully paid up upon incorporation. The NV must be incorporated before a notary. The shares must be held by two shareholders. If the shares are held by one shareholder as a result of acquisition of the shares of the other shareholders, such shareholder will have to transfer at least one share to another person or convert the company into a BVBA within one year. Afterwards he becomes jointly liable for all obligations of the NV created after the date on which he acquired all shares, until a second shareholder holds shares.[41]

The NV is managed by a Board of Directors consisting of three directors; it may be composed of two directors, if the shares are held by not more than two shareholders.[42] Daily management can be entrusted to a managing director or an executive committee operating under the supervision of the Board of Directors.

6 USE OF FOREIGN LEGAL CORPORATE FORMS

23. Belgian lawyers can join a foreign law firm. In general, and unless a special agreement with the bar of lawyers which is competent for such foreign law firm provides otherwise, the co-operation with a foreign law firm requires the prior authorisation of the Council of the Bar.[43] If such a law firm is located outside the European Union, it is furthermore required that the foreign lawyers are part of a legal or professional organisation which is recognised by the National Bar.[44] This condition is imposed to ascertain that the foreign lawyers are part of bar which has a minimum of ethical rules which guarantee the independence, discretion and reputation of the legal profession and professional secrecy.[45]

The possibility for Belgian lawyers to join a foreign law firm which is entitled to exercise the legal profession with professionals who are not lawyers, is discussed in another report.[46]

---

41 Art. 646 of the Code on companies.

42 Art. 518 of the Code on companies.

43 Art. 7 of the Regulation of the National Bar.

44 Idem.

45 See art. 307 of the Deontologische regels en huishoudelijk reglement of the Dutch-speaking Brussels Bar.

46 With respect thereto, please also refer to art. 308 of the Deontologische regels en hu-

The *Deontologische regels en huishoudelijk reglement* of the Brussels Dutch-speaking Bar require moreover, that the Articles of association of the foreign law firm provide that (i) the foreign lawyers may exercise the legal profession in Belgium through this law firm; (ii) each lawyer who is a partner in the law firm benefits from the independence required for Belgian lawyers; and (iii) the foreign lawyers and the law firm as an entity will comply with the rules of the ethical code of the Belgian bar with respect to matters who relate to co-operation and the exercise of the legal profession in Belgium.[47]

24. It follows that Belgian lawyers can exercise their legal practice in a foreign law firm. In consequence, a Belgian law firm can join a foreign law firm which wishes to operate in Belgium.

Whether the foreign corporate form chosen by the foreign law firm, and to which the Belgian lawyers wish to adhere, is acceptable, will depend on the ethical code of the Bar of which the Belgian lawyers are a member and, to the extent the applicable ethical code does not provide special rules, on the Council of that Bar. In certain countries, foreign law firms can be incorporated as a *naamloze vennootschap* or *société anonyme*. In that event the Council of the Belgian Bar cannot in general oppose the admission of Belgian lawyers to the foreign law firm. It can only do so if such corporate form if used by the foreign law firm in accordance with its ethical rules, is prohibited by the local rules of the Belgian Bar.

As indicated above (nr 21), the *Deontologische regels en huishoudelijk reglement* of the Brussels Dutch-speaking Bar require that the foreign law firm which admits Belgian lawyers who are a member of the Brussels Dutch-speaking Bar, comply with the ethical rules on partnerships. This would imply that such foreign law firms can only be set up in the form of a legal entity which is similar to the corporate forms admitted for partnerships of lawyers under the Regulation of the National Bar of 8 March 1990.[48] In consequence, a foreign *naamloze vennootschap* or *société anonyme* is only admissible if such corporate form under foreign law is similar to the BVBA under Belgian law, and does not constitute a capital driven company as the NV under Belgian law. A Dutch NV is generally considered to be very close as regards structure and management, to the BV (*besloten vennootschap*), with the main dif-

---

ishoudelijk reglement of the Dutch-speaking Brussels Bar.

47 Art. 309. Comp with Art. 11 of Directive 98/5/EC of the European Parliament and of the Council of 16 February 1998 to facilitate practice of the profession of lawyer on a permanent basis in a Member State other than that in which the qualification was obtained, which contains similar rules for foreign partnerships with foreign lawyers who wish to practice in another Member State. This Directive will be implemented in Belgian law; a draft of law is being discussed in Parliament: Parl. Doc. Chamber of Representatives, S. [2000/2001], nr. 1120/005.

48 See nr. 7.

ference being that the shareholding of a BV is closely held by law.[49] But the shareholding of an NV can also be closed by statutory provisions to such effect; in practice this is in most NV, which shares are not publicly traded, the case.

7 RULES APPLICABLE TO BELGIAN LAW FIRMS

7.1 Incorporation

25. Upon incorporation, the Articles of association of a law firm in which one or more Belgian lawyers participate must be approved by the Bar of which such lawyer(s) is (are) a member. In some Bars this prior authorisation is delegated to the President of the Bar (the *Stafhouder* or the *Bâtonnier*).[50]

Afterwards the Bar should be informed of any new partner who is admitted to the law firm. In some Bars, apprentice lawyers (*stagiaires*) can be admitted as partner under certain conditions.[51]

If the authorisation of the Council of more than one Bar is required, the Articles should comply with the most restrictive ethical code.[52]

26. A partnership must choose a name in order for third parties to be able to identify the partnership.[53] Under Belgian corporate law, partnerships have extensive freedom in the choice of a name; there is no obligation to mention the name of the partners or one of them in the corporate name. However, a corporate name should not be confusing with the name of another legal entity.[54]

Traditionally, the names of Belgian law firms include the names of all its partners. The National Regulation prohibits partnerships with partners belonging to different Bars from including names other than the names of

---

49 W.C.L. VAN DER GRINTEN, *Handboek voor de naamloze en de besloten vennootschap*, Tjeenk-Willink, Zwolle, 1989, 46.

50 See art. 293 of the Deontologische regels en huishoudelijk reglement of the Dutch-speaking Brussels Bar.

51 Art. 293(3) of the Deontologische regels en huishoudelijk reglement of the Dutch-speaking Brussels Bar; art. 85 of the Nouveau réglement d'ordre intérieur of the French-speaking Brussels Bar. As explained above, the National Regulation only applies to partnerships with lawyers admitted to several Bars (see nr. 15; D. VAN GERVEN, "Kan een stagiair vennoot zijn in een advocatenvennootchap?", to be published in a following issue of *Poelaertplein*).

52 Art. 10 of the Regulation of the National Bar of 8 March 1990.

53 Art. 65 of the Code on Companies.

54 See D. VAN GERVEN, "Grotere vrijheid in de keuze van de vennootschapsnaam voor de naamloze vennootschap", *T.R.V.* 2001, 125.

partners or retired partners in the corporate name.[55] This rule has been made applicable in most local Bars.[56]

If its corporate name consists of the names of some of its partners, this firm is required to mention the names of all the partners on the letter heading.[57]

However, in the Brussels Bars this is no longer an obligation. The choice of a fantasy name is admissible, subject to approval by the *Stafhouder*[58] or the Council of the Bar.[59] The fantasy name should be in accordance with the dignity of the Bar, and should not be confusing nor refer to professionals who are not lawyers.[60]

However, in these Bars special rules apply if the name of the partners are not all mentioned, or do not form part of the corporate name. In the Dutch-speaking Brussels Bar, the letter heading must state that clients can always request a list of the names of all partners.[61] This rule is in accordance with Article 5 of the Agreement of 6 August 1994 between the American Bar association (ABA) and the Brussels Bars, which entitles U.S. law firms to operate in Belgium and admit Belgian lawyers, without indicating the name of the Belgian lawyers on the letter heading. In the French-speaking Brussels Bar, the names of all partners must be mentioned in the letter heading.[62]

If the names of partners are included in the corporate name, the Council of the Bar may in certain situations, such as in the event of disciplinary sanctions, require the name of a partner to be removed from the corporate name.[63]

27. The Articles of association of a law firm, regardless of whether it has legal personality or not[64], should include at least the following provisions, in the event of a law firm with partners belonging to more than one Bar:

---

55 Art. 4 of the National Regulation of 8 March 1990.

56 See Chapter 4 of the Codex of the Antwerp Bar; art. 3.7.14 of the Deontologische Code of the Bar of Ghent. J. STEVENS, *Regels en gebruiken van de advocatuur te Antwerpen*, Antwerp, Kluwer, 1997, 511.

57 Art. 3.7.14. of the Deontologische Code of the Bar of Ghent.

58 Art. 293(6) of the Deontologische regels en huishoudelijk reglement of the Dutch-speaking Brussels Bar.

59 Art. 90 of the Nouveau réglement d'ordre intérieur of the French-speaking Brussels Bar.

60 Art. 293(6) of the Deontologische regels en huishoudelijk reglement of the Dutch-speaking Brussels Bar; Art. 88 of the Nouveau réglement d'ordre intérieur of the French-speaking Brussels Bar.

61 Art. 293(7) of the Deontologische regels en huishoudelijk reglement of the Dutch-speaking Brussels Bar.

62 Art. 88 of the Nouveau réglement d'ordre intérieur.

63 Art. 292(7) of the the Deontologische regels en huishoudelijk reglement of the Dutch-speaking Brussels Bar; Art. 67 of the Nouveau règlement d'ordre intérieur of the French-speaking Brussels Bar.

64 In general, as explained in nr. 15, a partnership of lawyers forms by law a maatschap or

a) The undertaking to comply with the regulations of the Bars of which the partners are a member, and the National Regulation of 8 March 1990.
b) The partners undertake not to represent a client which has interests which are in conflict with the interests of a client of the law firm or of a partner.
c) The provision that the partner who is required by a decision of the Council of one of the competent Bars to retire from the partnership, is by law no longer a partner of such firm.
d) All conflicts between partners are decided in last instance by one or three arbitrators designated in common agreement between the *Stafhouders* or *Bâtonniers* of the Bars to which the partners belong, and in the event of disagreement, by the President of the National Bar.
e) The allocation of cases is done in accordance with the instructions of the client.
f) In the event of liquidation, one or more liquidators are appointed in common agreement between the *Stafhouders* or *Bâtonniers* of the competent Bars, and in the event of disagreement, by the President of the National Bar.[65] The liquidator of the partnership must be a lawyer in order to comply with the criminally sanctioned requirement of professional secrecy.[66]

The above rule laid down in the National Regulation, also applies to law firms with partners only admitted to the Antwerp Bar[67], the Ghent Bar[68], and the French-speaking Brussels Bar, with the exception, for the latter Bar, of (d), which is formulated as a recommendation.[69]

Similar rules apply to law firms with partners who are only admitted to the Dutch-speaking Brussels Bar.[70]

The National Regulation[71], and most local regulations, such as the regulations of the Antwerp Bar[72], the Ghent Bar[73] and the French-speaking[74] and

a société with no legal personality. However, partners may choose to set up a legal entity in one of the corporate forms discussed above.

65 Art. 4 of the National Regulation of 8 March 1990.

66 Art. 292(4) of the Deontologische regels en huishoudelijk reglement of the Dutch-speaking Brussels Bar.

67 Chapter 4 of the Codex of the Antwerp Bar.

68 Art. 3.7.9 of the Deontologische Code of the Bar of Ghent.

69 Art. 89 of the Nouveau règlement d'ordre intérieur, which provides a few additional obligations.

70 Art. 293 of the Deontologische regels en huishoudelijk reglement of the Dutch-speaking Brussels Bar.

71 Art. 5 of the National Regulation of 8 March 1990.

72 Chapter 4 of the Codex of the Antwerp Bar.

73 Art. 3.7.9 of the Deontologische Code of the Bar of Ghent.

Dutch-speaking[75] Brussels Bars provide additional obligations for law firms which are incorporated in a legal entity (VOF, BVBA, CV or NV[76]). The Articles of association of the partnership should at least include, in addition to what is mentioned above, the following provisions:

a) The partner who is in charge of a matter, is jointly liable with the partnership for all obligations of the partnership towards the clients. This provision applies especially to liability for professional negligence. In this event the client is entitled to claim damages from the partnership. If the partnership is a VOF, or a CV with unlimited liability, this provision is of no particular importance, as the partners are jointly and severally liable for all obligations of the partnership, including professional liability due to negligence of one of the partners (or other lawyers working for the account of the law firm).[77] However this provision is important for partnerships with limited liability, such as the BVBA, the CV with limited liability and the NV. As the liability of the partners is limited to their contribution in capital, clients which suffer damages due to professional negligence cannot sue the partners except on the basis of tort. In most cases the professional negligence will constitute also negligence in tort, so that the limited liability will not protect the negligent partner. But the statutory provision also implies that the partner is liable for negligence of an associate or another partner who works in a case of which the first partner is in charge. The above provision raises another issue with respect to the CV with limited liability. Article 353 of the Companies Code explicitly prohibits the Articles of association of a CV making a difference between partners with respect to their liability. This prohibition is intended to make an end to CVs with several degrees of liability. Since 1991 only two types of CV: the CV with joint unlimited liability of the partners, and the CV with liability limited to the capital contribution. A provision, in the Articles, to the effect that a partner of a CV with limited liability has unlimited liability for professional negligence in a case handled under his control, is not compatible with Article 353. The Dutch-speaking Brussels Bar has changed its regulation in this respect, and provided that it is sufficient for the partnership to contract an insurance cover for professional negligence in matters handled for its account, and for this obligation to be inserted in the Articles of association.[78] This obligation should be read jointly with the obligation of any

---

74 Art. 90 of the Nouveau règlement d'ordre intérieur.

75 Art. 294 of the Deontologische regels en huishoudelijk reglement.

76 The latter corporate form only for the Dutch-speaking Brussels Bar; See above, nr. 15.

77 See nr. 19 above.

78 Art. 294(1) of the Deontologische regels en huishoudelijk reglement of the Dutch-speaking Brussels Bar.

lawyer and of each law firm to (i) subscribe to a professional insurance; and (ii) contract insurance cover which is in proportion to the type of legal practice of the insured lawyers.[79] A violation of this provision of the regulation of the Dutch-speaking Brussels Bar constitutes a tort.[80] In consequence, law firms with lawyers who are solely member of the Dutch-speaking Brussels Bar, are not required to insert an unlimited liability provision in the Articles of association of the BVBA, NV or CV with limited liability which they decide to incorporate, provided however, they undertake to subscribe to professional negligence insurance. Finally, it has been argued that the professional liability of the so-called "free professions" cannot be limited.[81] It is not clear, however, on what basis this argument is made. No law prohibits this. However, the client should be properly informed of any limitation of the professional liability.[82] This is the case if the law firm concludes a contract in this respect with the client, or if the law firm explicitly mentions any limitation professional liability on its letter heading.

b) The professional liability of the law firm and of the partners must be insured. This was discussed under (1).

c) The partnership is managed by one or more partners. The Dutch-speaking Brussels Bar is more liberal. Its regulation provides that the law firm can be managed by one or more lawyers who need not be partners, provided that a lawyer cannot be a manager in different law firms.[83] This is reasonable: in current times, larger law firms should be able to choose the most suitable manager among all lawyers working in the firm, without being limited to partners. It should furthermore be possible to find an external lawyer who is especially contracted to manage the firm. In large firms, the management of the firm can be a full-time job, which prevents the manager from handling cases for clients. There is no reason that such manager should have to be a partner of the firm. It may even be advisable that, in such cases, the firm looks for an external professional manager, who is solicited for his managerial skills. This will especially be so if none of the partners has the managerial skills

---

79 Art. 63 of the Deontologische regels en huishoudelijk reglement of the Dutch-speaking Brussels Bar.

80 L. CORNELIS, Beginselen van het Belgische buitencontractuele aansprakelijkheidsrecht, 1989, 266-267.

81 Art. 61 of the Deontologische regels en huishoudelijk reglement of the Dutch-speaking Brussels Bar, provides explicitly that lawyers may restrict their professional liability towards their clients.

82 Art. 62 of the Deontologische regels en huishoudelijk reglement of the Dutch-speaking Brussels Bar.

83 Art. 293(8) of the Deontologische regels en huishoudelijk reglement.

to manage the firm. This derogation from the rules imposed by the National Regulation applies, as explained above, only to law firms with lawyers who are a member of the Dutch-speaking Brussels Bar (see above).

d) The law firm is not dissolved because of the death of a partner. This rule is important as it confirms that the law firm is a separate legal entity, to be distinguished from its partners. The law firm should be able to survive its founders and its first generation partners. It implies that the Articles of association may not provide otherwise. However, it is permissible, but not advisable to provide that the law firm is dissolved upon the departure or retirement of a partner. The Dutch-speaking Brussels Bar has extended the above prohibition of dissolution to the departure of a partner.[84]

e) The rights and obligations of the partner or his successors should be defined upon departure or death of such partner. This provision tends to ensure that upon departure or death, the law firm pays such partner or his heirs an indemnity for the loss of value of his shares. This can be organised by a transfer of the shares to the remaining partners. The indemnification will of course depend on whether the partner is entitled to continue his legal practise elsewhere, and continue to work for the clients he worked with in the law firm.

f) The annual accounts of the partnership should be verified by an auditor who is a member of the Institute of Certified Auditors, or by an accountant, recognised by the Council of the competent Bars.

g) The transfer of shares (including upon death) to another partner requires a decision by a two-thirds special majority.[85] A transfer of shares to a new partner is regulated differently in the Dutch-speaking and the French-speaking Brussels Bars[86]: in the Dutch-speaking Bar, it is sufficient that the new partner has been admitted as a partner in accordance with the Articles of association[87]; in the French-speaking Bar, the unanimous agreement of all partners is required, provided that in the event of refusal, the existing partners must take over all shares of the partners

---

84 Art. 292(3) of the Deontologische regels en huishoudelijk reglement

85 Art. 294(2) of the Deontologische regels en huishoudelijk reglement of the Dutch-speaking Brussels Bar; Art. 90(c) of the Nouveau règlement d'ordre intérieur of the French-speaking Brussels Bar. This statutory requirement is not mentioned in the National Regulation of 8 March 1990.

86 Again, the National Regulation of 8 March 1990 does not require any specific statutory rules in this respect.

87 Art. 294(3) of the Deontologische regels en huishoudelijk reglement.

who proposed a transfer, or organise a partial liquidation by reimbursing the departing partner.[88]

7.2 Management

28. Management of a law firm will be organised in accordance with the rules applicable to the corporate form in which the law firm is incorporated. Thus a VOF, CV or BVBA, can have either a manager or a board of managers (preferably at least three, or alternatively with a chairman who has a casting vote). In a NV, a Board of Directors of at least three directors (or two if there are not more than two shareholders) is in charge of management, and daily management can be delegated to a Managing Director or an Executive Committee.

Larger law firms have tested several concepts of management. Initially, they seem to opt for a board of managers, with one executive manager charged with daily management. In such structures, the chairman of the board tends to be an older partner who spends part of his time in the amicable resolution of conflicts between partners.

It is difficult to define an ideal concept for the management of a law firm.

However, when analysing the manner in which partners behave when part of a law firm, some general guidelines may be suggested. Typically, (i) lawyers, when working together, prefer to keep their independence, (ii) they have little time to spend on management, and when they do, management issues are always handled after the cases (which is normal as work for clients generates income), (iii) most lawyers have no management skills, (iv) lawyers tend to entertain lengthy discussions before coming to conclusions and decisions; and (v) a partner feels excluded when he is not informed or consulted when management decisions are taken.

Given these facts, it is advisable to concentrate management with a limited number of managers. The rule is to try to limit the number of managers to the minimum, but by staying in regular contact with all partners. In other words, if management can be handled by one person, then this is the best solution. This will allow the firm to have someone who focuses on management, who will develop a consistent management style, and who will take responsibility for decision-making. The managers need to keep contact with all partners and heads of department within the firm.

This management should preferably be delegated to partners with management skills. If management skills are not available in the firm, the firm should look for external managers.

---

88 Art. 90(c) of the Nouveau règlement d'ordre intérieur.

Besides management, a General Assembly of partners is entrusted with a limited number of decisions, which are basically the decisions which are reserved for the Shareholders' meeting, such as approval of accounts and budgets, appointment and removal of managers, admission of new partners, changes to the Articles of association, the internal regulations and the structure of the firm.

Finally, in order to avoid management deciding on issues of general policy, a committee or supervision board can be set up which discusses strategy and examines together with management any issues which go beyond ordinary management. This committee will also entertain contact with the partners, to the extent that management fails to do so. The position of this committee will increase in accordance with a larger number of partners. In such latter case, partners will find it difficult to meet regularly.

29. In a large law firm with a large number of partners (exceeding 50), the General Assembly will meet very rarely. Nevertheless, some decisions require the approval of the partners because they concern the type and structure of the firm.

The admission of partners should be decided by the General Assembly of partners, because a law firm is always a partnership *intuitu personae* where the *affectio societatis* is entirely based on the good relation between the partners. A partner which feels isolated or has regular conflicts with other partners, will either leave or be forced to leave. It is therefore important that partners be able to give their opinion on the new candidates for partnership, and decide with a special majority on the admission.

Changes to the Articles, the internal regulation and the structure concern the manner in which the partners decide to work together. It is therefore advisable that it can only be changed by them.

The General Assembly should also approve a budget for the following year which will contain directives for the management.

Finally, management should justify its management decisions of the last year, by submitting the annual accounts for approval. The General Assembly should be able to remove any managers who no longer have the confidence of a large number of partners.

7.3 Admission, departure, transfer of shares

30. A law firm can only accept partners who are lawyers, i.e. members of a Bar or a similar foreign professional organisation, which guarantees the same ethical rules, including independence and professional secrecy.[89]

The admission of partners is regulated differently by each Belgian Bar. No National Regulation exists which defines general rules applicable to partnerships with lawyers of different Belgian or foreign Bars. If the law firm counts partners of different Bars, the most restrictive rule will prevail.[90]

The rules applicable to admission will therefore depend on what is agreed in the Articles of association within the limits of the applicable rules of the competent Bars.

31. Also the transfer of shares and in general the departure of a partner is differently regulated depending on the rules imposed by the competent Bars.[91]

But the rules on the transfer of shares and departure of a partner will also depend on the corporate form that the partners have chosen to incorporate the law firm.

32. The shares in a VOF cannot in general be transferred, unless the Articles of association provide otherwise. If the Articles do not provide anything in this respect, the unanimous consent of all partners is required for a transfer.

A partner can always leave the VOF. Under the Companies Code, the departure or death of a partner implies the liquidation of the company[92] unless otherwise provided in the Articles of association.[93] As indicated above in nr 27, the National Regulation and the regulations of the Dutch-speaking and French-speaking Brussels Bars require that the Articles of association provide that the death of a partner does not imply the liquidation of the law firm. The Articles should furthermore provide for a payment to a departing partner of his share in the law firm (if he leaves without his clients).[94]

In case of his death, the heirs are entitled to his share.[95] As indicated above (nr 27) the rights of the departing partner, or his heirs, should be defined in

---

89 See nr. 23 above.

90 Art. 10 of the National Regulation of 8 March 1990.

91 See for the French-speaking and Dutch-speaking Bars, nr. 27 in fine.

92 Art. 39, 3° and 5° of the Code on companies.

93 Art. 39, 3° and 5° of the Code on Companies. However, the departure of a partner does not result in the liquidation in VOF with a limited duration (Art. 43 of the Code on Companies), unless the number of remaining partners falls beyond two.

94 See nr. 27 in fine (e).

95 Art. 42 of the Code on Companies.

the Articles of association. It is indeed advisable clearly to define what the departing partner or his heirs are entitled to, in order to avoid long conflicts.

33. In the event of a BVBA, parties will have to take into account the restrictions on the transfer of shares which are provided in the Companies Code. However, these rules are no more restrictive than the rules provided in the regulations of the Dutch-speaking and French-speaking Brussels Bars.

The shares of a BVBA can only be transferred to a third party with the consent of half of the partners which hold three quarters of the capital (after deduction of the shares for which a transfer is proposed). This consent is not required for a transfer to (i) a partner; (ii) a spouse of the transferring partner or of the heir; (iii) to relatives in the ascending or descending line; or (iv) to persons defined in the Articles of association.[96] These rules may be rendered more restrictive; they must not be relaxed in the Articles of association. This is not an issue as the regulations of the Bars are in general (though not always) more restrictive (see above, nr 27 *in fine*). To the extent that they are not more restrictive, the Articles of association of the law firm which is incorporated in a BVBA will have to comply with the Code on Companies Code.

A transfer in breach of the above rules, is void; it has no legal effect.[97]

If a partner of a BVBA proposes to transfer his shares to a third party or a partner, and this transfer is refused in accordance with the above rules, such partner may challenge the refusal. If he can show that the refusal was arbitrary, the court will hold the other partners liable to take over the shares of that partner for a price and under the conditions defined by the court; if the Articles of association define a price and conditions, the court will have to apply such rules.[98] As indicated above, the regulation of the French-speaking Brussels Bars requires that in the event of a refusal of a proposed transfer to a third party, the other partners are bound to take over the shares of the partner who wishes to depart, or to partially liquidate the law firm in favour of that partner.[99]

If in the event of a decision of the court in favour of the departing partner but his shares are not taken over by the other partners within three months under the conditions determined by the court, the transferor is entitled to request the liquidation of the partnership, provided that he formulates his

---

96 Art. 249 of the Code on Companies.

97 See M. WYCKAERT, "De instemmingsvereiste bij de overgang van aandelen in een B.V.B.A.: opschortende of bestaansvoorwaarde? Een poging tot verantwoording van de mogelijke stellingnames", *T.R.V.* 1990, 184.

98 Art. 251 of the Code on Companies.

99 Art. 90(c) of the Nouveau règlement d'ordre intérieur.

request in court within 40 days after expiration of this above three-month period.[100]

It follows that a partner who wishes to leave, will have to find a transferee. Indeed under the Companies Code, the obligation to take over the shares only exists in the event of proposal of the refusal of a transferee. But the partner may also request the other partners to take over his shares for a price determined by the court, in the event of good reasons, *i.e.* events caused by the other partners which make it impossible to continue to work together.[101]

In the event of death, the heirs are entitled to the value of the shares of the deceased. In the event of disagreement as regards the price and conditions of transfer, the court will define the price and conditions; if the Articles of association contain rules in this respect, the court will have to apply such rules. If the remaining partners do not take over the shares within three months, the heirs may petition the liquidation of the company.[102]

34. Shares in a CV can be freely transferred to partners. But in general shares in a CV cannot be transferred to third parties. They can only be transferred to third parties (i) which are mentioned explicitly in the Articles of association; or (ii) which belong to a category of persons defined in the Articles of association, and subject to approval of the partners' meeting or any other corporate body designated in the Articles of association.[103]

Unless provided otherwise in the Articles of association, a partner cannot force his partners to take over his shares in the CV. This is only possible if the Articles of association provide that the other partners must take over the shares of the partner who wishes to leave. Under the regulation of the French-speaking Brussels Bar, the Articles of association must provide for an obligation to take over the shares in the event of refusal of transfer to a third party.[104]

Finally, partners can leave the company by reclaiming the value of the shares in accordance with the Articles of association (if that is provided for). Unless provided otherwise, such partners are entitled to the value of their shares as it results from the balance of the fiscal year, in which the partner has left the company.[105] The Articles may provide for another formula to determine the value.[106]

---

100 Art. 251 in fine of the Code on Companies.

101 Art. 340 of the Code on Companies. The request has to be filed with the President of the commercial court, and is handled as in summary jurisdiction.

102 Art. 252 of the Code on Companies.

103 Artt. 364 and 633 of the Code on Companies.

104 Art. 90(c) of the Nouveau règlement d'ordre intérieur.

105 Art. 374 of the Code on Companies.

106 Liège 23 March 2000, *J.L.M.B.* 2001, 816.

Also in the event of death of a partner, the partnership will have to pay the value of the shares to the heirs of the partner.[107]

35. As mentioned above, the Dutch-speaking Brussels Bar allows the incorporation of a law firm in a NV. The transfer of shares in a NV is allowed; the right to transfer can be restricted, but not excluded.[108] This means that the Articles of association have to provide for a pre-emption procedure allowing other shareholders to purchase the shares of the departing shareholder, combined with an obligation to take such shares over if at the end of the pre-emption procedure not all shares are purchased.

7.4 Conflicts

36. Working together on a daily basis in a law firm automatically creates conflicts: each partner has his own ambitions and requirements. Furthermore, lawyers have difficulty accepting a hierarchy. They generally do not accept that decisions made at a higher level are imposed, even to resolve conflicts.

It is therefore important to define a legal framework to resolve conflicts which may arise between partners.

There are three categories of conflicts, depending on their seriousness: conflicts which do not affect the co-operation between the partners; conflicts which render any further co-operation impossible, and conflicts which lie between these two extremes.

The first category, which includes daily irritations because of the decisions or attitude of another partner, must be solved without too many formalities. This can be done by appointing a partner who can be addressed on the subject to seek a solution.

The second category, *i.e.* conflicts which render any further co-operation impossible, can only be solved by the departure of a partner or by liquidation of the law firm. If no procedure for departure is provided, they will easily result in the dissolution of the law firm.

The third category of conflicts requires an adequate type of procedure, which makes it possible to find a solution without increasing the conflict and rendering any future co-operation difficult or impossible. This can consist of the designation of an older partner to listen to both parties and propose a solution through dialogue. However a special procedure should be provided in case this conversation does not lead to a solution. This can be organised internally, by appointing a settlement committee which decides after having

---

107 Art. 375 of the Code on Companies.

108 Art. 510 of the Code on Companies.

heard the partners. The members of the settlement committee are senior partners (who are not involved in management[109]) or retired partners. This does not constitute an arbitration procedure, but an alternative resolution procedure confronting the views of the parties, and proposing a decision.

If one of the parties does not agree, he can always turn to the *Stafhouder* or *Bâtonnier*, and, finally, to arbitration (see below).

37. The Articles of association of a law firm should provide for an arbitration procedure.[110]

Typically the arbitration procedures provides for two steps, where the first is not mandatory. In a first step, the partners submit their dispute to the *Stafhouder* or *Bâtonnier*. If the law firm consists of partners of different bars, the *Stafhouders* or *Bâtonniers* of all relevant bars are consulted, and will attempt to find a common solution. In serious cases, a meeting will be set up, or a common representative will be appointed who looks for a solution together with the parties.

In a second step, and if the first step does not lead to a solution, the dispute will be submitted to formal arbitration. The arbitral court should be composed by one or three arbitrators. In the event of law firms composed of partners of different Bars, the arbitrators must be appointed in common agreement by the *Stafhouders* or *Bâtonniers* of the different bars involved, and in the event of disagreement, by the President of the National Bar (the *Deken* or *Doyen*[111]). This rule applies also to partnerships falling under the authority of local Bars, such as the Antwerp Bar or the Ghent Bar, which have rendered the National Regulation applicable to the partnerships with members of their Bars. In the French-speaking Brussels Bar it is recommended to refer to the *Bâtonnier*.[112] The *Stafhouders* or *Bâtonniers* will appoint lawyers as arbitrator.

If the arbitrators are not appointed by the *Stafhouder* or *Bâtonnier*, the parties will make sure that a lawyer or a person who is equally bound by professional secrecy is appointed in order, to avoid disclosing any information covered by the professional secrecy of the parties involved in the arbitration procedure, and which may be disclosed in such a procedure.[113]

---

109 It may indeed be that the conflict opposes a partner to the managing partner(s) of the firm.

110 See nr. 27 above.

111 This clause will cause a problem when the National Bar wil disappear formally, and as long as the National Regulation of 8 March 1990 has not been replaced by regulations of the new regional bars.

112 Art. 89 (c) of the Nouveau règlement d'ordre intérieur.

113 See Art. 292(2) of the Deontologische regels en huishoudelijk reglement of the Dutch-speaking Brussels Bar.

The decision of the arbitral court is subject to review and can be annulled by the civil court of first instance for one of the reasons specified in Article 1704 of the Belgian Judicial Code.

38. Finally, some regulations provide that the Council of the Bar may intervene in firms in which the further co-operation between partners is impossible. For example the regulations of the Brussels Bars provide that the Council of the Bar may order a partner to leave the firm in the event that the continuation of the co-operation is seriously disrupted.[114] This regulation provides also that the *Stafhouder* or the *Bâtonnier* can take other interim measures if necessary.

7.5 Professional secrecy

39. The law firm is considered as one lawyer for the purpose of the rules of professional secrecy. Partners and associates working in an integrated law firm are supposed to work together and to share information in order better to serve the clients (and thus to act in the interest of the firm's client).

However, this does not mean that lawyers within the same firm are authorised to exchange information on clients or on matters without limitation. Lawyers are always bound by a duty of discussion which is inherent in the nature of the legal profession. They will refrain from disclosing information which is not useful to share, and from speaking about information they obtained in a matter where this is not necessary for the case in question.[115]

The same rule applies to the confidentiality of the correspondence between lawyers.

7.6 Disciplinary sanctions

40. If a lawyer breaches his obligations under the ethical code of the Bar to which he belongs, the Disciplinary Council of the Bar can take disciplinary sanctions. In such event the Disciplinary Council can order the lawyer to leave the law firm, or the deletion of his name from the corporate name of the firm. The National Regulation of the 8 March 1990 does not deal with these issues. In consequence, this will depend on the regulations of the local Bars, and the treaties between those Bars and any foreign Bars.

---

114 Art. 292(8) of the Deontologische regels en huishoudelijk reglement; Art. 87 of the Nouveau règlement d'ordre intérieur.

115 A. BRAUN and F. MOREAU, *La profession d'avocat*, Brussels, Bruylant, 1985, 142.

The regulations of the Brussels Bars provide that the Council of the Bar may order a partner to leave the firm in the event of serious infringement of the ethical code.[116]

The regulation of the French-speaking Brussels Bar provides that the Council of the Bar can order the deletion of the name of partner from the corporate name of the firm, if that partner is ordered to leave the law firm by way of disciplinary sanction.[117] The regulation of the Dutch-speaking Brussels Bar provides that the Council can order the deletion of the name of a lawyer from the name of the law firm in the event that maintaining the name would cause prejudice to the Bar, or to one of the partners or to third parties.[118]

7.7 Liquidation

41. The Articles of association of a law firm should provide that it is not dissolved by the death of a partner.[119] The Dutch-speaking Brussels Bar requires the Articles of association moreover to provide that the law firm is not dissolved by the departure of a partner either.[120]

In any event, the death or departure of a partner would not affect a law firm incorporated in a BVBA, CV or NV, unless otherwise provided in the Articles of association.

Other reasons for dissolution may be provided in the Articles of association. If the firm is incorporated for a limited duration, it will by law be dissolved upon expiration of the duration, unless the partners' meeting has prolonged the duration.

42. The partners may always decide to dissolve the law firm. In the event that the law firm is incorporated in a company with legal personality, such decision must be made by the partners in accordance with the rules applicable to the modification of the Articles of association, *i.e.* with the quorum and special majority required by the Companies Code for such decisions. The Articles of association may provide for more restrictive rules.

A special procedure must be complied with in order to decide to dissolve the partnership.

43. Upon dissolution, the law firm will enter into liquidation.

---

116 Art. 292(8) of the Deontologische regels en huishoudelijk reglement; Art. 66 of the Nouveau règlement d'ordre intérieur.

117 Art. 88 of the Nouveau règlement d'ordre intérieur. This also applies to the Ghent Bar: Art. 3.7.15 of the Deontologische Code.

118 Art. 292(7)(c) of the Deontologische regels en huishoudelijk reglement.

119 See nr. 27 above.

120 See nr. 27 above.

In such event one or more liquidators are appointed by the *Stafhouder* or *Bâtonnier* of the Bar to which the partners of the partnership belong or by the *Stafhouders* or *Bâtonniers,* in the event of a partnership with partners of different Bars. If the *Stafhouders* or *Bâtonniers* disagree on the names of the liquidator, the latter is appointed by the President of the National Bar. These rules must be provided in the Articles of association.[121] The French-speaking Brussels Bar provides a similar rule.[122]

The *Stafhouders* or *Bâtonniers* will ensure that the liquidator is a lawyer, in order to ensure that the matters are handled and transferred in respect of the obligations of professional secrecy.

The regulation of the Dutch-speaking Brussels Bar provides only that the liquidator should be a lawyer, without giving any authority to the *Stafhouder* to appoint the liquidator.[123] Of course, the Articles of association could confer this authority to the *Stafhouder* in the event that the partners cannot reach agreement.

44. The liquidator will pay all debts with the assets of the law firm, and make sure that the pending cases are transferred to the lawyer of the client's choice.[124] In the event that the dissolution is the result of the partners deciding freely to terminate the co-operation, each partner will take his clients.

---

121 Art. 4(e) of the National Regulation of 8 March 1990.

122 Art. 89(e) of the Nouveau règlement d'ordre intérieur of the French-speaking Brussels Bar.

123 Art. 292(4) of the Deontologische regels en huishoudelijk reglement of the Dutch-speaking Brussels Bar.

124 Art. 4(d) of the National Regulation; Art. 292(4) of the Deontologische regels en huishoudelijk reglement of the Dutch-speaking Brussels Bar; Art. 89(d) of the Nouveau réglement d'ordre intérieur of the French-speaking Brussels Bar.

LEXCEL: THE PRACTICE MANAGEMENT QUALITY MARK

John Pickup, Council Member of the Law Society and Chairman of the Lexcel Assessment Panel

Lexcel is the Law Society of England and Wales' Practice Management Certification Scheme. It is the quality mark awarded by the Law Society to practices and legal departments that have been independently assessed as having achieved the Law Society's Practice Management Standards.

Before I outline the Lexcel scheme to you, I thought it might be useful to take a step back and look at why management standards are important - not just within the legal profession, but for all organisations.

1 WHY DO WE REQUIRE MANAGEMENT STANDARDS?

It is becoming more and more important that legal practices are able to distinguish themselves from their competitors - not just competitors within the legal profession, but also external competitors, such as accountants providing competing services.

Practices are having to become far more efficient and economical, generating more and more revenue wherever possible.

Recently in England and Wales we have experienced an increase in the general number of complaints and claims against solicitors, costing the profession vast amounts of money year on year with increased professional indemnity insurance premiums. Though this year's figures are showing a downturn in the number of complaints received.

Today, all clients are far better educated about products and are demanding ever-higher levels of service. Whilst clients expect their lawyers to provide them with excellent legal advice, they will also certainly judge lawyers by the quality of tangible services, such as how frequently they are communicated with and how well informed they feel about their case.

2 WHY DO WE REQUIRE ACCREDITATION?

Accredited standards provide recognition from the professional body.

They provide an external check - for how else will practices know whether they comply?

And will also help with improved recruitment - after all who wants to work for a practice with poor systems and procedures?

3 HISTORY OF LEXCEL

So why were Practice Management Standards and Lexcel necessary? Well, in the early 1990s we noted that where lawyers were performing poorly was not in the quality of their legal advice, but in the way they delivered their services.

As part of our campaign to improve management within legal practices, we therefore encouraged practices to obtain quality kite marks such as ISO 9000 (the international kite mark you may well be familiar with) or Investors in People (which is a UK national standard focusing more on people management).

Eventually, we decided, that with all the expertise we had within the Law Society we should develop our own standards. And in 1993, the Law Society published a set of Practice Management Standards which were optional for practices to work towards.

Following publication of the Practice Management Standards, it was then decided to devise a certification scheme based on these Standards, which was to be called "Lexcel". This quality mark allows practices, the Law Society, and indeed clients, to know whether a practice is successfully implementing the standards. Lexcel was launched in 1998.

4 WHY SHOULD PRACTICES CONSIDER LEXCEL?

The main reason for Lexcel's success to date is that the scheme was written by lawyers for lawyers – thus meeting the unique needs of the legal profession. It incorporates the best of many of the other quality standards available and puts them into a legal practice setting.

Because the standards cover all the areas of practice management, there are a huge number of benefits involved in achieving Lexcel certification - benefits which not only relate to the practice, but more importantly to clients.

These include improved client care, efficient management and reduced costs, effective deployment of resources, reduced mistakes, effective risk management as well as improved morale and motivation of staff.

5 WHAT IS THE BASIS OF THE LEXCEL SCHEME?

So in terms of how Lexcel works, as I've mentioned Lexcel is based on a number of Practice Management Standards which were devised by the Law Society.

All types and sizes of practice can apply for the Lexcel award: including both public and private practices, from sole practitioners to the largest practices.

In order to protect the integrity of the scheme, applicants can choose to be assessed by one out of 12 independent Assessment Bodies who are either ISO 9000 or Investors in People assessment units, and are therefore experienced in this field. This was critical as we did not want the profession to see assessment as some sort of back door policing of the profession by the Law Society.

The Assessment Bodies are responsible for auditing Lexcel and internally verifying the process. Assessors will have undergone Law Society training on Lexcel and on what to expect of a legal practice.

Joint assessments with ISO 9000 and Investors in People are also possible.

Lexcel is not just about rubber-stamping good firms. It is also about improving the way in which practices manage themselves. Therefore, even if a practice has essentially failed an assessment, it is allowed a period of time in which to take corrective action and undergo a further assessment.

Once the Assessment Body is happy that the practice is ready for certification, it produces a report which is sent to the Law Society recommending certification. It is the Law Society which reviews the report and takes the final decision to award the practice. Once a practice is awarded Lexcel, the certificate is valid for three years, but is subject to Annual Maintenance Visits.

6 HOW DOES LEXCEL WORK?

Lexcel provides practices with an effective framework for good management.

It identifies all the areas of practice management which a practice must consider. Lexcel sets the standards for what to do, but does not prescribe exactly how to do it. Because the scheme needs to be flexible enough for sole practitioners, in-house legal departments, as well as both private and public practices, the structure of the scheme is such that each practice can determine the most appropriate procedures and systems it wants to put in place. But the standards are the same for everyone.

Lexcel helps to ensure consistently good standards of service not just within a practice, but for multi-site practices, also across all branches.

However, Lexcel does not monitor the quality of legal advice.

7 REVISIONS

The Lexcel Practice Management Standards were revised last year. In particular, revisions include new areas of client care, complaints handling, and IT, but the largest change relates to new requirements on risk management (which I'll come back to in a moment).

8 AREAS COVERED BY THE PRACTICE MANAGEMENT STANDARDS

The Practice Management Standards themselves cover 6 main areas which, when implemented, provide a better service to the client. They are a key part of the Society's policy of helping the profession deliver excellent service to the public:

These are set out in the following categories:

- *Management Structure* encourages an orderly approach to the way people work. It requires the practice to have a written description of their management structure and a named supervisor for each area of work. Practices can demonstrate this by having something as simple as a "family tree" of the practice showing where responsibilities lie.
- *Service and Forward Planning* encourages practices to have clear goals for the future and give thought to how they want to market their services. It is a key part of business planning which so many practices fail to do; yet it is simple and need not be complex.
- *Financial Management* focuses on enabling practices to gauge whether the time spent on caseloads is profitable. The practice has to show who is responsible for financial affairs and show that they have the management and financial information necessary for monitoring income, expenditure and cost, and for forward planning. Annual budgets, quarterly variance analysis of income and expenditure against budget, together with a profit and loss account and annual balance sheet, form part of the assessment. For many this proves to be a real eye-opener, introducing them to some of the basics of sound financial management.
- *Managing People* - By making sure its people have the proper skills and knowledge for the job, the practice ensures that it is best placed to provide the best possible quality service to its clients. Things assessors would look for include job descriptions, appraisals, good recruitment policies and adequate training.
- *Office Administration* is often overlooked when thinking about solicitors' services yet it is the key to the efficient running of the practice. To be accredited a practice must have in place an office manual which

records all of its procedures and clearly designates administrative responsibilities. They also have to ensure that fee-earners have access to up-to-date legal reference material and receive timely information about changes in the law relevant to their work - for example by circulation of law reports and journals. The key to success here is to "say what you do and do what you say".

- The largest section of the Standards relates to the most legally-specific area. *Case Management* controls everything the solicitor does from the opening to the closing of a case.

9 CASE MANAGEMENT

The scheme requires practices to maintain an index of matters; a system for identifying any conflict of interest; and monitoring to ensure that fee- earners are working within their capacity in terms of time and experience. A system for ensuring key dates are not missed is required and proper authorisation and monitoring of undertakings.

It is in this module that requirements are set out on client care and it also includes supervision and complaints handling. The focus here is very much on fostering good relations with clients which avoid problems rather than having an adversarial system in place.

10 RISK MANAGEMENT

Due to the recent changes in the provision of indemnity insurance within England and Wales (which has meant a move from a mutual fund to the open market) risk management is certainly a key topic for practices at the moment.

There is increased pressure on lawyers to take risks. Clients are more demanding, deadlines are perhaps tighter than ever, and tougher fee targets are being set.

It is important that all practices assess and manage risk and this is an area which is also being emphasised by providers of indemnity insurance. Since there is a clear relationship between good practice management and effective risk management, Lexcel has a very strong role to play. Lexcel is therefore being promoted as an effective risk management tool, and awarded practices are more likely to see favourable discounts on their indemnity insurance premiums.

11 CLAIMS ARISE MAINLY OUT OF POOR ADMINISTRATION

There are 7 key causes of claims against solicitors in England and Wales, most of which relate to practice management. These include areas such as diary control, training, supervision of staff and terms of engagement.

Practices also need to inform clients as to the costs and complaints procedure.

Lexcel covers all of these areas and thus forms the basis of our argument that Lexcel is a key risk management tool.

12 HOW DO WE ASSESS RISK?

Lexcel now includes specific risk management requirements:

- That the practice must appoint someone responsible for dealing with risk
- The practice must define what they consider to be risky and non-risky work and assess each case in turn

Where a case is deemed to be risky, but the practice wants to accept the work, additional systems and procedures must be implemented to deal with this additional risk

And, finally, that an annual audit of all risk management data is conducted.

13 AIDS TO ACHIEVING LEXCEL

In order to help practices, we have developed and produced a *Lexcel Practice Excellence Kit*. This was designed to make the process as clear as possible for practices and includes the Lexcel Assessment Guide and Lexcel Office Procedures Manual.

Also available is a more general text on quality entitled: *Quality Management for Law Firms.*

14 COSTS TO PRACTICES OF OBTAINING LEXCEL

By investing in Lexcel, awarded practices will reap numerous benefits.

There are two elements to the costs of Lexcel:

- Firstly, an annual registration fee which is paid to the Law Society. This depends on the size of the practice (*e.g.* £50 for a sole practitioner and £250 for an 8-10 partner size practice).
- And secondly, the largest element of cost is the fee for the actual assessment conducted by the Assessment Body. This amount will vary depending on a number of factors: the most important of which are

the size of the practice and the number of branches. Assessment Bodies usually charge around £500-£650 per day.

15 CURRENT PROGRESS

So how have we done so far?

Well Lexcel is certainly becoming *the* prestigious quality standard for the legal profession.

The acceptance of management and therefore practice management will take time, since a cultural shift is required.

However, more than 200 firms have now applied. These vary from sole practitioners to top 100 practices in England, as well as many in-house departments of local authorities.

We can certainly say that through Lexcel, practices are able to demonstrate effective management systems which are essential to help improve the delivery of legal services within England and Wales.

"CYBERLIABILITY" FOR LAWYERS - CONTRACTUAL AND OTHER ISSUES RELATING TO THE PROVISION OF ONLINE LEGAL SERVICES[1]

Mark Ford, Strategic Research Manager at Clifford Chance, London

1 INTRODUCTION

This article concerns the effect of so-called "e-business" - that is, the application of internet-based technologies to traditional businesses - on the legal industry. Increasing numbers of law firms are now embracing the World Wide Web and struggling to understand how they can best make use of this new technology.

With the new business models offered by the internet come a new set of challenges for firms to address, not least the issues of "cyberliability"; that is, how firms might be liable to clients or other entities for electronically delivered legal services. In addition, because these services can be provided to users virtually anywhere in the world (at least any location from which internet access is available) many countries' legal systems could potentially affect the provision of the service. This article highlights some of the key legal challenges which law firms entering the e-commerce arena face and suggests possible strategies for addressing them.

2 DIFFERENT TYPES OF ONLINE SERVICE

There is a vast spectrum of different online services which a law firm could choose to offer, from a basic web site to a highly sophisticated service providing access to a variety of online tools and knowledge resources. For present purposes, however, there are two broad types of online service to consider, namely technology- and knowledge-based services.

Technology-based services provide clients or users with some form of online tool to assist them in their work. For example, a secure extranet site that allows a client to see details relating to the files which the firm is working on for that client is a technology-based service. It may well be an extremely useful and valuable service for the client, but it does not contain any legal content.

The value of knowledge-based services, on the other hand, lies primarily in their content. The essence of this type of service is that the firm has packaged some element of its legal know-how and made it available to clients via the

[1] This contribution was previously published in the April 2001 edition of *Electronic Business Law*.

internet. For example, a service that gives clients guidance on how to incorporate a company in the UK is a knowledge-based service.

Of course, some services may both be rich in content and use sophisticated technology and therefore combine elements of both types of service. The reason for drawing the distinction here, however, is that the process of packaging legal knowledge and providing it to clients online is far more problematic from the point of view of legal risk than merely providing a technology-based tool to clients.

3 AN OVERVIEW OF THE KEY ISSUES

3.1 Professional conduct: conflicts of interest

Solicitors are bound by strict rules of professional conduct which govern the way in which they practise law. One rule which raises particular issues in the context of online services is that relating to conflicts of interest. Broadly speaking, this states that a solicitor may not act contrary to the interests of an existing client. Accordingly, a solicitor should not accept instructions where this would put him in a position of conflict.

The rule on conflicts, as well as the other rules relating to the professional conduct of solicitors, will apply to online activities in the same way as they apply to "offline" advice. From that perspective, therefore, the fact that the advice is provided online has no bearing on the situation. However, difficulties may arise where a law firm is using the internet to provide a type of service that is different from traditional one-to-one legal advice and where the firm wishes to avoid creating a solicitor-client relationship.

To give an extreme example of the problem, if anybody that visited a firm's public web site were regarded as being a client, the firm would be extremely limited in its ability to accept new instructions because of possible conflicts of interest. Nobody, of course, would argue that visitors to a law firm's web site do become clients, but consider the position of a law firm that wishes to package its knowledge and provide it to clients as an online "product". If the users of this product are drawn from the firm's existing client base, there is no problem (they are already clients). But would a user who is not already a client become a client merely by virtue of using, or subscribing to, a knowledge-based online service? The question is not an easy one to answer, but it is important for a law firm that wishes to provide services of this nature to a wider audience than its existing client base: indeed, the opportunity to expand the firm's client list may be one of the primary motivating factors for creating an online legal service.

A number of factors will need to be weighed against each other in making an assessment of whether users of online services become clients of a law firm. If the service provides detailed legal guidance to subscribers, is tailored to their specific situation and is charged for at a rate comparable to the cost of traditional consultative legal advice, it will be difficult to resist the conclusion that subscribers are indeed clients. On the other hand, a free service which provides summary guidance in exactly the same form to all users is less likely to create a solicitor-client relationship.

To some extent, this question will also depend on whether the law firm has, in all the circumstances, created a reasonable expectation in the mind of the subscriber that a client relationship exists. A law firm that wishes to avoid this conclusion may therefore wish to make this clear to the subscribers.

Another factor to consider is the extent to which the subscriber provides information to the firm through its use of the service. If the service is highly interactive - perhaps a form of expert system[2] - the conflict rules are again more likely to come into operation. In any event, they will certainly do so where the user provides confidential information relating to his specific circumstances to the law firm in question.

A possible solution to the conflicts issue is to obtain a contractual waiver from subscribers. This would permit the firm to act in relation to a particular matter even where doing so would be contrary to the subscriber's interests. Whilst this solution works in theory, however, conflict waivers have never been tested in the courts, so a significant degree of uncertainty regarding their efficacy remains.

3.2 Limiting liability

Law firms and their clients are accustomed to legal advice being provided with no limit on liability, although firms are obliged to arrange professional indemnity insurance to cover the cost of negligence claims. Whilst the concept of limiting liability in relation to traditional, one-to-one legal advice will be anathema to many lawyers, there are good reasons to consider imposing such limits in relation to the provision of online services. Apart from the fact that they represent a new form of legal service, law firms are potentially liable to many different subscribers at once, and so may consider it advisable in some circumstances to limit their liability in relation to online services. Whether this is appropriate will depend largely on the nature of the service

2 The aim of an expert system is to request input from the user on his or her specific circumstances and then, using the logic rules and knowledge base which have been programmed into the system, provide guidance tailored to the user's situation.

in question and, in particular, on the content which is provided to subscribers.

If the service constitutes legal advice provided to clients for which they are paying fees, it may be difficult to persuade clients to accept a cap on the firm's liability. Clients are generally unaccustomed to seeing limits on liability in their contracts for legal services and if the online service is closely analogous to traditional legal advice, this may prove problematic. The argument in favour of a cap on liability, however, is stronger where the legal advice or guidance is packaged, or "productised," and sold to clients at a lower cost than the charge for providing the same advice on a one-to-one basis. Here a cap may be justifiable on the grounds that the law firm potentially has many times greater liability - to all subscribers - and because the clients are paying less for the advice than they normally would.

One important factor must be borne in mind, however. Although there is no absolute prohibition on solicitors limiting their liability, Law Society rules currently prohibit solicitors from limiting their liability to clients for legal advice to less than the minimum level of cover required by the Solicitors' Indemnity Rules (currently set at £1,000,000). Under the current rules, therefore, solicitors could not impose a lower cap than £1M in relation to online services providing legal advice to their clients. This means that the issue of whether making a particular service available constitutes the provision of legal advice is an important one to determine, since this will restrict the law firm's scope to limit its liability in relation to that service. On the other hand, if the service does not constitute legal advice, it is unlikely that the minimum will apply.

At the other end of the spectrum from general legal information to specific legal advice,[3] it would seem entirely reasonable for law firms to impose a much lower limit on liability, or even to exclude all liability (at least to the extent permitted by statute). For example, it would be intolerable for a law firm to be prohibited from excluding liability in relation to a public web site that provides general information on the law. This is clearly not legal advice since it is not provided by the law firm to a specific client with knowledge of his or her specific circumstances. Indeed, in this example, it is hard to see how the law firm could be found to have any liability since it would almost certainly have no duty of care towards, nor contract with, visitors to its web site. A more difficult example would be one where there clearly is some

3 The difference between legal advice and mere "information" has been much discussed. The key distinction for present purposes is that legal advice is given by a solicitor based on knowledge of the client's specific circumstances. Legal information, on the other hand, is not based on knowledge of the recipient's situation, but analagous to giving the recipient a legal textbook to read.

duty of care, and/or a contractual duty to provide a given service, but where the value of the service is focussed more on the technology provided to the users than on the legal content itself. It is less clear whether the £1M minimum would apply in those circumstances.

There is a strong argument to the effect that legal knowledge which is "productised" and sold on a subscription basis constitutes a new category of legal service, falling somewhere between mere information and bespoke legal advice. Consider, at one extreme, an individual who buys a book from a legal publisher (who is clearly not getting, or at least expecting, legal advice) and, at the other, a client going to his or her lawyer for legal advice tailored to his or her specific situation (who clearly is getting legal advice). Packaged knowledge services seem to represent a new category, falling somewhere between these two extremes.

In essence, the success of this argument depends on an assessment of the reasonable expectations of the user - is he paying for, and does he think he is getting, legal advice, or does he think he is just buying the equivalent of a legal textbook? In the light of those expectations, an estimate must be made of the degree of responsibility which it is reasonable for a law firm providing this kind of service, rather than one providing bespoke legal advice or publishing a book, to accept.

3.3 Technology-related issues

These issues do not relate specifically to the provision of online legal services, but are worth mentioning because some lawyers who are embarking on online service projects may not have considered all of the technology-related issues that could arise. Examples of contractual provisions which it may be appropriate to include in an online service subscription agreement are set out below:

What uptime can the law firm guarantee? Apart from the reliability of the service itself, the ability of subscribers to gain access will depend on a number of factors outside the law firm's control, not least the availability of internet access by the users. In this context, it is important to manage the expectations of the subscriber and to set out clearly what the firm is promising, and what is outside the scope of its control and responsibility.

What equipment does the subscriber need? Related to an uptime guarantee is the question of whether the subscriber needs any particular equipment or software on his PC in order to access the service. For example, if the online service supports only certain platforms, or specific browsers, this should be clearly stated.

What level of support is the firm offering? What is appropriate here will depend mainly on the nature of the service. If it provides business-critical support for key clients of the firm, a high level of support (possibly 24 x 7) will be appropriate. Equally, a service that provides "nice to have" information but that is not time critical may warrant only a much lower level of support (perhaps normal business hours only). Again, the scope of the law firm's obligations in relation to support should be clearly stated.

A related issue to consider is the contract between the law firm and any relevant service providers. A number of third parties may be involved both in the development and the maintenance of an online legal service, and it is important to ensure that those contracts contain obligations that mirror those of the law firm to the end user. For example, if the service is hosted by a third party, the level of support and uptime guarantees provided by the host will clearly affect the promises which the firm can make to its subscribers.

In addition, intellectual property considerations are important. Software development and/or web site design may also be carried out wholly or partially by third parties, and it is important for the law firm to ensure that it retains sufficient rights to be able to develop and expand the service, to provide it without infringing anybody else's rights, and to change to a new service provider (or bring the design or development in-house). It is important to ensure, therefore, that these contracts contain the necessary provisions to allow the law firm the flexibility that it needs.

3.4 Managing the subscribers' expectations

From the point of view of a law firm providing an online service, it is important to set out clearly the extent of the law firm's obligation to users of the service - principally what the service will provide, and when and for how long it will be available. For example, what subject area and/or jurisdictions does the service cover? What kind of guidance can a user expect to get from the service (*e.g. a* high level "issues list", or much more detailed advice)? When will the service first be made available and for how long?

Related to the matter of the law firm's obligations is the question of when a service, or part of a service, can be withdrawn, and in what circumstances. Some firms or their clients may feel that including a right to withdraw a service demonstrates a lack of commitment to the project and gives the client an unacceptable level of uncertainty regarding the continued availability of the service. It may be prudent, however, to include a right to withdraw a service, at least where the provision of the service becomes infringing in relation to a legal or regulatory requirement. (An online service provided via the internet could easily infringe, say, a local regulatory requirement in the subscriber's jurisdiction.)

In the case of subscription services paid for in advance, it may be reasonable to offer a *pro rata* refund of the subscription fee where the service is withdrawn by the firm.

3.5 Passwords

The administration of passwords can be a significant burden. Equally, of course, this task is vital to ensure that access to the online service is properly protected and that only authorised organisations and individuals have access to it - at least where the firm is concerned to protect the perceived value of the content provided via the service. However, the twin desires to minimise the law firm's administrative burden in setting up passwords and to ensure adequate security can be conflicting. An important issue to determine here is whether to issue a password to each individual user, or merely one password for each subscriber organisation.

It is tempting to take the latter option because this avoids the need to set up what could be tens or even, in the case of large organisations, hundreds of users for each subscriber. Consider, however, what happens when an individual user leaves the subscriber's organisation. He or she will take the password with him or her and could potentially continue using it. This problem does not arise with individual passwords because a user's password can simply be deactivated when he or she leaves the organisation.

The corollary to that, however, is that a system must be put in place to ensure that the law firm is notified when any authorised user leaves the organisation. One way of achieving this goal is to impose an obligation on the subscriber to notify the law firm whenever one of its employees leaves. A more proactive solution would be to conduct a regular audit of subscribers to ensure all active users are still employed by the relevant subscriber.

The other main disadvantage of opting for a "group" password rather than individual passwords is that it does not permit the law firm to monitor individuals' use of the service. This kind of information can provide invaluable feedback on the service that will help in future development efforts.

3.6 General web issues

In addition to the issues discussed above, a number of more general considerations arise in relation to the provision of online services. Two of these are discussed below.

Intellectual property issues. The law firm providing the service will clearly have invested a significant amount of resources into the project and will be keen to ensure that its rights are properly protected. The scope of the licence granted to users in respect of the service should therefore be carefully drafted. What use is reasonable will depend on factors such as the nature of the service and the subscription fee charged, but the firm providing the service should impose appropriate contractual limitations on subscribers' use of the service in order to ensure adequate protection of its know-how.

Data protection. As mentioned above, it may be desirable to monitor subscribers' use of a particular service. Where the information collected during the course of this type of monitoring relates to an individual user, this is likely to have data protection consequences. A law firm that wishes to do this may need to obtain consent from each of the individual users to ensure that this information may be collected and used in the manner intended. Care should be taken to define the scope of the purposes for which the data will be used as this may affect the validity of the consent if there is a later change of purpose. For example, suppose that users give their consent to the law firm processing personal data relating to their use of an online service for the purpose of analysing usage of that service. It may then be a breach of the Data Protection Act for the firm to use that information for general marketing purposes, which are not covered by the consent.

4 CONCLUSIONS

The provision of online services by law firms represents a new business model for law firms, as well as a new form of legal guidance for clients / subscribers. It is not only appropriate to reconsider the terms on which these services are provided, but important that law firms enter into service contracts that are appropriate in all the circumstances.

It is to be hoped that the Law Society will provide guidance on these issues at some point in the near future. In the absence of such guidance, however, it is up to law firms embarking on such projects to consider the factors involved - some of which are highlighted in this article - and adopt their own stance.

ETHICAL ISSUES AFFECTING MDPS FROM A EUROPEAN PERSPECTIVE

John G. Fish, Partner Arthur Cox, Dublin and President, CCBE

1 INTRODUCTION

1.1 General remarks

It would be difficult to imagine an issue affecting the practice of law which has generated as much interest, if not emotion, on the part of the legal profession globally, as the issue of MDPs, and in particular the ethical issues which have been hotly debated by either proponents or opponents of MDPs. Supporters of the need to liberalise regulatory regimes where restrictions exist, have resolutely argued that the provision of legal services through an MDP should be permitted, as this would be of benefit to consumers, clients and society in general. Opponents have equally resolutely argued that the provision of legal services through an MDP would irrevocably endanger the core values of the profession, resulting in adverse consequences for the consumer.

Let me state therefore at the outset that, notwithstanding the amount of ink which has been spilt and passion spent on the topic of MDPs, I do not propose in the course of this address to enter into a polemical discussion on the pros and cons of MDPs, but to concentrate on examining, as the title of this address implies, the ethical issues which do arise, and how significant to the legal profession these may or may not be in the context of MDPs. Whilst such issues are universal in nature, I intend to consider them also in a European context.

1.2 Conflict of interest

Before doing so however, I should at least declare any professional conflict of interest which I may be perceived to have! After all, conflict of interest is one of the core values I will be discussing later on. No doubt there will be those who will consider that because of my role in the CCBE as its First-Vice President, and indeed as Chairman of a Task Force which was established by the Law Society of Ireland, to examine the issues involved, that I would have a certain bias against the creation of MDPs!

It is of course true that a number of Bars and Law Societies who are members of the CCBE have adopted positions that MDPs are not in the interests of the profession or of the consumer. I have to say therefore that, although I will endeavour to deal with the issues as dispassionately as possible, my overall view is that any opposition on my part to the creation of MDPs is not motivated by an opposition to MDPs as such (I can well understand the benefits which from a purely commercial point of view, would accrue to both the members of the profession, and for their clients) but is motivated by a conviction that the "core values" which I will endeavour to analyse in this address, could be adversely affected, not just from the point of view of the members of the legal profession, or indeed consumers, but from the very fundamental role which lawyers play in the course of the administration of justice.

It is important to bear in mind however, that the CCBE is a representative body, whose members comprise the national Bars and Law Societies of the European Union, including a number of Bars and Law Societies who are classified as observers from other European States. Whilst the CCBE enjoys a particular status by representing the interests of the Bars and Law Societies before the various institutions (in particular the European Commission, the European Court of Justice in Luxembourg and the European Court of Human Rights in Strasbourg), positions which are adopted by the CCBE Plenary Sessions reflect invariably a common position agreed by the Bars and Law Societies.

Thus, in the case of the position adopted by the CCBE at its Plenary Session in Athens on 12 November 1999, on integrated forms of cooperation between lawyers and persons outside the legal profession, it should be noted that the CCBE, after reviewing various aspects of the issue, advised that there are overriding reasons for not permitting forms of integrated cooperation between lawyers and non-lawyers with relevantly different professional duties, and correspondingly different rules of conduct. The CCBE in this position document went on to state that those countries where such forms of cooperation are permitted, lawyer independence, client confidentiality, and disciplinary supervision of conflicts of interest rules must be safeguarded.

It will be noted from this that, whilst there is a generally agreed position within the CCBE as to forms of integrated cooperation between lawyers and non-lawyers, nevertheless it is acknowledged within the CCBE that where such forms of cooperation are permitted, then the essential core values, which I will address in greater detail in this paper, must be safeguarded.

2 SOME DEFINITIONS

2.1 Nature of an MDP

Whilst most legal practitioners would tend to consider an MDP as principally a partnership between lawyers and individuals from other professions, most notably the accountancy profession, the term has also been used to include any other form of association or practice with other professions whereby lawyers carry on practice in conjunction with one another.

I can well understand that given the many ways in which associations can be developed, whether by way of joint venture, parallel partnerships, exclusive referral arrangements, or whatever, I think that it does not really matter what you call the relationship, so long as (and looking at the arrangement from the point of view of a lawyer) the following elements are present; namely:

- where the practice carried on by the legal professionals to the arrangement is financed by non-lawyers;
- where the net profits of the lawyer's practice are shared with, or losses borne, by the non-lawyer members to the arrangement; and
- where the right to make decisions in relation to specific client matters are influenced by the non-lawyer members.

If any of these key elements are present, then in my view, an MDP in respect of which the core values of the legal profession must be taken into account, has come into existence. Any other arrangement, whether it includes forms of cooperation between lawyers and non-lawyers, the provision of non-legal services to clients, the investment of lawyers in entities providing non-legal services in which other professionals have an interest, falls outside the scope of this address. Nor do I make any comment on any ethical or Bar rules which might apply in these circumstances.

2.2 The question of "control"

As I have mentioned above, one of the key elements in an MDP is whether or not the decision making process can be influenced by the non-lawyer members of the MDP. As you can see, I have used the less precise word "influence" rather than "control". Indeed, as many of you will know, certain Bars and Law Societies have approached this issue on the basis that if the entity is "controlled" by members of the legal profession, then that would be sufficient to "protect" the core values of the profession. I think this is illusionary. The reality is that whilst partnership decisions often require varying levels of votes in order to be adopted, nevertheless the influence, by a minority of the partners can result in effective control of the entity concerned. We must bear in mind that in most instances we are talking about individuals rather than corporations where the decision making process is conducted through strict rules of procedure.

It is interesting to note that in Directive 98/5/EC[1] (commonly referred to as the "Establishment Directive"), Article 11 dealing with joint practice, provides that:

> *"... a host Member State, insofar as it prohibits lawyers practising under its own relevant professional title from practising the profession of lawyer within a grouping in which some persons are not members of the profession, may refuse to allow a lawyer registered under his home-country professional title to practice in its territory in his capacity as a member of his grouping. The grouping is deemed to include persons who are not members of the profession if:*
>
> *- the capital of the grouping is held entirely or partly, or*
>
> *- the name under which it practises is used, or*
>
> *- the decision-making power in that grouping is exercised,* de facto *or* de jure, *by persons who do not have the status of lawyer within the meaning of Article 1(2)".*

2.3 Definition of "legal services"

It seems to me that before one can even begin to tackle the subject of ethical rules and the role of lawyers in an MDP, the thorny subject of the nature of legal services, and what may be described as the practice of law, needs to be addressed. Even following a cursory review of the expansion in commercial legal services, especially when specialisation is taken into account, and the expansion of services by other professionals, it was always likely that the services provided by such professionals would overlap with one another.

The question therefore arises - What is so special about the nature of the services provided by lawyers and the manner in which those services are delivered to the client, that ethical standards over and above such ethical standards as would apply to any professional, such as standards of honesty and integrity, are essential?

The problem I believe is compounded by the fact that the provision of legal services is not always within the exclusive remit of the legal profession. Some jurisdictions do not impose any restrictions on persons from practising law such as Finland, whilst others operate on a fairly liberal regime such as in the United Kingdom and in Ireland, where in the case of the solicitors' branch of the profession (save in respect of the preparation of documents relating to land transactions, the winding up of personal estates and the

---

1 Article 11(5), Directive 98/5/EC of 16 February 1998, to facilitate practice of the profession of lawyer on a permanent basis as a Member State other than that in which the qualification was obtained. OJL 14 March 1998.

preparation of papers in Court proceedings), there is no restriction at all other than the non-lawyer providing a service cannot hold himself out to be a solicitor.

This can be contrasted with the United States, where lawyers have a monopoly on the practice of law, and difficult issues arise from time to time as to what is or is not the unlawful practice of law.

Might I suggest therefore that when considering these issues, rather than attempting to define what may turn out to be the indefinable, it might be better to concentrate on the role of the lawyer in providing a service regardless of the activity to which it relates.

Approaching the issue from this point of view then it is, I believe, relatively easy to identify areas of practice where such issues arise, namely:

- the representation of clients in Court and Court related work; and
- in the provision of legal advice to clients.

The first area, namely the representation of clients in Court proceedings, is I think straight forward, and there should be little argument in respecting such principles as the independence of the lawyer, conflicts of interest and confidentiality where Court proceedings are involved. The question which I will address is whether or not such core values are compatible with the ability of the lawyer to provide those services within an MDP.

As regards the second point, namely the giving of legal advice, this of course can range over a vast area of activity where the lawyer is called upon to give opinions, which so far as the client is concerned, should be opinions untainted by any other influence. Clearly, as legal services or indeed quasi-legal services expand, the role of the lawyer in providing legal opinions and advice becomes limitless. Again I would argue that the core values are relevant to the capability of the lawyer to provide that legal advice, and that any opinion should not be compromised by any influence which could be brought to bear by others.

3 ETHICAL ISSUES

3.1 General remarks

In terms of the specific ethical issues which require to be considered, it seems to me that these fall under the general headings of confidentiality, conflict of interest, and independence of judgement which, as noted by Advocate-general Léger in his opinion in the so-called NOVA Case[2], form part of "the very essence of the profession".

3.1.1 *Confidentiality*

Lawyers maintain that their obligations of confidentiality, i.e. an obligation not to disclose any information concerning their clients or their affairs, to any third party, save with the client's consent, is an obligation which is fundamental to the lawyer/client relationship. Lawyers will also maintain that because of the emphasis which, during the training of lawyers and during their professional careers, is placed upon the need to respect confidentiality, lawyers appear to have developed a highly tuned sensitivity to the need to maintain the absolute confidentiality of information revealed to them by their clients. It has often been suggested that members of the legal profession are unique in that respect.

The concept of confidentiality finds expression in many lawyers' codes of conduct. For example, Rule 2.3 of the CCBE Code of Conduct[3] provides that:

> *"It is of the essence of a lawyer's function that he should be told by his client things which the client would not tell to others, and that he should be the recipient of other information on a basis of confidence. Without the certainty of confidentiality there cannot be trust. Confidentiality is therefore a primary and fundamental right and duty of the lawyer.*
>
> *The lawyer's obligation of confidentiality serves the interest of the administration of justice, as well as the interest of the client. It is therefore entitled to special protection by the State."*

Similarly the principle of confidentiality is expressed in the Council of Europe's recommendation on "The Freedom of Exercise of the Profession of Lawyer"[4], where it states at Principle III (role and duty of lawyers at paragraph 2):

> *"Professional secrecy should be respected by lawyers in accordance with the internal laws, regulations and professional standards. Any violation of this secrecy, without the consent of the client, should be subject to appropriate sanctions."*

You will note however that in this recommendation, professional secrecy is qualified to the extent that it is in accordance with "internal laws" regulations and professional standards".

---

2 Case C-309/99 Opinion of Advocate-general Léger delivered 10 July 2001

3 Amended Code of Conduct for lawyers in the European Union adopted by the CCBE, 28 November 1998

4 Council of Europe Recommendation No. R (2000) 21 of the Committee of Members to Member States on the Freedom of Exercise of the Profession of Lawyers, adopted 25 October 2000.

Is there any reason to assume therefore that a lawyer who enters into an MDP, could find himself in a position whereby his ethical standard of confidentiality could be compromised? I fear that this could be the case. It is the duty of a lawyer always to act in the best interests of his client, and sometimes difficult decisions will arise based upon the information revealed by a client. These may include for example, the giving of legal advice to a client which the client might subsequently find unpalatable or unacceptable, resulting in the client seeking advice from another source, or the lawyer himself having to refuse to act, or to continue to act.

It is I believe unrealistic to assume that such decisions would be taken by the lawyer without reference to his colleagues in an MDP. Insofar as such decisions can affect the reputation, or even the profitability of the firm, it would be quite common in a partnership of lawyers for any decisions to be discussed amongst the partners. Given that under partnership law, a partner not only shares in the profits of the firm, but also in their losses, the partners have a very healthy reason for having all facts relating to the matter, to be disclosed to them.

Partnership agreements will invariably contain a provision that in the management of the firm, partners will act amongst themselves in good faith. It is also in my view unrealistic to assume that the non-lawyer members would have nothing to say, or that the non-lawyer would not be in a position to make any contribution regarding such significant decisions. How then can the lawyer in an MDP rationalise his obligation of confidentiality to the client, with his obligations to his partners?

Another point which I think arises in relation to the issue of confidentiality within an MDP, relates to the question of compliance with internal procedures which are put in place in relation to the MDP as a whole.

Insofar as the legal practice would be part of a larger network, then one must assume that in order to achieve the strategic objectives of the MDP, or in order to comply with internal requirements, as for example in relation to accounts and client accounts generally, or external requirements, such as money laundering obligations, full disclosure of all relevant information relating to the lawyer's client would be required to be disclosed to the non-lawyer members of the MDP. Thus it would be difficult to see how such requirements could be complied with in the context of the legal practice, without inevitably breaching lawyer's obligations of confidentiality.

Presumably the MDP as a whole would wish to ensure that adequate financial controls were in place on the principle that one weak link in the chain could endanger the strength of the entire.

An added complication arises in connection with the common law concepts of legal professional privilege, as applied in the United Kingdom, and the principle of professional secrecy as applied in civil law jurisdictions. It should, in passing be noted that whilst the obligation of professional secrecy is one generally imposed by law on lawyers in most of the Member States of the European Union, the right to assert privilege (as that term has been defined) is a right of the client rather than that of the lawyer.

3.1.2 *Conflict of interest*

Compliance with rules relating to conflict of interest is not, of course, an ethical issue which is confined solely to members of the legal profession. The question however, is whether the requirements imposed upon lawyers, and which to a greater or lesser degree impose obligations not to act or to act, following full disclosure to a client, are likely to be affected one way or another against the interests of the client in the context of MDPs.

Whilst it is perhaps beyond the scope of this address, to examine the way rules relating to conflict of interest are dealt with in various codes of conduct of each European Bar and Law Society (which do vary to some extent), I would nevertheless refer to the CCBE Code of Conduct Rule 3.2, which deals with conflict of interest as follows:

> "3.2.1 *A lawyer may not advise, represent or act on behalf of two or more clients in the same matter if there is a conflict, or a significant risk of a conflict, between the interests of those clients.*
>
> 3.2.2 *A lawyer must cease to act for both clients when a conflict of interests arises between those clients, and also whenever there is a risk of a breach of confidence or where his independence may be impaired.*
>
> 3.2.3 *A lawyer must also refrain from acting for a new client if there is a risk of a breach of confidence entrusted to the lawyer by a former client, or if the knowledge which the lawyer possesses of the affairs of a former would give an undue advantage to the new client.*
>
> 3.2.4 *Where lawyers are practising in association, 3.2.1 and 3.2.3 above shall apply to the association and all its members."*

Although this rule may well reflect the predominant national approach to the treatment of the conflict rule in many of the European jurisdictions, it is not nor does it claim to be, an all-embracing definition of the conflict of interest Rule. For example in the United Kingdom and Ireland, principles relating to conflict of interest are also bound up with the fiduciary duty of disclosure. Nevertheless, and subject to the difficulty in defining what is actually meant by the expression "a conflict of interest", the CCBE Rule can be regarded as a sufficient template for our purposes.

Just as ethical standards relating to confidentiality of information are in the interest of the client, not only from the point of view of ensuring the quality of legal advice, particularly in the context of litigation in the interests of the administration of justice, similarly other standards relating to conflict of interest are also so regarded. In terms of litigation, the concept seems to be fairly obvious, and certainly in common law jurisdictions, Courts have taken a fairly strong line. For example, in dealing with the issue of the duty of good faith, Mr. Justice Megarry stated that:

> *"A solicitor must be remarkable indeed if he can feel assured of holding the scales evenly between himself and his client"*[5]

It is I believe, in the field of commercial transactions that identifying the nature of a conflict can give rise to the most difficultly. Thus it is not uncommon for law firms, and indeed accountancy firms for that matter, to resort to "Chinese walls", where with the consent of the client, different lawyers from the same firm will act on behalf of different clients in the same matter.[6]

Individual firms will develop internal conflict procedures so as to ensure that as far as they are concerned, any conflict or potential conflict is identified, and the appropriate decision taken as to how it can be dealt with.

The question however, is whether in the context of an MDP, conflict of interest rules which apply to a lawyer, in the sense that they are a matter of professional regulation, will be adversely affected simply by virtue of being a member of an MDP.

The New York State Bar association in its excellent report on "Preserving the core values of the American legal profession"[7] when dealing with the subject, and after commenting that although most professionals confront conflict of interest, American lawyers have evolved far more detailed and stringent rules to regulate them than have members of other professions (or indeed lawyers abroad), concluded that

> *"in all these situations, multi-professional firms can avoid violating any professions' conflict rules by following the most restrictive rule applicable to any of its members.*
>
> *In most but not all cases, that will be the rule governing lawyers. The only questions therefore are whether all those involved are willing to accept the burden of this solution and whether, if not, a more lenient approach would undermine unacceptably the principles that conflict of interest rules promote."*

Still remaining on the other side of the Atlantic Ocean, a report prepared by the Charles River Associates of Canada, who had been commissioned by the "big five" professional services firms in Canada, to prepare an evaluation of

---

5 SPECTOR v AGEDA [1973] *Ch.* 30, 47

6 The concept of "Chinese walls" came under severe criticism in the House of Lords' Decision Prince Jefi Bolkiak v KPMG, 1999 1 *ALL E.R.* 517.

7 NYSBA, Albany, New York, April 2001

the economic advantages and disadvantages to clients of multi-disciplinary professional practices[8], identified the following in relation to conflicts of interest, namely:

- firstly, it is argued that in large and professionally diverse multi-disciplinary firms, conflicts of interest are inherently likely to become more pervasive;
- secondly, it is argued that some professions have different cultures and traditions than other professions in relation to the regulation of conflicts of interest, and that lawyers who are subject to stringent conflict of interest rules in order to ensure uncompromising fidelity to individual clients' interests, are specially likely to find their commitment to these ethical norms in jeopardy in MDPs with non-lawyer professionals; and
- thirdly, it is also argued that divergent legal and ethical duties of lawyers and non-lawyer professionals may create insoluble dilemmas within MDPs, and at this point refer to the rule of auditors and their obligations to disclose information publicly.

Whilst the report concludes that all these concerns have merit, it suggests that few of them are novel, or *sui generis* to the multi-disciplinary form of practice. In effect, the report suggests that whilst these concerns exist, in practical terms they should not of themselves be a cause for excessive concern.

The essential question to my mind is not in fact whether professional rules relating to conflict of interest would be compromised in an MDP, but that as in the case of confidentiality, whether in the context of the decision making process within an MDP, such rules could be breached.

3.1.3 *Independence*

When I was the Chairman of the Irish Law Society's Task Force on MDPs, I was very struck by the number of occasions on which this expression was used, and indeed within our own Law Society we had taken the view that independence is perhaps an ephemeral concept, easily understood but more difficult to express succinctly. Adherence to independence in the provision of professional legal advice, requires the lawyer to pursue without fear or favour his duties to his client, subject only to his duties as an officer of the Court and as a member of the legal profession. In particular, the lawyer's duty to give best advice to the client, must be pursued free from outside pressure.

---

8 Multi-Disciplinary Professional Practices. A Consumer Welfare Perspective, 4 August 1999.

In the New York State Bar association previously referred to which, after reviewing the specific role of the U.S. bar, goes on to state (at page 324):

> *"Unrestricted multi-disciplinary practice would pose a substantial threat to the roles and independence of the bar. The major accounting/professional service firms characterise themselves as MDPs. The rules of the accounting profession, focused on the audit function, play a relatively minor role in the regulation of those firms today. How will lawyers maintain their professional culture if many of their daily colleagues and partners come from other professions with differing functions and values? How will lawyers join as a profession if many of their professional links are with non-lawyers? How will lawyers interpret between private clients and the Government if the working firms, many of whose members lack that intermediary tradition? How will they resist pressure, whether to cut ethical corners, to reduce pro bono commitments, or to relax the professions rules, if colleagues from other professions with other standards call on them to do so? How will disciplinary bodies be able to determine whether a lawyer's independent judgement has been bent or displaced by the concerns of non-lawyer partners or stockholders? If positive answers to these questions cannot be found, the Bar will enter into new forms of practice only at the cost of injury to its independence and to the rule of law?"*

I would also draw your attention to Rule 2.1 of the CCBE Code of Conduct, where the principle of independence finds expression in the following terms:

> "2.1.1 *The many duties to which a lawyer is subject to require his absolute independence, free from all other influence, especially such as may arise from his personal interests or external pressure. Such independence is as necessary to trust in the process of justice as the impartiality of the Judge. A lawyer must therefore avoid any impairment of his independence, and be careful not to compromise his professional standards in order to please his client, the Court or third parties.*
>
> "2.1.2 *This independence is necessary in non-contentious matters, as well as in litigation. Advice given by a lawyer to his client has no value if it is given only to ingratiate himself, to serve his personal interest or in response to outside pressure."*

Again in the Council of Europe Recommendation previously referred to on the freedom of exercise of the profession of lawyer, the concept of independence is linked to the role of Bar associations or other lawyers' professional associations where it states at Principle 111.1:

> *"Bar associations or other lawyers' professional associations should draw up professional standards and codes of conduct and should ensure that, in defending the legitimate rights and interests of their clients, lawyers have a duty to act independently, diligently and fairly."*

This statement, and indeed other statements referring to the independence of the legal profession, I believe reveals two aspects, namely:

- the "independence" of the lawyer himself, i.e. in the sense that where acting on behalf of a client, he can exercise judgement independently of others; and
- the independence of the profession in a collective sense, which in effect really means the self-regulatory role of Bars and Law Societies.

I would suggest that whilst the issue of independence can easily be identified in the context of the individual lawyer, it is less clear in the context of the legal profession itself.

Certainly in a common law jurisdiction, from which I come, the concept of the Bar or Law Society exercising self-regulatory control over its members, is a well established feature. Self-regulation in this context means the right of the Bar or Law Society to set standards for admission to practice, albeit subject to Governmental approval, and the discipline of members where there has been a failure on the part of the member of the Bar or Law Society to comply with the Law Society's regulations, both in connection with the compliance of ethical standards, and the manner in which the practice of the lawyer concerned is conducted. For example, in relation to the solicitor's profession both in the United Kingdom and Ireland, there are very significant regulations in place regarding the holding of clients' funds, and powerful committees have been established relating to compliance with controls for the maintenance of solicitors and clients' accounts, and the approval of compensatory payments where funds are missing.

4 CONCLUDING REMARKS

As I have stated at the beginning of this address, I have endeavoured to highlight the ethical issues which must arise in the context of an MDP. I am not suggesting that these are insurmountable. Indeed it may well be that if MDPs are to become a reality, then it would be in the interests of the professions concerned, to jointly examine ways and means by which such ethical standards can be protected and interprofessional issues resolved.

It should be noted of course that since the publication of the NYSBA Report, New York has become the first State in the United States to adopt new provisions dealing with cooperative business relationships between lawyers and non-lawyers.[9] The new rules (which came into affect on 1 November

9 Joint Order of the Appellate Division, State of New York "Disciplinary Rules of the Code of Professional Responsibility" adopted 23 July 2001

2001) are constructed around two basic precepts, namely the preservation of the core values of the legal profession, and the best interests of the client.

From a European point of view, it is interesting to note that the rules make it clear that non-lawyers cannot direct or regulate the professional of judgement of lawyers in rendering legal services, or take any action which would compromise an attorney's ability to protect client confidences. In addition, non-legal professionals may not have any ownership or investment interest in a law practice, or have any managerial or supervisory power over the practice.

A key statement of the new rules is that multi-disciplinary practice between lawyers and non-lawyers is incompatible with the core values and the legal profession, and therefore a strict division between services provided by lawyers and those provided by non-lawyers is essential to protect those values.

Furthermore, it would only be fair to say that other Bars and Law Societies, most notably the Law Society of England and Wales and the Law Council of Australia, have taken the view that ethical considerations in an MDP, can be protected within an MDP.

For example, a Working Group established by the Law Council of Australian dealing with the issue of independence, took the view that apart from recognising that individual lawyers should be entitled to choose in whatever style they wish to practice, they must also comply with their ethical obligations of integrity and fidelity, and above all their individual commitment to the administration of justice.[10]

Furthermore, the Working Group pointed out that large legal firms already have to address and resolve on a daily basis core ethical issues, including conflicts of interest. The Working Group went on to note that the legal profession in Australia accepts without question the employment of lawyers by non-lawyers - such as the case of the in-house Corporate Council, or the public serving Government. The Working Group went on to pose the question that if the employment relationship does not detract from the professional responsibility of individual lawyers, why should a less subservient role, such as a lawyer being in partnership with a member of another profession, such as an accountant, give rise to concerns about independence?

In relation to confidentiality, the Working Group having first of all pointed out that the lawyer's duty of confidentiality in respect of information received in acting for a client is vital, proposed that it should be the obligation of the lawyer partners to ensure that their non-lawyer partners abide by that

---

10 Law Council of Australia Working Group Response adopted 20 January 1998.

requirement, and that this should be an irrevocable contractual relationship within an MDP.

Finally, I would like to leave the last word to Advocate General Léger, when he concluded that it was not contrary to the EC Treaty for a professional association of lawyers, such as in the particular case the Dutch order of lawyers, to adopt a binding measure prohibiting lawyers practising in the territory of the Member State concerned, from entering into multi-disciplinary partnerships with members of the professional category of accountants, if that measure is necessary in order to safeguard lawyers' independence and professional secrecy. It is a matter for the national Court to determine whether that is the case. It will be extremely interesting, if not crucial, to see whether the Court of Justice will endorse the opinion of the Advocate General.

A BAN ON MULTIDISCIPLINARY PARTNERSHIPS IN BELGIUM

Jo Stevens, Former Dean of the Antwerp Bar, Member of the Board of Directors of the Vereniging van Vlaamse Balies.

1 LAWYERS AND THEIR GOVERNING BODIES IN BELGIUM

1. Although in Belgium the lawyer has never been designated as an officer of the court, in practising the profession he is seen as associated to the public function of administering justice.[1]

He is a protector of civil rights and liberties. He is at the same time an organ of the power of state and a counter-power.[2]

In a democratic civilised society he facilitates the citizens' access to justice and is instrumental to their knowledge of their rights and their obtaining from the social body what is due to them. Therefore the objective of the lawyer's activity is of public interest.

That is the reason why professional rules regarding lawyering are laid down in legal statute.

In effect it is in the Judicial Code, containing all rules concerning civil proceedings, that are comprised the professional rules applicable to lawyers, in particular rules relating to organisation, qualification, professional ethics and supervision.[3]

Advocacy is defined in Belgium as part of the judiciary.

2. In Belgium the lawyer is seen as an independent professional, who freely exercises his mission "in defence of justice and truth".[4] Lawyers are independent agents.

There are no lawyers who exercise as employees of other lawyers or third persons, private or public bodies.[5]

Their mission related to the public service of justice, confers to lawyers special duties and prerogatives (*e.g.* attorney - client privilege) and imposes upon them strict ethical duties beyond these that are imposed on other citizens (*e.g.* independence, integrity, confidentiality, etc.).

---

1 C. CAMBIER, *Droit judiciaire civil*, t. I, Précis de la faculté de droit de l'université catholique de Louvain, Brussels, Larcier, 1974, 686.

2 C. PANIER, "A la fois organe du pouvoir et contre-pouvoir. Réflexions d'un magistrat" in X (ed.), *L'avocat à la recherche de son âme*, Liège, Ed. du Jeune Barreau, 1990, 122.

3 Gerechtelijk Wetboek/Code Judiciaire, Law of 10 October 1967, Boek III, art. 428-508/23.

4 Article 444 Judicial Code.

5 Article 437, 4° and 477ter Judicial Code; J. STEVENS, *Regels en gebruiken van de advocatuur te Antwerpen*, 2nd ed., Antwerp, Kluwer, 1997, p. 428-508, nr. 23.

Those duties are circumscribed in the Judicial Code as "the principles of dignity, probity and delicacy that are the fundamentals of the profession".[6]

Independence is the quintessence of the profession.[7]

It is a right and an overriding duty of the individual lawyer, and most of his ethical duties emanate from this right and duty, and find their cause and justification in the need to protect this independence.

As the IBA Resolution on MDPs[8] puts it: the ethical duties "are in many ways unique to the legal profession because they differ from similar aspects peculiar to other professions in that other profession do not play the pivotal role in the administration of justice and the upholding of the rule of law which the legal profession plays".

3. The individual lawyers' right and duty of independence is reflected in and is enhanced by the independence of his public professional bodies. They add to the independence of the lawyer "*la force d'une institution*".[9]

The independence of the advocate is seen as "an indispensable corollary to the independence of the judiciary".[10]

4. Each lawyer has to be a member of his local bar[11] and all local bars together formed until recently the Belgian Bar association.[12] The latter has been split up recently in a Flemish Bar's Association and an Association of the French- and German-speaking Bars.[13]

Each of these professional bodies has a public character, and its general councils and administrators (consisting exclusively of lawyers) are elected by the local lawyers.

As everybody knows, linguistic criteria are omnipresent and of overwhelming importance in Belgian public life.

---

6 Article 456, Judicial Code.

7 R. MULLERAT, MDPs and the public interest, is there a possible solution?, in X. (ed.), *L'avocat et son nouvel environnement concurrentiel*, Liège, Ed. du Jeunne Barreau de Liège, 2001, 2.

8 Vancouver, 13 September 1998.

9 B. LIBIEZ, "L'Ordre en question?", *J.T.* 1977, 13.

10 P. LEMMENS, "Independence and responsibility of members of the bar", in: *Rôle et organisation de magistrats et avocats dans les sociétés contemporaries*, IX° congrès mondial de droit judiciaire, Antwerp, Kluwer, 1992, 134.

11 Ordre des avocats/Orde van advocaten, article 431 Judicial Code; there are 29 local bars in Belgium.

12 Ordre National des Avocats de Belgique/Nationale Orde van advocaten van België, article 488 Judicial Code (in its former wording).

13 Law of 4 July 2001, to come into effect probably at the end of this year.

There are currently 12.672 Belgian lawyers, 7.233 of whom are Dutch-speaking lawyers, 5.410 are French-speaking and 29 are German-speaking lawyers.

5. The local bars have juridical powers over their members and visiting lawyers as disciplinary courts[14] and both local bars and the Belgian Bar association (in the future: the two associations created by the new law of 4 July 2001) have the mission to ensure the proper practice of the profession, and the power to adopt measures to that end.

6. They both have the legal power to issue regulations, which, in the case of the Belgian Bar association, are legally binding on each and every individual member of a Belgian bar.[15] In the future each of the regional associations' regulations will be binding to individual lawyers pertaining to the Dutch-speaking, respectively to the French- or German-speaking bars.[16]

2 THE BELGIAN BAR ASSOCIATION'S RULE ON MDPS

7. The situation in Belgium as to MDPs is not unlike that in the Netherlands.

Pursuant to article 8 of the Belgian Bar association's regulation on *"samenwerkingsverbanden"* (regulation on joint professional activity) of 1 October 1990 it pertains exclusively to this body (and more precisely to its General Council) to indicate those professionals with whom a Belgian lawyer may establish an MDP.[17]

This rule applies as well to integrated practice, where the participants practise their profession for their joint account, at their joint risk and by sharing control of final responsibility for that purpose, as to practice where "*means of production*" are put together by the participants who share only the costs of their joint activities.

8. As a matter of fact the Belgian Bar association has never indicated any profession that could prove eligible. On the other hand, the recent law on notaries public (the professionals deemed by the lawyers most indicated to associate with), expressly forbids them any integrated collaboration with other professionals.[18]

---

14 Article 456 Judicial Code.

15 Article 501 Judicial Code. These regulations are regarded as laws for the profession by the country's highest court, the Cour de Cassation/Hof van Cassatie; Cass. 12 December 1985, *Arr. Cass.* 1985-86, 533, *Pas.* 1986, I, 462 en *R.W.* 1986-87, 45.

16 Article 498 (new) Judicial Code, as amended by the law of 4 July 2001.

17 The rule reads in translation: "Only the General Council may indicate the other liberal professions, with which lawyers in Belgium can associate or group together".

18 Article 50 § 2 of the law of 4 May 1999 tending to the reform of the office of notary

9. It appears from this rule that joint professional activity was considered possible uniquely with other liberal professions. The rule does not show that as a matter of principal MDPs of any kind or with anyone should be banned. It simply says that MDPs are conceivable but that further regulation will indicate on what terms and with which professionals joint activity will be allowed.

In attendance of such further regulation MDPs remain forbidden in Belgium de jure et de facto.

10. This rule prohibits in no way occasional, non-integrated collaboration, or even referral commitments between professionals of different profession, as long as the professionals do not share profits, or do not bring means together to share costs for what appears externally as a joint activity.

11. Taking opportunity of difficulties in the Belgian Bar association (which were to end with the regional splitting up of this up till then unitarian public professional body) the French-speaking Brussels bar signed agreements with the professional bodies of the accountancy professions.[19]

The MDPs, which may be incorporated, that are allowed to the professionals of the three professions, are limited to sharing premises and equipment ("*société de moyens*"); fee-splitting remains prohibited.[20]

There is little doubt that these agreements of the Brussels French-speaking bar are contrary to the already mentioned regulations on this matter by the Belgian Bar association, a higher authority, whose regulations are legally binding for each and every individual advocate, and which may not be altered by a local and hierarchically lower professional body.[21]

12. As a matter of fact, until the present day authorisation for this kind of collaboration has not been applied for in the Brussels bar, since accountancy partnerships are not interested in the collaboration on a pure cost-sharing

---

public; A. DELIEGE, "Les sociétés de notaires", in X. (ed.), *L'exercice en société des professions libérales et les pratiques multidisplinaires*, Liège, Ed. du Jeune Barreau de Liège, 2000, 281; A. MICHIELSENS, *De nieuwe notariswet*, Antwerp, Kluwer, 1999, 330.

19 Convention entre l'Ordre français des avocats du barreau de Bruxelles et l'Institut des Réviseurs et Entreprises, 6 January 2000; Convention avec l'Institut des Experts-Comptables et des Conseils Fiscaux, 7 April 2000.

20 R. KROCKAERT, "Les experts-comptables et les conseils fiscaux", in X. (ed.), *L'exercice en société des professions libérales et les pratiques multidisciplinaires*, Liège, Ed. du Jeune Barreau de Liège, 2000, 308-310. See also in the same book: A. KILESSE, "Les activités du réviseur d'entreprises dans un cadre associatif", 356-357.

21 Article 501 Judicial Code. P. RAMQUET, "Mirage ou mariage, Libre propos sur la coopération de l'avocat avec les professions du chiffre", in X. (ed. .), *L'avocat et son nouvel environnement concurrentiel*, Liège, Ed. du Jeunne Barreau de Liège, 2001, 5; M. MERSCH, "Les avocats: état des lieux et perspectives", in X. (ed.), *L'exercice en société des professions libérales et les pratiques multidisplinaires*, Liège, Ed. du Jeune Barreau de Liège, 2000, 375.

basis. Secondly most lawyer partnerships in Brussels comprise French-speaking and Dutch-speaking lawyers, the latter resorting under the Dutch-speaking order of the Brussels bar, which has never made similar agreements with the accountancy professions.

13. Nevertheless, the mere existence of the illegal conventions incites some lawyers and some accountants to believe that in the near future MDPs between the two professions will become legal, are unavoidable, and so to say are written in the stars.[22]

14. In fact the Brussels conventions permit and even promote a certain hypocrisy. If one permits the two professions to practise under the same roof, in the same or adjacent premises, making use of the same personnel, hardware and software, it is improbable that the participants in this cost-sharing scheme would abide thereby.[23] There is some ambiguity in the press releases and declarations of leading accountancy firms personnel, that their firm has set up or is to begin MDP activities with or has taken over this or that Belgian lawyer firm (which declarations are seldom or never denied by the lawyers in question), and the affirmations of these same lawyers to their disciplinary authorities that there exists nothing but a not binding referral system, or a limited but close collaboration between the two firms.[24]

---

22 M. VANDEMEULEBROEKE, "La multidisciplinarité", in L. MARLIERE (ed.), *Quel avocat pour le 21° siècle?*, Brussels, Bruylant, 2001, 231. Laurent MARLIÈRE, secretary general of the Fidal Firm, the biggest MDP (KPMG) in France, is a fervent propagator of integrated collaboration with the accountancy professionals.

23 P. RAMQUET, "Le grand frisson de l'avocat", in X. (ed.), *L'exercice en société des professions libérales et les pratiques multidisplinaires*, Liège, Ed. du Jeune Barreau de Liège, 2000, 421-422.

24 See to this the comments of P. RAMQUET, *l.c.*, 424, note 20, who says that in Belgium the situation is clear: "sur le plan des principes en tout cas; ne lisait-on pas dans l'Echo du 29 février 2000 (sous le titre non exempt d'ambiguité "Avocat et Conseil: ne dites pas associés, mais clients priviligiés") un entretien avec Me Pascal Minne relatant le rapprochement du cabinet Bogaert and Vandemeulebroeke avec la firme d'audit Pricewaterhouse Coopers en refusant toutefois le concept d'association au sens juridique du terme pour décrire une relation d'étroite collaboration; nous observons que, depuis lors, le nom du cabinét a été débaptisé en Landwell qui est, on le sait, la dénomination sociale internationale des activités juridiques de PwC ...; le même journal d'ailleurs, en ses éditions du 12 au 14 février 2000, annonçait le début d'une collaboration entre le cabinet bruxellois Caesteker and Partners avec Arthur Andersen Réviseurs d'Entreprises, articulée celle-là, il est vrai, sur la toute récente alors résolution de l'Ordre de Bruxelles Français autorisant les associations de moyens entre avocats et réviseurs; les avocats concernés n''hésitaient toutefois pas à revendiquer leur prochaine intégration à Andersen Legal (2800 avocats, 100 établissements dans 34 pays)".

3 THE INTERNATIONAL BACKGROUND

15. It is a known fact that in the past opposition to MDPs was primarily led by the American Bar and the British Law Societies. MDPs found their way through the weak underbelly of Europe.

The debates held during two years in the House of Delegates of the ABA (American Bar association), came to an end when on 16 July 2000 in New York delegates voted to reject the advice of the commission ad hoc to admit MDPs.

Recently, and effective on 1 November 2001, the Appellate Division of the Supreme Court of New York, has made new regulations regarding non legal services, stating that multidisciplinary practice between lawyers and non lawyers is incompatible with the core values of the legal profession and that therefore a strict division between services provided by lawyers and those provided by non lawyers is essential to protect those values.

A lawyer may maintain a contractual relationship with a non-lawyer for offering both legal and non-legal services provided that:

a) the profession of the non-legal professional is included in a list to be established by the court;
b) the non legal professionals may not be granted nor obtain from the lawyer, hold or exercise, directly or indirectly, any ownership or invested interest in, or managerial or supervisory right, power or position in connection with the practice of law by the lawyer, nor share legal fees or receive any monetary or other tangible benefit for giving or receiving a referral;
c) the client must beforehand be told and agree in writ to the contractual relationship between the lawyer and the non lawyer and sign a Statement of clients' rights in co-operative Business Arrangements, drafted by the Court of Appeals.

The Council of the Bars and Law Societies of the European Union (CCBE), which is by all means the most representative body of the European lawyers, issued a declaration in 1993 banning MDPs for a variety of reasons connected to the lawyer's independence, legal privilege and avoidance of conflicts of interest.[25]

---

25 R. MULLERAT, *o.c.*, 4-5. See also the stringent conditions put forward by the Union Internationale des avocats in their "Résolution sur les pratiques multidisciplinaires" (New Dehli, 3 November 1999), J. LEROY, "Le niveau international: l'Union internationale des Avocats et le défi des pratiques multidiciplinaires, in X. (ed.), *L'exercice en société des professions libérales et les pratiques multidisplinaires*, Liège, Ed. du Jeune Barreau de Liège, 2000, nr. 435.

Partly as an answer to the position taken by the FEE - Fédération d'Experts comptables de l'Europe, the CCBE voted the resolution of Athens of 12 November 1999, saying that there are overriding reasons not to accept MDPs in countries where they are not allowed at the moment, and that in countries, where they exist, there is reason to give special protection to the independence, confidentially and disciplinary control over conflicts of interest.

16. CCBE also dressed a review of the factual situation[26] that shows a confounding multiplicity of situations and divergent rules.

There are countries (like Belgium, Finland, Liechtenstein, Luxemburg, Portugal, Spain and - limited to barristers - the U.K.) where no integrated or institutionalised collaboration with other professions is allowed.

Other countries (like the Netherlands, France, Denmark, Germany, Iceland, Italy, Norway, Sweden and - as regards solicitors - the U.K.) accept integrated or more limited forms of MDPs with specific professions.

Where MDPs are accepted, the accountancy profession, tax advisers, patent offices, financial advisers and notaries public belong to the chosen ones, although some countries exclude some of the named professionals.

The intensity of the collaboration, and its exteriorisation varies from country to country. Some countries accept that the various professions use a common denomination (Denmark, the Netherlands, Iceland, Norway), others preclude this practice (France, reason why the "lawyering section" of KPMG is named Cabinet Fidal in France; Ireland, U.K. Solicitors) or limit this possibility (Germany only with notaries public, Italy only with accountants, Spain with patent offices).

Some countries accept that the joint practice be located in the same premises, others do not. The same goes for fee- and profit-sharing, and taking a share in the stock of the lawyers' companies (forbidden in Denmark, France, Iceland, Italy, Ireland, Sweden, The Netherlands and the U.K.).

Some countries (Germany and Italy) have regulated that joint practice is possible provided that the other professionals abide with the professional rules of the lawyers.

17. With all this, it is clear that this review of national rules says nothing about the practical elaboration of the rules, and furthermore the question remains if in fact the rules and restrictions are observed by the practitioners.

---

26 "National situations regarding multidisciplinary partnerships".

There may exist a difference between the formal rules and their enforceability, viz. the degree in which their respect is effectively enforced by local authorities.

18. There are those who, pointing out the globalization or Europeanization of the profession and legal counselling in general, say that nothing should be prohibited to Belgian lawyers (or foreign lawyers desirous to join the Belgian Bar) that is already allowed in the surrounding countries at least.

There exists a European and even global profession, that has to have fundamentally identical rules.

The deontology of Belgian lawyers should therefore not be different from that of other lawyers in countries where MDPs are permitted. One cannot say that in those countries lawyers are less independent, dignified, honest or delicate, do not respect the duty of professional secrecy, or do not let the interests of their clients prevail.

19. Others think that advocacy remains primarily a national question and that, in view of differences in national or local traditions, perceptions and even sensitivities, differences in deontological viewpoints make sense, and are even necessary.

The principle of subsidiarity, recognised by the European authorities *i.a.* in respect to (auto) regulation of the legal profession, must prevail.

According to community law each member state is at freedom to regulate the professional status of lawyers on its territory and to issue its own rules of conduct.[27]

4 EUROPEAN AND BELGIAN COMPETITION LAW

20. It is constant that as to Belgian and European competition law the advocate's activity (as goes for all other liberal professions) is considered an economic activity, and that the professional bodies are viewed as associations of undertakings.[28]

---

27 Court of Justice, Case Reisebüro Broede, 12 December 1996, *TRD & I*, 1997, 02, 80; decision which refers to the Klopp Case, 12 July 1984, 107/83.

28 The European Commission has taken three decisions concerning the liberal professions: Decision 93/438/EEC of 30 June 1993 relating to a proceeding pursuant to article 85 of the EEC Treaty (IV/33.407 - CNSD) (OJ 1993 L 203, p. 27); Decision 95/188/EC of 30 January 1995 relating to a proceeding pursuant to article 85 of the EC Treaty (IV/33.686 - COAPI) (OJ 1995 L 122, p. 37); Decision 1999/267/EC of 7 April 1999 relating to a proceeding pursuant to article 85 of the EC Treaty (IV/36.147 - EPI Code of Conduct) (OJ 1999 L 106, p. 14). That last decision was in part annulled by judgement of the Court of First Instance of 28 March 2001 in Case T-144/99, "Institute of Professional Representatives before the European Patent Office v Commission" (2001), ECR II-000, "IPR; C.

21. When associations of undertakings take a regulation which has as its object the restriction of competition, or as its effect the prevention, restriction or distortion of competition, this regulation is contrary to competition rules, contained in article 85 (1) of the Treaty.

Even a "recommendation" without binding effect by the professional authorities must be censored, if the acceptance of that recommendation by the undertakings in question (the lawyers) would have a significant effect in the relevant market (of lawyers).

A call upon the special character of the liberal profession, its deontology, the duties of dignity, probity and delicacy, the quality of the services rendered, or the independence of the profession or the professionals, does not automatically provide justification. Furthermore these regulations or understandings must be notified to the European Commission in view of an exemption. If not they would be void *ab initio* pursuant to the direct effect of article 85 (1) EC, and article 2 (1) of the Belgian Competition Law[29] and the association of undertakings may be fined for issuing the said regulations.

Disciplinary authorities can only organise or promote those restrictive practices, which may be accounted for by reason of the necessity to guarantee the independence of lawyers, the quality of their services and the respect of their deontology.[30]

22. The Belgian professional rules being resemblant to those of the Dutch lawyers, it is clear that the outcome of the proceedings in the case C-309/99

EHLERMANN, "Concurrence et professions libérales: antagonisme ou compatibilité?", *Revue du marché commun et de l'Union européenne* 1993, 136; L. MISSON and F. BAERT, "Les barèmes d'honoraires des avocats sont-ils illégaux?", *J.T.* 1995, 485; L. IDOT, "Quelques réflexions sur l'application du droit communautaire de la concurrence aux ordres professionnels", *Journal des tribunaux de droit européen* 1997, 71; H. NYSSENS, "Concurrence et ordres professionnels: les trompettes de Jéricho sonnent-elles?" *R.C.B.* 1999, 475; A.M. VAN DEN BOSSCHE, "Voor economische vrijheid en mededigingsrecht: hoe vrij is de plichtenleer in het beperken van de economische keuzevrijheid van vrije beroepers?", *T.P.R.* 2000, 13; L NEELS, *Vrije intellectuele en dienstverlenende beroepen: deontologie, concurrentie en publiciteit. Een complexe driehoeksverhouding.* Studiedag F.V.I.B; Cass. 7 May 1999 (pharmacists' association case), *R.W.* 1999-2000, 112; Nederlandse mededingingsautoriteit, 21 January 1999, *N.J.B.* 1999, 231.

29 Law of 5 August 1991, of which many rules are literal translations of European competition regulation and jurisprudence of the Court of Justice. D. SZAFRAN, "La loi sur la protection de la concurrence économique - réforme de 1999", *J.T.* 2000, 474-475. For a more specific study on European and Belgian competition law as related to lawyers, see H. LAMON, *De advocaat in de 21ste eeuw: een ondernemer?!*, paper for the Limburgh Lawyers' Conference, 17 May 2001.

30 Belgian Arbitration Court (Arbitragehof/Cour d'Arbitrage i.e. Belgium's Constitutional Court), Tambue-case, Decision nr. 23/97 of 30 April 1997, 17.000; Opinion of the Adv. Gen. Dubrulle for the Pharmacists' case, Cass. 7 May 1999; Opinion of the Adv. Gen. Cormas of 12 February 1998 in case -35/96, Commission/Italy, par. 71.

Wouters, Savelbergh and Price Waterhouse vs. the Netherlands Bar association are of utmost importance to Belgian lawyers too.

The position taken by the CCBE and even more by the Commission and the Advocate-General Léger's Opinion[31] confirm the Belgian Bars in their attitude towards MDPs.

The Commission's opinion was that the ban on MDPs can be justified by coaxing reasons of public interest, being: the independence of the lawyers, professional secrecy and the active protection of clients. The Commission sees no less restrictive means to protect these aims and obviously does not believe in the efficiency of the famous "Chinese Walls", since the contradiction and conflicts of interests between the two professions remain unchanged.

Adoption of a clause of independence in the collaboration contract would be insufficient since the accountants' partnerships are to remain under control of the accountants, pursuant to article 2 of Directive 84/253/EC.

Accountants, as legal auditors of the accounts, have an obligation to inform the authorities and the public. This obligation makes the difference between them and other professionals.[32]

In his Opinion Advocate-General Léger says *i.a.* that application of the Community competition rules may be liable to "*obstruct the performance of the particular tasks assigned to lawyers*"[33], who must, to carry out their "public service tasks", respect duties in relation to their independence, respect of professional secrecy and the need to avoid conflicting interests.[34]

The Advocate-General comes to the conclusion "that the restriction of competition caused by the (Dutch) Regulation is necessary if features which form part of the very essence of the legal profession in the Netherlands are to be protected".[35]

It should be pointed out that the Advocate-General proposes to refer the examination of these matters back to the Dutch Raad van State[36] to decide if the prohibition measure as regards accountants is necessary in order to safeguard lawyers' independence and professional secrecy, whereas multidisciplinary partnerships are authorised in the Netherlands with notaries, tax advisers and patent agents.

---

31 Delivered on 10 July 2001.

32 Report of Judge Wathelet, p. 89.

33 Par. 179.

34 Par. 180. Those duties and their specific aspects are determined further by the Advocate-General in par. 181-186.

35 Par. 187.

36 Par. 200 and 258.7.

The difficulty consisting in the difference of treatment in the Dutch regulation between accountants and notaries, tax advisers respectively patent agents[37] does not exist in the Belgian situation since no profession has been elicited as yet to qualify for MDPs with lawyers. There is therefore no difference of treatment in the Belgian regulation.

5 THE DECISION OF THE "VERENIGING VAN VLAAMSE BALIES" OF 13 DECEMBER 2000

23. In the process of splitting up the Belgian Bar association two regional de facto associations have been created by the Flemish resp. French and German speaking Bars.[38]

It is these two associations that have been recognised recently by law, as the successors of the Belgian Bar association.[39]

The council of representatives of the (at the time not yet legally recognised) Flemish Bar association - the representative body of the Flemish advocates consisting of 58 directly elected members - have studied the MDP-problem, after suggestions were made to alter the Belgian Bar association 1990 prohibition rule on MDPs.

The question was raised in the Flemish Bars after the agreements of the French-speaking Brussels Bar with the accountancy professions' governing bodies.

24. The Green Paper[40] and discussions led the representatives with an overwhelming majority to the decision that the matter could not be postponed till the Court of Justice's decision, and that the Belgian Bar association's rule would not be altered. Integrated MDPs even limited to sharing costs in the joint activity, remain prohibited.

25. The discussions pointed out the already "classic" pros and cons.

25.1. It is said that MDPs will promote innovations, that closer contact between different professions might lead to greater appreciation of the needs

---

37 Pointed out by J.C.J. WOUTERS, "Conclusie A.-G. Europees Hof (2), Riskante ontsnappingsroute uit Europees mededingingsrecht", *Advocatenblad* 2001, 52.

38 The Vereniging van Vlaamse Balies, and the Conférence des barreaux francophones et germanophone, having each 14 local bars as their members, the bar at the Cour de Cassation remaining a bi-lingual institution.

39 Law of 4 July 2001 creating the Flemish Bar association and the Association of the French- and German-speaking Bars, to enter into effect after approval by the King of their intern governing rules.

40 J. STEVENS, Nota betreffende de multidisciplinaire samenwerkingsverbanden (MDPs), which was later to be presented to the Belgian parliament (5 May 2001) during its discussion on the implementation of Directive 98/5/EC of 16 February 1998 (Parliamentary Documents, House of Representatives, Doc. 501120/004, 29 June 2001, 19).

of the clients and to the provision of new improved and innovative products. That the one-stop approach corresponds to the user's needs for integrated professional services, and will allow to offer a mix of services not currently available or to offer services at price and quality conditions which would represent an increase in the current level of competition. It would widen the consumers' choice, and lawyers and accountants working together in joint practices could benefit from each other's experience, and improve the quality of their services.

Economies of scale could be achieved in common structures, having positive effects for consumers in terms of price.[41]

Those are sloganesque affirmations; but I am prepared to accept that each offer creates its own demand, especially if the offer is made to those who are already clients of the shop. The shop just selling another product by means of its former employees who have become lawyers.

Propagators of the MDP idea tend to say that although deontology is important for the liberal professions (it is also a selling argument, deontology being used regularly in marketing for the professions), it is not that different for the two professions involved and anyway the strictest of the two rules of the professions must prevail over the less strict.[42]

Further that independence is before all a state of mind, although the professionals have to uphold the apparent independence as well, i.e. the appearance as seen from the exterior.[43]

As to professional secrecy, referral is made to the theory of the "*secret partagé*"[44] with express assent of the client, and, where needed, the separation of files and computer data by "Chinese Walls".

The core problems of independence, secrecy and conflicts of interest can be tackled, since it is the client who at every moment controls the multidisciplinary assignment, who can take back parts of the tasks, who can limit be

forehand who may have access to certain privileged information, and can decide nevertheless to consult an MDP if a problem of possible conflicting interests arises.[45]

41 Opinion of the Advocate-general Léger already mentioned, in the NOVA-case, par. 117-119; R. KROCKAERT, *o.c.*, 316.

42 R. KROCKAERT, *o.c.*, 312-313; M. VANDEMEULEBROEKE, *o.c.*, 248.

43 A. KILESSE, *o.c.*, 353.

44 A. KILESSE, *o.c.*, 354; M. FRANCHIMONT, "Le secret professionnel du réviseur d'entreprise", *C.B.N.R.*, 2-1986, 32; E. JAKHIAN, Intervention at the Congress (Paris, 27 May 1999) of the Institut des droits de l'homme of Brussels and Paris, Lettre du bâtonnier, 1998-1999, nr. 5, 306.

45 M. VANDEMEULEBROEKE, *o.c.*, 249.

25.2. Those against MDPs stress the need for independence, control of the firm by lawyers, abidance with lawyers' ethical rules, strong supervision by the bars and exclusion of incompatible professions, i.e. professions such as lawyers and auditors, whose professional duties not only conflict but are incompatible.[46]

As the Advocate-General Léger puts it in the Nova-Case, the existence of multidisciplinary structures including lawyers and accountants is liable to constitute a threat to the independence of the lawyers, and a major obstacle to the observance of the lawyers' professional secrecy.[47]

The argument of the one-stop shopping is refuted as a "geographical advantage"[48], a marketing device, or publicity stunt, since multidisciplinary teamwork can perfectly be done (if and when it could prove useful to the client) on a punctual basis, and without the professionals sharing each other's profits, with all the risks of rent seeking and dichotomy involved, in a market that will always be characterised by its asymmetric information.

---

46 R. MULLERAT, *o.c.*, 11; LEGER, Opinion NOVA-Case, par. 185.

47 In par. 185 he indicates: "There is a certain incompatibility between the "advisory activities of a lawyer" and the "supervisory activities of an accountant". The written observations submitted by the Association show that accountants in the Netherlands have the duty to certify accounts (185). They undertake objective examination and scrutiny of their clients' records, so as to be able to impart to interested third parties their personal opinion concerning the reliability of those book-keeping data. Lawyers might no longer be in a position to advise and defend their clients independently if they were to belong to an organisation that had also to give an account of the financial results of the transactions in which they acted. In other words, setting up a body with financial interests in common with members of the professional category of accountants poses the risk of tempting - even forcing - lawyers to take account of considerations other than those exclusively linked to their clients' interests."
And in par. 186: Once members of the two professional categories have undertaken to share the profits, losses and financial risks connected with their association, they will obviously have an interest in exchanging information about the clients they have in common. An accountant may be tempted to ask for and obtain information from a lawyer relating to, for example, negotiations conducted by the latter in a certain dispute. A lawyer may, vice versa, be tempted to ask questions of an accountant in order to obtain evidence which would help him to make a better presentation of his client's case in court. The risk of violating legal professional secrecy is the greater because, in some circumstances accountants are required by law to impart to the competent authorities information concerning their clients' activities.

48 M. MERSCH, *o.c.*, 382. See also the opinion of M. GOUT, former president of CCBE in L. MARLIERE (ed.), *Le marketing du cabinet d'avocats*, Paris, Organisations, 1999, 129. It may be pointed out that with the ever-increasing extension of communication facilities of all sorts, the "geographical advantage" to be located on the same spot in order to bring one's expertise together is a feeble argument.

In fact clients could benefit more from having two separate independent professional views, where one professional could control the other and if necessary criticise any possible irregularity.[49]

This opinion inscribes itself in the world-wide discussion concerning cumulation of control- and advisory functions by professionals, who are participants in the same integrated organisation.

The Green Paper of the European Commission[50], the position taken by the U.S. Securities and Exchange Commission (S.E.C.), parliamentary initiatives in Belgium and abroad, and not the least recent scandals that, for evident lack of control, caused personal and financial damage to thousands of investors in Belgium (Lernout and Hauspie, Kempische Steenkolen) demonstrate that these questions and problems have not a merely theoretical character.

If moreover, the auditing professionals, apart from their collaboration with advisory services of their group (which they introduce to their clients), collaborate on a fee-sharing basis with lawyers in the same group, they call into existence an additional confusion of tasks and interests, which is detrimental to the integrity and independence of the professions concerned, and detrimental to the quality of the professional services rendered by the different professions, and, eventually, as has been made clear by various recent scandals, to the public itself.

The independence of lawyers in MDPs with accountants, where pursuant to directive 84/253/EC the majority of the shares and in the board of directors must be in the hands of accountants, cannot be guaranteed. This independence, however, is one of the core values of the profession, and lack of professional independence can be sanctioned by the local Bars, who can decide disbarment, or other disciplinary sanctions.[51]

The independence of lawyers is mandatory and pertains to the Belgian public order.[52]

Even if conflicts of interest could be regulated and if professional secrecy could be protected by some kind of Chinese Walls, it is felt that control by professional authorities will be hazardous if not impossible.[53]

---

49 R. MULLERAT, *o.c.*, 13; F. GLANSDORFF, "Aperçu général des avantages et des inconvénients des pratiques multidisciplinaires", in X. (ed.), *L'exercise en société des professions libérales et les pratiques multidisciplinaires,* Liège, Ed. du Jeune Barreau, 2001, 406.

50 The role, position and responsibility of the accountant in the European Union (24 July 1996, COM/96/338 def.); see also CCBE's Consultative Paper on Statutory Auditors' Independence (7 March 2001).

51 Article 437, al. 2 Judicial Code; J. STEVENS, *o.c.*, nr. 306.2. This recently was done by the Antwerp Bar on the 22nd of October 2001, when access to the bar was denied to two members of KLegal, the advocacy network of KPMG (judgement under appeal).

52 Cour d'Appel de Bruxelles, 1 October 1987, *Jur. Liège* 1987, 1453.

It is therefore felt that such safeguards are based on unfounded expectations.[54]

Ultimately it is a choice for a unique non-split[55] and independent profession, with its own identifiable specificity and ethical rules, its own vocation in the spirit of a public service linked to the judiciary, that is made by those opposing MDPs in Belgium with regard to the traditions and specifications of the Belgian Bars.[56]

6 THE IMPLEMENTATION OF THE ESTABLISHMENT DIRECTIVE (98/5 EC)

26. When discussing the implementation of the Establishment Directive 98/5/EC of 16 February 1998 the Belgian Parliament indicated that, whereas at the present time MDPs are prohibited by article 8 of the Belgian Bar association's regulation on joint professional activity[57], this issue will come under the competence of the two new professional bodies (the Flemish Bar association, and the Association of French- and German-speaking Bars[58]).

One knows that the predecessor of the Flemish Bar association has already voted, almost unanimously, on 13 December 2000 that no alterations be made to the existing ban on MDPs.

A committee was set up by the French- and German-speaking bars to study the problem once more. The Brussels French speaking bar seems to be the only one to want the introduction of MDPs at a cost-sharing basis.

It is understood that in the future the Flemish Bar association will by means of new regulations specify more in detail the ban on MDPs, and the factual

---

53 As already set forth in footnote 24, the lawyers who collaborate with the big five in Belgium have set the tune by obscuring the real content and conditions of their collaboration.

54 R. MULLERAT, *o.c.*, 13, par. 4; F. GLANSDORFF, *o.c.*, 402-406, where the "solutions" for remaining problems like the "secret partagé", Chinese Walls, the "independence as a state of mind", and the like are criticised.

55 R. MULLERAT, *o.c.*, 15, par. 6.

56 M. VAN DOOSSELAERE, "L'avocat belge dans le marché unique", in L. MARLIERE (ed.), *Quel avocat pour le 21° siècle*, 2001, Brussels, Bruylant, 182; P. RAMQUET, *o.c.*, 19, says: "Le mirage de la fusion interdisciplinaire perdrait la profession d'avocat à l'instant où le professionnel de la confidence épouserait le contrôleur, en se soumettant d'ailleurs, sans doute, à sa puissance financière. L'avocat est différent, et doit le demeurer.".

57 Report to par. 2.1 of this paper.

58 Belgian Parliament, House of Representatives. "Bill to facilitate the practice of the legal profession and the establishment in Belgium of lawyers practising in member States of the E.U.", discussion of 29 June 2001, Doc. 50 1120/004, pag. 12, 17, 19 and 26.

and occasional collaboration with other professionals, so as to close the loopholes currently existing in the national regulation.[59]

27. From the parliamentary debate on the new establishment law it appears that the Belgian Parliament will simply make use of the possibility given by the Establishment Directive[60] to prohibit MDPs for foreign lawyers who wish to enter the Belgian Bar, in the exact wordings of the Establishment Directive itself.[61]

This way equality of treatment between Belgian and European Union Lawyers will be assured, and any reproach of discrimination avoided. It is therefore to be expected that in the foreseeable future in Belgium the ban on MDPs will be maintained, at least for MDPs with the accountancy professionals.

---

59 *E.g.* sharing the same or adjacent premises, or receptionist facilities, networking, joint marketing, various remunerations paid by the lawyers to their accountant partners for goodwill, for the use of the premises, library facilities, personnel, hard- and software, expert assistance and other so-called at-arm's-length invoicing.

60 Article 11.5.

61 Doc. 50 1120/001, 16-17, article 477octies § 5 (new) of the Judicial Code; Doc. 50 1120/005, 12-13.

MDPS: WHERE CLIENTS ARE KING

Marc Vandemeulebroeke, Senior Partner Bogaert & Vandemeulebroeke, Member Landwell[1]

1 INTRODUCTION

1.1 The general context

Multidisciplinary practice[2] in our view is where a lawyer or a law firm practises its profession alongside other professionals in order to offer clients, who more often than not are common to them all, a range of legal and non-legal services that is as broad as possible and practised in as integrated a manner as possible. It is therefore a synergy effect that is sought, based on a joint vision of the clients' needs and on a group culture in which everyone works as a function of the others but in the interests of the client. Each of the members of an MDP generally constitutes a point of access to the services offered by the others.

Two different forms of MDPs would appear to exist[3]: on the one hand, a true, operational integration accompanied by a sharing of losses and profits and, on the other hand a close cooperation at an operational level, albeit based on a broad "structural" autonomy amongst the partners. The first model is generally called a "multidisciplinary partnership"; the second model is dubbed a "multidisciplinary *practice*". This article essentially concentrates on this second model.

Advocates of MDPs see in them, as far as lawyers are concerned, a unique opportunity to better serve clients who have need of advice in certain areas, particularly those going beyond the legal sphere, and the chance for them to service their clients in a more pro-active and global manner.

Opponents of multidisciplinary practice fear that lawyers will lose their independence and disregard the conflicts of interests rules to the prejudice of the profession's image. Moreover, lawyers would become hostage to a "mercantile" culture that would be hard to reconcile with the so-called traditional characteristics of the lawyer's craft.

Advocates and opponents of MDPs confront one another with slogans whilst the professional authorities misjudge the contours of the questions and, *de facto*, have allowed powerful multidisciplinary firms to set up in Belgium.

---

1 The opinions here expressed are those of the author only
2 Generally known internationally under its English abbreviation "MDP".
3 N. SPEECHLY, "Accountants and the Legal Business", *Lafferty*, 1999, p. 6.

Modern lawyers want to profile themselves on a market that is increasingly open and hence competitive. One has to be better, faster, more creative and cheaper; advice has to contribute a value-added and find solutions. With this in mind, proximity to one's clients is essential, as is a perfect understanding of the challenges with which they are confronted. It is for that reason that the central position that the client is thus accorded in the modern lawyering profession has entitled me to subtitle this presentation "MDPs: where the client is king".

1.2 But what do clients expect from their lawyers?

What clients fundamentally want from their lawyers[4] is at one and the same time assistance in their transactions and the assurance of an identified and verified legal risk. They want solutions and no longer just an opinion that leaves them alone to face the decisions to be taken. The lawyer does have to play the role of a guide enabling his clients to circumvent the obstacles without risk and to bring their business strategies to fruition.

The players in the economic world do not lack legal assistance and they can generally rely on internal legal advisers or a breadth of practical experience in helping them to reduce their risks. In this context, clients expect their lawyers to contribute a value-added to their own analysis. Lawyers therefore will have to come up not only with technical knowledge but also with an excellent understanding of their client's trade. This latter factor means having knowledge of the business sector, the competitive restrictions, and changes in the field of technologies and in the market etc. The presence of a lawyer within an MDP from this point of view constitutes an important advantage, since it allows him to get a better appreciation of the economic stakes and to play a more active role in his advisory brief.

When working within an MDP, a lawyer is able to set his vision of the client's needs (essentially a request for legal advice and legal support for certain transactions) against that of other professions that are just as indispensable for the client's prosperity (tax advisers, consultants, actuaries, computer engineers, auditors, risk managers, etc.).

Clients have global needs that are very rarely limited to an isolated legal question. For instance, the acquisition of a company frequently entails the involvement of a variety of professionals: auditors, specialists in computer or environmental risks, tax advisers, computer technicians, notaries public, bankers, various consultants, etc. The client will build his team of advisors either by selecting them individually or by calling on multidisciplinary

---

4 This applies to lawyers who are not members of the bar.

teams that already have wide, common business experience and will save him the difficulty of coordinating each of their tasks. It is obviously in this latter situation that MDPs assume their great significance.

1.3 What do the lawyers propose?

In the face of these needs, Belgian lawyers have, for the most part, remained extremely fearful, preferring to carry on their profession around their traditional monopoly of appearing in court, thus leaving room for a number of the largest firms, banks and advisors in all realms, some of them known as the Big Five.

The question of whether alliances had to be formed with other professions has of course arisen with greater intensity. Hence we have seen a number of European firms broadening the perimeters of their activity to notaries public, tax advisers, (non-legal) specialists in trademarks and patents, and to corporate finance specialists and consultants.

Many of these alliances have representatives in Belgium, which has certainly provided food for thought on the question of multidisciplinary practice. In particular, the presence of Dutch notaries and German auditors in the largest law firms that have set up in Belgium means that the subject can no longer be ignored.

Nowadays, nearly every large-scale law firm in Belgium is an MDP, working in Belgium or abroad alongside other professionals, mainly notaries public and company auditors.

Whatever the criticisms are that have been levelled against MDPs, they have existed for a long time and have progressively taken a share in the market. In its listing of the 50 largest law firms, the IFLR[5] classifies 4 firms linked to the Big Five amongst the first 20.

As has very recently been written, and quite rightly:

> *"Some lawyers and bar associations will likely never be convinced that there is market demand for MDPs. But MDPs are already operating. Clients and public interest would both clearly be better served by admitting that MDPs already exist, by allowing them to exist openly, and then to regulate them in a manner consistent with the core values of the profession. The call to demonstrate that the market is demanding MDPs wholly misses the point. MDPs are not only inevitable, they already exist openly in some parts of the world, and undercover in the rest of it".*[6]

---

5 IFLR1000 50 largest Law Firms in the World.

6 *International Bar News*, December 1999, "Protect the Clients, Not the lawyers".

1.4 And what do the clients think?

A number of surveys have been done in order better to gauge client opinion.

The American Chamber of Commerce[7] and the American Corporate Counsel Association[8] (ACCA) thus did a market survey in January 2000. The principal message was: nearly 70% of Americans would like to see the rules changed in order to allow lawyers and other professions, like accountants, financiers, etc., to work within the same firm. As the vice-president of the of US Chamber of Commerce has emphasised, *"this provides clear evidence the public supports the idea that they want more options for where and how they get legal services"* and the president of the ACCA has stated that *"MDPs will provide a broader range of choice for clients seeking solutions to complex prolbems."*

A recent poll conducted by the Financial Times has shown that more then 50% of the largest "buyers of legal services" in the United Kingdom and the United States are prepared to use the services of firms whose members simultaneously include lawyers and accountants. For American companies, this percentage even exceeds 75%.[9]

The bulletin of the American Bar association recently devoted an article to MDPs: "The legal profession must be market driven, and market demand appears to be calling for and receptive to more consolidation of legal business expertise in terms of multi- and cross- disciplinary schemes."[10]

In an interview that attracted a lot of attention, Digby Jones, the new director general of the Confederation of British Industry (CBI) stated[11] *"the ban on multidisciplinary partnerships should be lifted as soon as possible, allowing the corporate clients the ability to pick and choose the right professional service provider for the specific needs. The market – not the regulators – should be the deciding factor in whether MDPs survive as a realistic form of practice. ... MDPs are inevitable and it would be better for the profession to espouse them and deal with them."*

Nor is there any shortage of public stances to the same effect.[12] Very recently nearly 40 American consumer associations insisted that the American Bar

---

7 Which represents some 3 million members.

8 Which, for its part, covers 11.000 members and 4.000 organisations.

9 Financial groups support multi-disciplinary firms.

10 Law Practice Quarterly, February 2000.

11 *The Law Society Gazette*, "Industry Chief Puts Weight Behind MDPs", January 2000.

12 In particular: "Touting For Fear: MDPs and In-House Lawyers", *European Counsel*, Volume IV, Issue 10, Dec. 99; "The importance of Multi-Disciplinary Practice", *Law Practice Quarterly*, February 2000; "Industry Chiefs Puts Weight behind MDPs", *The Law Society Gazette*, January 2000; "Financial Groups support multi-disciplinary firms", *Financial Times*, September 1999; "Hybrid Law Practices in US Debated", *The Wall Street Journal*, 31 May 2000; C. ARNHEIM, "Multidisciplinary law firms?", *Managing Partner*, January 1999, p. 3; "Stretching the Law", *The Economist*, 29 August 1999; "Can the Big

association at last change its rules and cease its practice of only taking account of the interests of attorneys.[13]

In France, the MEDEF (formerly CNPF) takes the view that, if MDPs exist, "it is that they are a response to a demand for services. Their rapid development goes hand in hand with market needs and they offer a major advantage to expatriate firms due to their presence in the majority of countries".[14]

Still in France, a recent survey carried out amongst 524 businesses shows that 77% of them use MDP networks, especially the larger companies. In addition these businesses have a tendency to use a number of networks. Of the companies using MDPs, more then half also ask for legal advice; their main reasons are, in descending order of importance, international geographical coverage (54%), multidisciplinary skills (34%), the personal relationship with their legal adviser (27%), and presence at a national level (9.4%).[15] The same survey puts into proportion the supposed decisive advantage of a "one-stop shop": large companies in particular are far from systematically requesting legal advice just because they are audited by an auditor who is part of an MDP. That is true in only about one-third of cases. However, if these same companies consult MDPs, it's above all for their unmatched networks and their efficiency in the practical deployment of solutions.

In Belgium, an older survey, which has been kept extremely confidential, has revealed an identical tendency and the same demand on the part of business.[16] A recent survey[17] has highlighted a certain number of interesting tendencies in Belgium, showing that the liberal professions want to be able to create multidisciplinary alliances:

- 57% of accountants, 59% of notaries public, 68% of auditors and 72% of lawyers questioned think that MDPs will allow for acceleration in the advisory process (and therefore a reduction in prices);
- more then 60% of lawyers cite the existence of a multidisciplinary link with a notary public, accountant, auditor or tax advisor;

Five hire every lawyer in the US?", *Worldlaw Business*, April 2000, p. 39.

13 Press release "Consumer groups praise ABA panel for hearing client voices", 1 June 2000, unpublished.

14 See the Nallet report, p. 97.

15 Nallet report, pp. 100 et seq.

16 See E. JAKHIAN, *o.c.*, II, E, and the reference made to discussions with the Institute Company Auditors; on the same lines see also K. BARREZEELE, "Samenwerken", *Financieel Economische Tijd*, 4 September 1999, 2.

17 STV InNOVAtie and Arbeid, "De weg naar multidisciplinaire kantoren" by S. HELLINGS.

- nearly 82% of the lawyers questioned would in the future like to have a multidisciplinary alliance with at least one other liberal profession, in particular a notary public.

2 THE STATUTORY AND REGULATORY FRAMEWORK

2.1 In Belgium

Article 8 of the Regulations of 8 March 1990 issued by the national Bar association grant exclusive power to the general assembly of the national association to decide which other professions lawyers may form a grouping or association with. No such decision has ever been taken. Quite the contrary, certain local bar associations have taken the view that, as far as they are concerned, they can on their own initiative to take a negative position vis-à-vis MDPs and, what is more, decide on their own what "association" or "grouping" signifies.[18]

This Article 8 is now in contradiction with Article 11 of the EU Directive 98/5/EC (see hereafter) which allows exclusively Member states to rule on MDPs; the national Bar association is not part of the Belgian State and has no valid ruling power on the MDP issue. Article 8 is therefore a "measure" as meant in articles 43 and 49 of the EU Treaty and can be challenged by any concerned party. The all Regulation is not any more enforceable in domains already covered by the EU Directive. The same situation will apply to any possible new regulation to be decided by the two new Bars associations ("OVB" and its French speaking counterpart).

From the said Article 8, assuming it is enforceable - *quod non,* it is quite obvious that MDPs are allowed *in principle* in Belgium, although the technical provisions needed for them to operate properly are still missing. It is highly relevant to read in the foreword of the National Regulation of 8 March 1990 that it also intends to cover "multidisciplinary partnerships", thus showing that their mere existence and validity cannot be challenged.

Article 8 of the Regulation of 8 March 1990 issued by the national Bars associations has been challenged before the Belgian Competition Council. The outcome of this proceeding is not expected before long.

Moreover Article 8 only concerns multidisciplinary associations and groupings but does not cover the other forms of multidisciplinary practice, such as "correspondent relationships" that might be established between a law firm and company auditors or, all the more, "occasional multidisciplinary prac-

18 Unpublished resolution taken by the Dutch Order of Attorneys at the Brussels bar.

tice" which is particularly present in innumerable fiduciaries and notaries' offices.

Any attempt to use the said Article 8 would also infringe Article 81 of the EU Treaty and Article 2 of the Belgian Law on Competition because there is no list of professions made, even after such long period of time.

The Brussels (Flemish) Bar produced a Working Document in the summer of 2000 aimed at taking stock of (but not regulating) MDPs. This document came to the following conclusion:

- *Integrated MDPs* are forbidden;
- *Cost-sharing* and *non-integrated MDPs* are allowed with some safeguards: professional secrecy must be guaranteed, the MDP lawyer must have direct contact with the client, the client has freedom to choose his lawyer, no profit-sharing with non-lawyers, no commission to non-lawyers on legal fees, cost-sharing must be done in an objective and fair way and at market prices, the client must see the MDP link on the stationery, no confusion in branding, no joint marketing, strict conflict of interests policy (lawyers can do little work for auditors' clients);
- *Correspondent arrangements* and *networks*: same conditions as above will applied, but mutatis mutandis.

There would also be controls and a sort of Master Agreement (for MDPs) to be validated by the local Bar; a statement under oath from lawyers and non-lawyers in the MDP will be requested in order to confirm compliance with the Bar rules.

This Working Document has not been approved by the VVB and has not been made into an official Regulation; however it has received the support of a vast majority of Bar Council members and was drawn up after a short hearing session with some (alleged) MDP lawyers.

One of the most shocking sets of rules in Brussels (the Dutch-speaking Bar) is the so-called "Rules of Vervins" also nicknamed "the anti-Big Five provisions".[19] These provisions state that a lawyer practising in Belgium can enter into cooperation ("samenwerking") with a lawyer from another EU country who, in his country, has a cooperation with a non-lawyer (MDP), but on condition that (1) that MDP complies with local rules and (2) the non-lawyer from the MDP is neither directly nor indirectly active in Belgium and does not cooperate with a non-lawyer established in Belgium.

This (believed) subtle and fine combination of provisions is aimed at shifting any MDP ban from the largest Belgian law firms who have consultants, ac-

19 See article 308 par. 2 DRHR – Brussels Flemish speaking Bar

countants or auditors present in their partnership (or in their network) outside of Belgium. Needless to say, such discriminatory provisions would seem to be invalid and would likely be challenged in they event they were used.

On 6 January 2000, the French Order of Attorneys at the Brussels Bar signed an agreement with the Institute of Company Auditors founded on a twin realisation that independence is a principle common to both professions and that the public interest dictates that joint services can be offered. Under the terms of this agreement, lawyers can create cost-sharing associations along with auditors provided they have authorisation from the Council of the Order and there is no profit sharing. A similar agreement was subsequently signed with the Institute of Chartered Accountants and Tax Advisers.

Article 11.5 of EU Directive 98/5/EC of 16 February 1998 allows Member States to regulate MDPs but only refers to situations where lawyers are practising "within a group". Therefore, it does not regulate MDPs' contractual group arrangements such as "correspondent cooperation" or non-integrated MDPs (with only joint operational services or referral agreements, for example). In other words, there is nothing in Directive 98/5/EC that could be used as a basis for a ban on non-integrated MDPs, and any such ban would likely be viewed as an unlawful restriction of competition unless it successfully passed the usual EU tests on proportionality, etc.

A Parliament member's bill draft was lodged on 29 March 2000 by 3 members of Belgian parliament (belonging to the VU and ID) seeking to transpose directive 98/5/EC into Belgian law. This bill was to be combined with the bill amending the provisions of the Judicial Code with a view to the creation of two (Community) orders of attorneys.

This proposed bill contained a draft new article 437 *bis* of the Judicial Code prohibiting lawyers from carrying on their profession within a group containing persons outside the profession unless a Community regulation allowed. The mischief of this bill requires no commentary. "In effect we are unable to resist the large foreign multidisciplinary groups, who risk absorbing us".[20] This draft bill has not been enacted.[21]

On 26 February 2001, the government tabled a draft bill "intending to facilitated the practice of the legal profession and the establishment in Belgium of lawyers who are nationals of another Member State of the European Union".[22] The government's aim is to use the powers accorded it by Directive 98/5/EC to regulate the practice of the legal profession within groups of

---

20 *Doc. Chambre* 1999-2000, Doc. 50 0547/001, p. 985.

21 See Financieel Economische Tijd, 15 June 2001

22 *Doc. Chambre* 2000-2001, Doc. 50 1120/001, p. 2459.

which persons from outside the profession are members. Belgium wishes to make use of this restriction and enable the bar authorities, which have sole jurisdiction with regard to ethics, to refuse to allow lawyers to carry on business in Belgium within a group of which persons from outside the profession are members. It is thus local Bar associations that have the last word (clause 477 *octies* (5)) but within strict limits in accordance with the directive.

Thus, under the government draft bill, registration of a Community lawyer can only be refused if he is a member "of a group of which persons from outside the profession are members". A "group" contains persons from outside the legal profession if at least one of the following conditions is satisfied:

- the group's capital is held in whole or in part by non-lawyers;
- the group's name is used by non-lawyers;
- power of decision is exercised *de iure* or *de facto* by non-lawyers.

In the context of this draft bill, there are few specific cases where multidisciplinary practice can be banned.

The provision would in no way appear to hinder the development of MDPs in Belgium; it obviously pre-supposes that MDP lawyers have power of decision, *de iure* and *de facto*.

On 13 December 2000, the "Vereniging van Vlaamse Balies" adopted a negative stance with regard to MDPs and condemned any form of collaboration between lawyers and non-lawyers. This condemnation is excessive to such a degree that it will certainly be appealed against and the object of court action if it ever one day becomes a compulsory rule (which it presently is not given the purely private nature of the VVB).

2.2 Abroad

Foreign professional bodies have also endeavoured to examine the question.[23]

In France, in September 1998, the Prime Minister asked Mr. Nallet, a member of parliament, to draw up a report clarifying the current debate on *"the compatibility of network structures with the professional and ethical rules of the various professions that they cover"*.[24] In his voluminous report, Mr. Nallet made a certain number of suggestions that were intended to set the framework for multidisciplinary practice: *"Working in a network, in cooperation be-*

---

23 No attempt will be made here to show the contradiction between many of the "regulations" and other "decisions" by bar associations and Community or Belgian competition law.

24 L. Jospin, letter of commission to Mr. Nallet MP, 14 September 1998.

tween lawyers and other professionals, is set to develop in all forms. Rather than dreaming of a return to a status quo ante that has never existed, it is necessary to create a number of strict rules intended to ensure that, that which makes a lawyer the indomitable defender of individual freedom is staunchly guaranteed. And, for the rest, to offer the means to all those that so wish to show that they are as good and as efficient as their international competitors".[25]

Amongst these suggestions, we would highlight:

- a legal framework for multidisciplinary networks based on the freedom of association;
- a national body ensuring compliance with ethical rules and supervising accords between professions;
- a reinforcement of the independence of lawyers and auditors;
- clear rules governing conflicts of interests, professional confidentiality and advertising;
- structural and fiscal assistance to traditional firms.

The Law Society of England and Wales has also taken a decision in principle in favour of MDPs and is working on a draft text "[a]llowing solicitors to provide a legal service through any medium to anyone while still providing the necessary safeguards to protect the public interest". According to the Council's recommendation:

> *"Recognising that full MDPs require legislation and time to implement, the Council plans two interim solutions. The models which the working party hopes to implement in a matter of months are a legal "Practice Plus model", which would permit solicitors to bring in non-solicitor partners, and "Linked Partnerships", which might permit fee-sharing between solicitor's practices and other business (e.g. accountants) – this would be a development of the present strategic "alliances" arrangements with the Big 5, but could also be extended to other professional service providers."*

The American Bar association (ABA) has set up an MDP committee, which has prepared a report recommending far-ranging changes to the rules applicable to attorneys such as to allow them to join an MDP. This report initially drew vigorous opposition. It was not adopted in plenary assembly and the MDP committee has resumed its work and drawn up a second report, still recommending that MDPs be permitted. Thus, lawyers would be able to share their fees with non-lawyers provided that the lawyers had control and sufficient power to ensure their independence. In the interim, various American bar associations have passed reforms to this effect.

---

25 Nallet Report, Introduction, p. 7.

The Philadelphia Bar association, in terms of a decision taken on 23 March 2000[26], has authorised certain forms of MDPs that entail a sharing of fees, provided that the lawyers retain control of the firm, refrain from offering legal and audit services to the same clients and ensure that only attorneys carry out legal business.

On 24 July 2001, the New York Bar association[27] saw its new rules in the area of multidisciplinary practice validated by the four New York Appellate Division departments:

- non-lawyers with whom New York attorneys wish to enter into contractual relations have to have "certain minimal educational standards and enforceable rules of ethical conduct";
- the non-lawyers cannot have control over the lawyers;
- complete information must be given to clients for whom lawyers and non-lawyers work together;
- particular care must be taken for marketing non-legal services.

Similarly, the Canadian Bar association has just adopted a favourable position of principle with regard to MDPs and has decided to pursue its consultation procedure to this effect. The initial results show general support for authorising MDPs, while nonetheless regulating them.[28]

In Australia, a new statute applicable in New South Wales allows fee sharing with non-lawyers and permits law firms to raise capital and apply for listing on the stock market.[29]

In Spain, the government has also decided to adopt legislation allowing lawyers to belong to an MDP (which had already de facto been possible).[30]

The Union Internationale des Avocats (UIA) also adopted a paper in favour of MDPs on 3 November 1999. The UIA, which is visibly concerned to fall into step with other decisions in the area of multidisciplinary practice, does not make any pronouncement on the principles themselves but suggests a number of rules where MDPs are permitted. The UIA rightly insists that there should be a duty to provide the client with information but manifests strong reluctance in not authorising lawyers to do work for the clients of the MDPs auditors: how can such practice be called multidisciplinary? Is this not in total contradiction with what clients expect? And why weigh lawyers

---

26 <Law Money.com>, 28 March 2000, "First approval for MDPs in the United States".

27 Which has nearly 67.000 members!

28 CANADIAN BAR ASSOCIATION, Striking a Balance: The Report of the International Practice of Law Committee on Multi-Disciplinary Practices and Legal Profession, August 1999.

29 See the numerous references under the Recommendation by the ABA, <http://www.abanet.org>

30 *Legal Week*, 5 July 2001.

down with the restrictions incumbent on auditors without any evidence being adduced of the alleged conflict of interests?

Only the Council of the Bars and Law Societies of the European Union (CCBE) has issued negative recommendations with regard to MDPs.[31] It is true, the CCBE does not forbid all forms of MDPs but does proscribe those in which the lawyer's independence might be threatened. Its position becomes indefensible when it views working together or sharing any infrastructure (a building, a company restaurant, telecommunications, etc.) as classic evidence of a lack of independence[32] on the part of a lawyer.

In the Statement it made in Athens in November 1999, the CCBE did not rule on "non-integrated means of cooperation", leaving the way open for MDPs to opt to operate in a non-integrated way.

2.3 EU law and the NOVA case

Community law has been progressively enriched with a number of texts of direct interest to lawyers:

- directive 77/249 of 22 March 1977[33] is intended to make it easier for European lawyers to carry on the legal profession and contains the principle of mutual recognition;
- directive 89/48 of 21 December 1988[34] contains the principle of the mutual recognition of qualifications;
- directive 98/5 of 16 February 1998[35] completes this construction by making it easier for lawyers to establish within the European Union.

The European Commission does not seem to be determined to propose a regulatory framework for multidisciplinary networks. The Bangemann project for the creation of a company under European law bringing together various professions has been abandoned. The Commission seems to be more inclined to allow the general principles of free competition and free establishment to govern.

In November 1999, the Commission[36] expressed certain views on the question of whether a ban on MDPs might be considered as a restriction of competition.[37] The Commission recognises that, in an international context,

---

31 "Position of CCBE on integrated forms of co-operation between lawyers and persons outside the legal profession", 27 September 1998.

32 Point 1.4.

33 *O.J. L.*, 78/17 of 26 March 1977.

34 *O.J. L.*, 19/16 of 24 January 1989.

35 *O.J. L.*, 77/38 of 14 March 1998.

36 Directorate-General IV (Competition).

37 At the request of the Law Society of England and Wales.

MDPs could play a great role in terms of innovation, assistance in adapting to fast-changing markets and meeting users' increasing needs for integrated professional services, facilitating the entry of newcomers into markets for professional services, and increasing the quality of service and lowering prices, etc. The Commission also refers to fears about threats to confidentiality and the need to prevent conflicts of interests.

The Commission believes that:

- only on a case-by-case basis could the Commission conclude whether a ban on MDPs amounted to a significant restriction of competition going beyond that which is necessary for the legitimate objectives pursued;
- the Commission would of course welcome the endorsement of MDPs by professional bodies.

The Court of Justice of the European Communities will soon give a preliminary ruling on a question referred by the Dutch Raad van State relating to the validity of a prohibition by the Dutch Bar associations against lawyers' forming an association with other professions within a single legal structure.

The NOVA case relates to integrated MDPs in a profit-sharing situation: this is not something that seems to exist in Belgium and it is likely to be a very exceptional and extreme form of MDP. Therefore, for me, the NOVA case is not relevant to MDPs in Belgium. Of course, should the European Court rule that any kind of ban or restriction against any form of MDP were prohibited, then, following an "a fortiori" reasoning, it would impact (positively) on the issue surrounding MDPs.

The EU Directive 98/5 does not apply to MDP using the form of networks or cost-sharing arrangements ("groepering") and only targets situation where MDP lawyers are partners with non-lawyers in the same legal entity. This is not a situation that exists in Belgium.

The Office of Fair Trading (OFT), the British competition authority, has announced its intention to commence an inquiry into anti-competitive practices within the legal profession with regard to the difficulty of establishing MDPs where there is no apparent reason for depriving the market of such professional structures. For its part, the American Antitrust Institute (AAI) has issued similar criticisms with regard to the American Bar association for its hesitation in respect of MDPs, which seem to it to be anti-competitive, contrary to consumers' free choice and a possible violation of the antitrust laws.

In Belgium, professional organisations are now subject to competition law, thus exposing them to supervision by the Competition Council.

As Mr. Jakhian, a former president of the Brussels Bar (F), so correctly writes, "[i]n Community law, the lawfulness of the prohibition therefore remains uncertain at this stage. It seems to me that a lawyer could as of now challenge the prohibition against his participating in a form of inter-disciplinary firm".[38]

3 WHAT LIMITS ARE DESIRABLE?

When practising their profession within a multidisciplinary structure, do lawyers have to have absolute freedom? Or, on the other hand, is it necessary to lay down a number of specific rules?

A variety of fundamental values of the legal profession might in theory be affected: professional confidentiality, independence, and the absence of conflicts of interests. Is there any issue or not?

3.1 Professional confidentiality

According to some, multidisciplinary structures favour - even require - the exchange of information in accordance with the - supposed - culture of auditors, whose legal duty in effect relies on the cross-collection of information on the undertakings audited. As a result of this, the lawyer would no longer be able to abide by his professional duty of confidentiality and would inevitably submit to pressure to denounce any fraud or risk that the auditor might have to look into.

Such fears appear to be based only on a misplaced supposition as to what is truly intended. Whether he does or he doesn't work in an MDP, a lawyer has to adhere to professional confidentiality and knows very well that any breach in this regard will cause serious harm to his reputation and, therefore, to his professional future. Moreover, is it conceivable that, say, an auditor would present or recommend an MDP lawyer to one of his clients and run the risk of jeopardising his own relationship with his client as a result of a breach by a lawyer who failed to adhere to professional confidentiality given that this fundamental rule of the profession is its hallmark?

In truth, the issue of professional confidentiality has hardly any connection to MDPs. Where a client engages the services of an MDP, it is because he wants there to be an exchange of information between professionals and a coordinated solution as a function of the various problems encountered. The value-added of an MDP, which a client is seeking, is precisely the depth of this dialogue between different professions, which is in the exclusive inter-

38 E. JAKHIAN, *o.c.*, VI.

ests of the client. The client at all times has control over the multidisciplinary assignment and its performance.

Furthermore, the professional confidentiality of lawyers is tending to diminish as the fight against serious crime is increasing.[39] In France, the Court of Cassation rejects confidentiality for the negotiation or preparation of documents and confines it to the activity of prosecuting court cases.[40] Nowadays, "[t]he professional confidentiality of lawyers is now in practice no different to that of the other liberal professions who are bound by professional confidentiality i.e. subject to exceptions or deviations. It has lost its force, which was drawn from its categorical and vehement nature".[41]

MDPs can therefore perfectly well make use of the notion of "collective" or "shared" professional confidentiality[42]: each professional applies his own rules and, in cases of difficulty, it is the most restrictive rule that prevails under the joint surveillance of the various professional authorities. The solution thus sketched out is ultimately the same as that which applies between lawyers admitted to different bar associations or from different countries and grouped within one and the same structure. It is a fact that lawyers constantly work with other professionals in performing services for a client. Thus they are used to share privileged information with other professionals, as for an example in IPO's. Is there any issue there: clearly not.

3.2 Independence

It is clear to what extent independence is viewed as a traditional cardinal principle of the lawyer's profession. It is said this independence would be compromised by belonging to a multidisciplinary structure since, within that structure, lawyers would be in such a link of subordination that they would no longer be able exclusively to defend the interests of their clients; they would in effect also - at least partially - have to bear in mind the interests of their partners, any lapses by whom they would not - it is believed - want to denounce.

Moreover, where lawyers work alongside auditors, the auditors would also be lacking in independence as a result of legal advice given to the company being audited that would not have to be contradicted: it is said this would be jeopardising the duty that has been devolved upon auditors to provide the shareholders with information.

---

39 E. JAKHIAN, *o.c.*, III, B.

40 French Court of Cassation 30 September 1991, Gaz. Palais, 4-8 April 1999.

41 E. JAKHIAN, *o.c.*, IV, A.

42 E. JAKHIAN, *o.c.*, IV, C.

Finally the economic weight of lawyers working within a multidisciplinary team is said to be weak compared with the other professions represented, who are said to dictate operations rather than be true partners.

All these fears appear to be based on misunderstandings or to have been unwarrantedly placed in an emotional context.[43]

I do not believe that "independence" is of the essence of the legal profession except in advising clients on assignments: the lawyer, member of a Bar or not, must always give, based on his expertise in Law, an independent advise in the sense that the opinion given to the client cannot reflect other views than those of the lawyer himself. If a transaction is not seen as valid, the lawyer must say it regardless any influence from the client himself, the regulators or ... from his partners or colleagues.

But that's all. Outside that there is no true independence. Every lawyer is dependent from his relation with his client, with his own firm, with his boss, with his local community, with his previous opinions made on a specific legal issue, etc. How can we see independence for lawyers who are working in large firms where the strategy, the pricing, the team of associates, the conflict of interests are imposed to the lawyer? Is this an issue? Clearly not. Both lawyers and clients are well aware of this. In other words the situation is now changed: lawyers are well dependent, as any other businessman, because they work in open business context but maintains a full sense of autonomy when performing services for clients.

Clearly lawyers are agents and owe fiduciary duties to their principal.

The debate focuses too much on Big Five while it seems to us that multidisciplinary practice is most often carried on within small local structures[44] in which a few lawyers decide to ally with a firm of auditors or chartered accountants. Their objective is to share not only infrastructure but also to procure privileged access to the clients of the other professionals. Ultimately, they will be able to find specialist partners with the ability to implement their advice. If a large local business wanted to carry out a reorganisation, such MDPs would provide it with partners working close at hand, far from the anonymity of large structures.

As regards the impact of fee sharing on lawyer's independence, the financial pressures of such arrangements are not dissimilar to lawyers who work in traditional firms. In these circumstances professional rules rely on the lawyers to resist such pressures. In the context of professional pressure, existing professional rules rely on the lawyer working in-house or in government to

---

43 See the outstanding article "Multidisciplinary Practice" by D.R. FISCHEL, *The Business Lawyer*, Vol. 55, May 2000, p. 954

44 E. JAKHIAN, *o.c.*, II, E.

resist these pressures also. As such it is wrong to assume that lawyers, merely because they join an MDP will have their status compromised. Indeed it seems to actually in the best interest of MDPs to allow all their members to abide by their individual professional rules.

The general view is that the independence of lawyers is a wide subject. In reality, it is simply a matter of ensuring that a lawyer advises his client without seeking personal gain as a priority and provides the client with his best advice. There is no direct link with multidisciplinary practice. For example, in Belgium, many insurance companies, semi-state organisations and government departments will consult a lawyer at the eleventh hour, submitting to him draft pleadings which he would hardly be in a position to refuse to countersign. Where is the lawyer's independence in such a context?

Do we need to say that the independence of a lawyer will also be jeopardised where one of his clients represents too large a share of his business?

Once again, for me the most important value to preserve is to have lawyers advising clients in their sole and exclusive interest. This is not issue for MDPs only but for the all profession.

As one will see, these issues, important though they are, bear no relation to MDPs to the extent that lawyers working within such a structure make sure they deal directly with the MDPs clients (who thus also become their clients) and avoid confining themselves to anonymous sub-contracting.

"Operational" independence therefore has nothing to do with the issue and MDPs" lawyers will therefore ensure they give a precise contractual framework to joint services.[45]

Finally, in the situation where profitability criteria were to be agreed within an MDP, this situation in no way differs, as far as independence is concerned, from a cross-border firm of lawyers whose Belgian member was subject to such criteria.

3.3 Conflicts of interests[46]

By their size and the presence of a number of professions in their midst, multidisciplinary structures are said to be confronted with numerous conflicts of interests. The cohabitation between regulated professions (auditors, lawyers, accountants and tax advisers) and non-regulated professions (con-

---

45 Against this: standard 2 of the UIA.

46 See for an overview of the various rules on conflicts of interests in Europe: "Divided we stand", *The European Lawyer*, May 2000, 71, and for a remarkable general and highly documented analysis: "Conflicts of interest, Chinese walls and the Changing Business of the Law", CHESTER, ROWLEY AND HARRISON, *Business Law International*, January 2000, especially, pp. 73 et seq.

sultants, computer specialists, financial advisers) is said to render the settlement of conflicts of interests uncertain and opaque.

It is very probably here that MDPs face their greatest challenge. The difficulty comes are said not to come from lawyers but from auditors, whose assignment is often regarded as hard to reconcile with that of lawyers. The latter exclusively defend the interests of their clients, whilst the former are charged with the task of providing information to the general public.

It is first of all pointed out that the Belgian Law on Companies provides that non-audit fees earned by persons with whom statutory auditors are in co-operation must be reported in the annual report made by the board of directors. This shows clearly that the Belgian law allow auditors to work with other professions for joint clients. Further, it is allowed for them to work in the same group, provided that the shareholders received fair information on fees gained by the auditors and the non-auditors.

Moreover, articles 30 and 31 of the Royal Decree of 10 January 1994 clearly contain an authorisation to create inter-disciplinary companies amongst regulated professions.

The auditing profession is therefore far from being confined by the statutory provisions applicable to it in an isolation that is detrimental to the practice of the profession. That is all the more understandable given that an auditor cannot expected to possess universal knowledge that would enable him to identify all risks in all areas. It is when he surrounds himself with specialists - consider in particular legal and tax risks - that he is better able to fulfil his assignment.

Next, one must be sure not to forget that lawyers and auditors are at one in respect of the principle of independence. It is true that auditors' role is to be linked with the interests of the shareholders and employees as well as those of the general public. But it is no less true that both professions share an exacerbated concern to preserve their independence. A priori, therefore, there is no conflict of interests.

Where the question of conflicts of interests is raised within the domain of MDPs, it is in reality work on behalf of the same clients that is at issue. Can a lawyer advise a client of the auditor? Can a lawyer advise a client in a sector in which one of his MDP colleagues has already taken a stance contrary to that preferred by the client?

Another issue is to deal with situations where the client wants the lawyers not to speak with the auditor: but this is a matter of professional secrecy rather than related to conflict of interest.

In our opinion it is the client who must decide: does he want to consult an MDP lawyer for his expertise, whilst accepting the fact that other members of the MDP advise his competitors and opponents? Or, on the other hand, does he want advice from somebody who has no potential conflicting connection with the desired transaction? Does he want advice that is totally independent[47] of his auditor? As we see it, it is up to the MDP lawyer to explain to his client his personal position within the MDP, any conflicts of interests, and the measures taken to redress them.

First, professional rules on conflict of interest brings with it responsibilities on both auditors (or accountants, or tax advisors) and lawyers to avoid such conflicts. Second, their professional rules have the mechanisms to avoid it and for dealing with such issues. Third, MDPs have existing procedures in place (*e.g.* separate internal reporting lines, different partners and staff, Chinese walls, consent of the parties). To this multi-tiered security systems can be added regulation by the market itself, were a firm would rapidly lose its market position if such conflicts arose.

If the client is satisfied with that, the question of a conflict of interests no longer arises.

Anticipating their clients' legitimate questions, MDPs will obviously ensure that they construct Chinese walls[48] and other systems that protect work done in following up cases from any detrimental influence. This must be of state of the art.

What would happen if a client wants to misrepresent its financial information and tells its auditor to go along or lose the mandate? This threat would in theory more affect MDPs where there is more to lose than the single audit mandate. A MDP faced with such situation might think to balance the loss of revenues with the damage to its reputation if it participates in the scheme. But there will even be no such discussion: the true culture and mindset of auditors is to keep up high there sense of fair reporting; they will also be protected by the number of their clients and mandates making the loss of one of them (and not an honest one) economically affordable. From this perspective, the larger the firm, the lower its incentive to compromise its reputation. This shows that auditors and lawyers share common core values.

Some are arguing that there is an alleged conflict between lawyer's duty to maintain confidentiality and the auditor's duty to disclose information to shareholders. This argument misses two points.

First auditors are not "information providers" but are expected to certify the accuracy of the annual accounts as set by the Board of directors. They are not

47 What is meant here is the "perception" of independence: it goes without saying that an MDP lawyer will always give independent advice but it will be conceded that the client's perception may differ.

48 In the United States, the term used is "ethical walls".

at all expected to search for information in order to make it public. When they believe there is an issue with the financial statements they have to refuse to certify the board's decision. Not to take up its role. On top of that they have neither the budget nor the means to check everything in - say - a large multinational company. Recent events show that there is a misunderstanding on auditors' role.

Second, auditors usually seek information from clients and their lawyers when deciding to certify financial statements. Clients and lawyers must then decide whether to provide the information requested or refuse based on the attorney-client privilege. It is exactly the same situation within a MDP.

All this is not all related to MDPs but is of interest for all auditors and all lawyers.

At a practical level, it would appear that at least three measures have to be taken to ensure harmonious cooperation between lawyers and auditors.

First of all, the MDP must ensure that the client is given correct information. He has to know that his auditor and his lawyer work closely together whilst each of them makes sure that he adheres to the cardinal principles of his respective profession.

Then, before entering in to relations with its clients, the MDP has to lay down clear and precise joint working rules, by which the economically stronger party is prevented from tacitly imposing its views. By accepting legally restrictive rules, the MDP in reality safeguards the independence of each of its members.

It goes without saying that an MDP lawyer will not serve proceedings against the clients of his partners. This would be contrary to the common rules of the professions in question.

4 FUTURE PROSPECTS

4.1 Self-regulation

Multi-disciplinary structures should likely start self-regulation efforts and continue implementing techniques to prevent conflicts of interests. The absence of complaints from clients and other lawyers against multidisciplinary networks is a notable feature that is worthy of emphasis.[49]

It seems to me that MDP law firms in Belgium should set themselves ethical standards together (on top of those already applicable to Bar members) and erect firewalls as needed. As it is quite obvious that the Bar authorities do

49 See the Nallet Report, p. 118.

not fully understand what an MDP is, there is no better solution than to opt for a self-regulation process. This type of process has proved to be efficient, flexible and reliable in the worlds of banking and capital markets. Obviously, this self-regulation should be complemented with input from the Bar authorities, and external independent legal advice should be sought before laying down rules.

Such rules should cover practical arrangements and aspects of MDP operations including: rental agreements, access to offices, pay-roll and accounting support, knowledge management tools, use of IT, financial flows within the MDP, marketing, communications to the press, recruitment at universities, data protection and IT security, support staff, means of funding, audit reports, branding, etc.

Further in this process of self-regulation, there should also likely be a firm commitment from MDP law firms (not only from those close to Big Five) on transparency in information to be provided to the Bar. It seems to me a good idea that each year the relevant Bar authorities should be provided with:

- a report from the accredited auditor on the financial flows between lawyers and non-lawyers: are services rendered by the lawyers duly invoiced to the non-lawyers? At what rate? How quickly are payments made? Is there any discount? How are support services invoiced to lawyers? At what rate? Is there any income support? or any other forbidden funding technique? etc.;
- a report from a certified IT security engineer describing the measures taken by the lawyers to protect their data and comply with their professional secrecy obligations;
- a special report by the partners in the law firm (1) explaining how they deal with conflicts of interests vis-à-vis non-lawyers in their MDP, (2) explaining how they market their joint services and (3) describing any kind of contractual arrangement they may have with non-lawyers in their MDP.

4.2 Information

In our view it is the provision to the client of information on the MDP itself and the service that he is entitled to expect from the MDP that is the most important factor in multidisciplinary practice. Clearly, MDP lawyers must ensure that they demonstrate to their clients that all measures have been taken within the firm to ensure the independence of its advice and professional confidentiality.

It is of crucial importance to provide the clients with full and fair information. Therefore, MDP lawyers should be allowed to refer to their MDP-type activities (correspondent to a Big Five firm, accounting practice, tax advisers' office, etc.).

This would allow the clients to decide whether or not they wanted to get advice from the MDP and to check whether a conflict of interest's policy was in place. Such information should appear on all lawyers' documents and stationery.

4.3 Verification after the facts

As MDPs are a new way of practising the legal profession, there should be an MDP Commission in place within each Bar association concerned, with people fully aware of what does MDP means and how it can be operated. These commissions would be given the task of following up on MDP matters and making sure our main values are preserved, but with enough flexibility to address the clients' needs.

5 LOOKING FORWARD

The MDP debate is one of the most important facing the professional market today, which has been precipitated by the fundamental changes that have occurred in the way in which goods and services are delivered to clients.

The issue of MDPs is, therefore, not one exclusive to legal services and accountants, which this case focuses on, but involves the whole service sector.

Due to the changing global business environment it is an obvious fact that the demand for MDPs has grown rapidly allowing MDPs to be successful. This is also true in Belgium with almost all Top 10 large law firms being MDPs and with 3 of them having a close link with the Big Five. There are about 1000 lawyers working in MDPs in Belgium.

MDPs will improve the quality of services which are available to clients, will increase competition in the professional services sector and will increase consumer choice. More and more, consumers are looking for integrated, workable solutions to a problem with legal components. Consumers are no longer satisfied with the Bar's requirement that they hire - and pay for - a lawyer for only one part of the problem.

Therefore this is good time to open a fair discussion, to listen to the market, to look to the competitors abroad, to get input from non-lawyers and to come up with adapted solutions. Should this process fail then it will be necessary to make a difficult choice: change the rule or change the rule maker. The latter option would lead to a separate Bar organisation available to business law firms[50] and in-house lawyers, all merged in one body and one profession. But this is our next debate.

---

50 See L. MARLIERE, "Un Barreau belge à plusieurs vitesses", *Echo*, 12 February 2000

BRINGING THE GOOD NEWS FROM GHENT TO AIX

Avrom Sherr, Woolf Professor of Legal Education at the Institute of Advanced Legal Studies, University of London

How They Brought the Good News from Ghent to Aix
[16--]
Robert Browning (1812–1889)

I sprang to the stirrup, and Joris and he;
I galloped, Dirck galloped, we galloped all three;
"Good speed!" cried the watch, as the gate-bolts undrew;
"Speed!" echoed the wall to us galloping through;
Behind shut the postern, the lights sank to rest
And into the midnight we galloped abreast.

Not a word to each other; we kept the great pace
Neck by neck, stride by stride, never changing our place;
I turned in my saddle and made its girths tight,
Then shortened each stirrup, and set the pique right
Rebuckled the cheek-strap, chained slacker the bit,
Nor galloped less steadily Roland a whit.

This paper considers what we know about clients' views of their lawyers from recent research work in Scotland and England and Wales. It also considers what we know of how clients view advice agency workers providing similar services. New forms of litigation, including conditional fee agreements, set up new areas of difficulty between lawyers and clients and there is a concern that current ethical rules may not cover the needs of the new forms of service agreement. The paper asks whether conduct rules are applicable to these issues. Finally it considers whether all of this is "good news" and whether Robert Browning's poem has any relevance.

1 WHAT DO WE KNOW ABOUT WHAT CLIENTS THINK OF THEIR LAWYERS?

First, a hasty gallop through the recent literature. Two recent pieces of research from Scotland and from England and Wales each provide an updated view on what clients think of lawyers in criminal and civil cases.

In Scotland the new pilot system for a public defender was treated to independent evaluation research.[1] Earlier research noted the passivity of criminal clients with lawyers "processing hopeless, confused people through the system in a routine, ritualised way, often owing greater loyalty to the prosecution and the court than to their clients." Criminal defence lawyers were involved in "a confidence game" which involved lowering clients' expectations, making extravagant claims of inside knowledge and play acting in dramatic but superficial pleas in (Blumberg, 1967). Some research suggested that clients judge mainly on outcome (Ericson and Baranek, 1982 in Canada), whereas others feel that a sense of fairness (Caspar, Tyler and Fisher, 1988), or "being listened to and given voice", (Tyler, 1990) are important. Sommerlad and Wall (1999) and Davies (1998) seem to suggest that a good rapport with clients is essential in order to elicit enough information to perform a technically competent service.

The Edinburgh study showed that many private practice solicitors had established long term relationships with their criminal clients.

> *"She's my father's lawyer as well. She's like a family lawyer. It was my Dad who says to get in touch with her." (Client interview – private solicitor client 2000).*
>
> *"I've been practicing in Edinburgh for 27 years... it's just by reputation...over the years...it's the sons of fathers...I'm waiting for my first grandson...that's how we get our business." (Private solicitor interview, 1998).*

Clients tended to speak of their solicitors as being an individual rather than a firm and it was mainly people from families who were used to the criminal process who had a longer term relationship with a solicitor. These relationships appeared beneficial to both solicitor and client and clients expressed that benefit.

From the ethical point of view lawyers in this position might find it difficult to differentiate between their clients' interests, their duty to the court, duty to the profession and their own interests and there could be a temptation to work more for the client than for their sense of "social justice". It is interesting to contemplate whether public defenders might differ from private practitioners.

Contrary to Ericson and Baranek, clients in Edinburgh did not in general appear to make judgements on their lawyers based only on the outcome of their cases, but also on the process. This was helpful for public defenders since they pleaded their clients guilty earlier than their private practice

---

1 *The Public Defence Solicitors Office in Edinburgh: An Independent Evaluation*, GORIELY, MCCRONE, DUFF, KNAPP, HENRY, TATA, LANCASTER and SHERR (Scottish Executive Central Research Unit, 2001).

counterparts and this led to a larger number of convictions. Perhaps this served the lawyers' duty to the court and to the public purse. But it did not help a small percentage of their clients (c.7%) whose cases might have been abandoned later by the prosecution.

Although the clients may not have been able to judge the professional proficiency of their lawyers, their interpersonal skills were closely watched and their mastery (or otherwise) of the details of their case were carefully considered. Treating clients as people, rather than "bill fodder" was important, so was giving robust advice, providing clients with a voice in court and the confidence with which the lawyer dealt in court.

Providing clients with a voice in court could conflict considerably with a lawyer's other obligations and may even be a conflict with the lawyer's duty to act in the interest of a client, rather than following their expressed desires.

In the Scottish study it was enormously important to clients to be able to choose their own lawyer. In the Scottish pilot clients had been for the first year directed to the pilot public defenders system and were not allowed to use a previous lawyer, or another lawyer of their own choice.

The Scottish clients of criminal lawyers were asked what they thought of their lawyers through a questionnaire study and also in private interview. In general the clients of private practitioners thought their lawyers had done a better job, told them what was happening more, "were there when I wanted them" and had "enough time for me" and "told me what would happen at the end". "Volunteer" clients who went to the pilot Public Defender Office without compulsion had slightly lower ratings for all of these than private practice lawyers. The clients of the Public Defender Office who had been directed to that office had the lowest ratings of their lawyers for all of these items. Broadly, the picture was the same in relation to "knew the right people to speak to", "told the court my side of the story", "treated me like I mattered" and "stood up for my rights". But, interestingly, it was the private practice lawyers who were thought to be "too friendly with the other side" more than either directed or volunteer PDSO clients. Although there were clients who were very happy with their Public Defender lawyers, in general clients valued the ability to choose a lawyer and resented being directed towards one.

"Twas moonset at starting; but while we drew near
Lokeren, the cocks crew and twilight dawned clear;
At Boom, a great yellow star came out to see;
At Düffeld, "twas morning as plain as could be;
And from Mecheln church-steeple we heard the half-chime

So Joris broke silence with "Yet there is time!"

At Aerschot, up leaped of a sudden the sun,
And against him the cattle stood black every one,
To stare through the mist at us galloping past,
And I saw my stout galloper Roland at last,
With resolute shoulders, each butting away
The haze, as some bluff river headland its spray

And his low head and crest, just one sharp ear bent back
For my voice, and the other pricked out on his track;
And one eye's black intelligence,—ever that glance
O"er its white edge at me, his own master, askance!
And the thick heavy spume-flakes which aye and anon
His fierce lips shook upwards in galloping on.

2 QUALITY AND COST IN ENGLAND AND WALES[2]

Two approaches were used in the English and Welsh study to obtaining a "clients' eye view" of their lawyers and legal work. The (more traditional) client survey approach was used with over three thousand clients of both private practice lawyers and not for profit advice agencies, all carrying out advice and assistance work under legal aid contracts. Additionally, for the first time in academic socio-legal research, "model clients" were sent out, posing as real clients, to both solicitor and NFP groups who were involved in the study. All the lawyers and advisers had previously been warned that they might be visited in this way. Amusingly, some advisers had already claimed they had noticed the "model clients", long before any had been sent out.

Client survey results among professionals, unless there is a forced or persuasive return methodology, are normally affected by low response rate. In this case, since we could compare the responding sample with the non responding sample we are able to say that there are no major differences and therefore that their responses were not affected by sample bias, even though the response came from 28% of those surveyed. Overall the clients showed fairly high satisfaction with their lawyers with positive results for "listening to

[2] *Quality and Cost, Final Report on the Contracting of Civil, Non-Family Advice and Assistance Pilot*, MOORHEAD, R., SHERR, A., WEBLEY, S., ROGERS, L., PATERSON, A. and DOMBERGER, S. (Stationery Office, London 2001).

what they had to say", "telling them what was happening", "being there when I wanted them", "having enough time for them", "telling them what would happen at the end", "knew the right people to speak to", "really stood up for their rights", "paid attention to their emotional concerns", "did what they wanted" and "treated them like they mattered", all ranging between 74% and 86% positive.

Clients seemed to prefer cases to be handled by one individual rather than more than one adviser and thought that cases were handled better when they were. There were also problems about not explaining properly to clients the need for the involvement of more than one adviser. In general the not for profit agencies satisfied their clients more than the solicitors in seven out of ten headings. There were also differences between different payment systems within the solicitors' groupings. White clients rated their cases as "excellent" in 50% of matters compared with only 28% for clients who were not white. Many of the latter rated their advisers as "very good". A similar proportion of white and non-white clients rated their advisers as poor or very poor.

One major difference in client satisfaction was the effect of a positive financial result. Where there had been a positive financial result, 59% of clients rated the case as excellent and 23% as very good, whereas the equivalent figures for no positive financial result were 43% and 28%. Recommendation was also an important element in satisfaction, and those who had been recommended to an adviser were more likely to be satisfied with them. On multiple regression the highest effect on satisfaction was having only one adviser handling the case. Failure to give advice on the likely length of the case also had a major effect.

Complaints were also an interesting issue. 10% of those clients who responded said they had complained. 76% of those remained unsatisfied with the outcome of their complaint. As might be expected there were strong relationships between dissatisfaction and whether a complaint was made, and whether a complaint was adequately dealt with once made. It was clearly possible to regain some of the confidence of a client by reacting well to a complaint.

It is therefore possible for lawyers and advisers, through the management of their cases, and the ethical conduct of their work to control a number of the issues which cause satisfaction or dissatisfaction from clients. However, some of these may affect the costing and organisation of work.

45 model client visits were organised, divided as between the different sectors of the study. Model clients are only able to assess early aspects of service including access and quality of advice and immediate follow up at initial interview. However, these are crucial aspects of service. The methodol-

ogy was enhanced by being able to send the model clients' notes of their interviews to peer reviewers for assessment. The model clients noted how difficult it was, especially with some of the not for profit agencies, to gain access to advice and make initial contact with advisers, getting them to make appointments and getting them actually to give advice. Additionally there were also other difficulties in the manner in which advice was given.

The model client system was a new form of methodology which provided a useful opportunity to give insight into service delivery at and before an initial interview. It also allowed a direct comparison between what a client (or model client) thought about a particular interview and what a peer reviewer might think. In one case, the model client said:

> *"The adviser showed an impressive level of concern for my job security, understanding that I could not afford to lose my job. Made a point of telling me that it can be quite common for part time women workers to encounter unfair bosses because they know how much they need the job and think that they will be able to get away with it (i.e. treating them unfairly). Overall he was very helpful, reassuring and personal and tried to think of as many other organisations I could turn to as he could. The people he suggested were a CAB, ACAS, a local law firm, a trade union"*

The peer reviewers, however, were much more concerned about this visit and the following comment shows up the distinctions between what clients might think and how a lawyer might assess the same interaction:

> *"Although very clearly empathetic, this adviser does not really know enough about the law to be using legal aid money. A good example of touchy feely advice."*

The quality of the advice given as assessed by the peer reviewers was not very strong. In all personal injury cases correct advice was given, but in half or more of debt, housing and employment cases poor advice was given or the clients failed to access advice at all.

3 SUMMARY

From these two pieces of research, looking at both criminal law and civil law subject areas and looking at both private practice and publicly employed lawyers and advisers, we have a fair idea of current views of lawyers and advisers from their clients. Although clients are pleased with the quality of the work carried out for them and in general are satisfied with their lawyers, there are a number of areas of dissatisfaction – some of which show up important issues of competence, ethics and management of legal professionals.

Explaining to clients who will actually be carrying out the work is an important element of the English and Welsh Law Society Solicitors' Conduct Code

Rule 15. Also included in Rule 15 is the need to explain to clients how long their cases will take and what is happening on them. Complaints handling is also a conduct issue which comes under that rule. Clearly, not all lawyers and advisers are able to satisfy clients' complaints quickly and reasonably.[3]

By Hasselt, Dirck groaned; and cried Joris, "Stay spur!
Your Roos galloped bravely, the fault's not in her,
We"ll remember at Aix"—for one heard the quick wheeze
Of her chest, saw the stretched neck and staggering knees,
And sunk tail, and horrible heave of the flank
As down on her haunches she shuddered and sank.

4 NEW, OR DEVELOPING FORMS OF PRACTICE - THE ETHICS OF CONDITIONAL FEE ARRANGEMENTS[4]

The development of new forms of legal service or conditions for legal practice also produces new ethical dilemmas. In England and Wales conditional fee arrangements have been legislated as a new means of funding certain types of litigation.[5] Previously, these areas of litigation, including particularly personal injury litigation, could be funded initially under the legal aid scheme, although most cases settled and funds were paid back into the scheme when the defendants accepted the claimants' costs.

Conditional fee arrangements (CFAs) set up a rather new set of conditions between lawyers and clients. The lawyer will assess the likelihood of success of the case and may include, as part of the contract, an uplift in the lawyer's fees of up to 100%, if the case is particularly risky. The lawyers, in general, fund their own work and sometimes disbursements, from their own funds, until the case is settled or won.

The Report suggests that opponents of this approach will see it as inevitable that the direct financial interest of the lawyers in their clients' success or failure will involve:

- A conflict between the lawyers' own interest and the lawyers' duty to their clients.

---

3 See also MOORHEAD, R., ROGERS, S., SHERR, A., *Willing Blindness? OSS Complaints Handling Procedures,* (2000) Law Society, London.

4 The Ethics of Conditional Fee Arrangements, January 2001, The Society of Advanced Legal Studies - Ethics and Lawyer Fee Arrangements Working Group, Chairman, Richard Southwell QC, Convenor and Author, Richard Moorhead.

5 Courts and Legal Services Act 1990 and Access to Justice Act 1999.

- A conflict with the over-riding duty owed by lawyers to the court, i.e. to the public interest and the administration of justice, and to their professions.
- A marked decline in the ethical standards of lawyers in England and Wales (by reference to the worst practices of contingency fee lawyers in the United States).
- The shifting of financial risk or compromise access for expensive or risky (but worthy) cases, difficult clients or cases where a client might withdraw. Therefore there would be more "cherry picking" of easy cases.
- And therefore reduced access to lawyers.

The working group found that there were some real problems remaining in the new conditional fee arrangement system. There was some real concern about the role of insurance companies in the litigation process, who would be involved partly as insurers of the litigation on the claimant's side and might also be involved as defendants. The Report suggested that a compulsory "period of contemplation" should be required between the explanation of a draft CFA and the client being asked to sign, except in cases of urgency. The CFA was a fairly complicated agreement and it could well be that a client might have a better deal from one lawyer than another. The Report suggested that an explanatory video might be prepared so that clients could see this and understand more clearly what they were involved in. The Report also said:

> *That success and win should be defined in terms of damages actually recovered.*
>
> *That there should be rules about how and when lawyers can recover costs from clients*
>
> *That the Law Society's practice rules should make clear that the solicitor's duty to a client under Practice Rule 1 puts the solicitor in a situation of conflict with their client if the solicitor is aware that litigation insurance they advise the client to take out is unnecessary or unnecessarily expensive.*
>
> *That the Bar's Code of Conduct should include stronger provisions requiring barristers to act in accordance with their clients' interest rather than the personal interest of the barristers.*

So we were left galloping, Joris and I,
Past Looz and past Tongres, no cloud in the sky;
The broad sun above laughed a pitiless laugh,
"Neath our feet broke the brittle bright stubble like chaff;
Till over by Dalhem a dome-spire sprang white,

And "Gallop," gasped Joris, "for Aix is in sight!"

"How they"ll greet us!"—and all in a moment his roan
Rolled neck and croup over, lay dead as a stone;
And there was my Roland to bear the whole weight
Of the news which alone could save Aix from her fate,
With his nostrils like pits full of blood to the brim,
And with circles of red for his eye-sockets' rim.

5 W.L.F. FELSTINER'S "TOUR D'HORIZON" ON LAWYER CLIENT RELATIONS RESEARCH

A recent talk[6] provides a highly developed picture of the current research together with some different focus and two points of analysis. Felstiner first suggests that "justice" may be defined in lawyer-client relations in both substantive and procedural terms. "Substantive justice" is that lawyers counsel clients to do "the right thing". "Procedural justice" is that lawyers treat their clients properly.

Many ethical codes set up the *substantive justice* position by privileging the lawyer's duty to the court, duty to the profession or duty to society above the lawyer's duty to the client or the lawyer's own interests. There is usually some form of regulation to this effect, which tends to differ between jurisdictions but, in general, supposes that it is possible for the lawyer to identify "the right thing" and that a lawyer may counsel clients to do it. This is a fundamental assumption of the ideology of professionalism which transcends changes in patterns, procedures and management of legal work.

Procedural justice, in Felstiner's terms suggests that "lawyers treat clients well - that lawyers are accessible, responsive, empathetic, communicate effectively, pay prompt attention to their clients' affairs, and are motivated by professional values rather than financial returns." These elements of legal conduct are quite different from the elements of *substantive justice* conduct which were more frequently found in early versions of the English and Welsh Solicitors' Code of Conduct. Those precepts dealt primarily with "professional issues" - how the lawyer reacted to other lawyers, how the lawyer had a duty to the court and a duty to justice, including the *substantive justice* approach referred to above.

---

6 *Synthezing Research on Lawyer-Client Relations*, Plenary by Professor WLF FELSTINER at the W.G. Hart Workshop, June 2001, Institute of Advanced Legal Studies.

In this respect *procedural justice* is only a recent input into ethical and conduct rules and appears to be the result of consumerism, growing democracy between professionals and lay clients, class and education standardisation etc.

Felstiner then goes on to show that the research on lawyer client relations paints a poor picture of both *substantive* and *procedural* justice. The socio-legal research suggests that corporate lawyers in general follow what their clients want, or what they assume their clients to want and Galanter suggests that there is not even any "angst" about this in Britain as compared with the United States where at least the lawyers often confess that they shirk this responsibility. Lawyers have become "dehumanised, unable to relate to clients with compassion".

Lawyers working in the "personal services hemisphere" of the profession have more problems regarding the *procedural* side of justice. Felstiner says that the *substantive* side has never been high on their "agenda". The question is whether criminal and indigent civil law clients experience "neglect, rejection and disrespect" from overloaded and harassed lawyers who are "impatient, highly focused on the instrumental dimensions of their work and little inclined toward caring, empathy, responsiveness, co-operation, sharing and patience."

Felstiner then goes on to query how reliable the socio-legal literature is in painting such a depressing picture of the profession and suggests that his own recent research leaves the profession looking a little better than previously thought. However, what is most important for this paper is the question whether different, or differently policed, conduct rules would make any difference to the ways in which lawyers behaved.

Then I cast loose my buffcoat, each holster let fall,
Shook off both my jack-boots, let go belt and all,
Stood up in the stirrup, leaned, patted his ear,
Called my Roland his pet-name, my horse without peer;
Clapped my hands, laughed and sang, any noise, bad or good,
Till at length into Aix Roland galloped and stood.

6 THE CONFERENCE THEME

The conference theme suggests three levels of approach to ethical behaviour: the professional association, the firm and the individual lawyer. This paper has shown that the needs of clients might be addressed at all three levels.

Lawyer competence in producing effective quality can be dealt with by encouraging more effective modes of qualification and more effective monitoring or policing by the professional association. It can also be achieved with better training and experience in-house in firms and encouraging the individual professional responsibility to ensure that lawyers work only on cases in which they are competent, or they make themselves competent to do so.

Some other issues might be dealt with at each of the three levels. Management issues such as organising that only one adviser deals with one case, where possible, are clearly to be organised at the firm level, although there may be questions which arise for individual lawyers as well. It is clearly for individual lawyers to provide proper information on how long a case is going to take and what is happening in it. Systems for handling complaints are designed and policed at the professional association level, but it is at the firm and individual level that the problems associated with complaints and handling these properly all occur.

And all I remember is, friends flocking round
As I sat with his head "twixt my knees on the ground;
And no voice but was praising this Roland of mine,
As I poured down his throat our last measure of wine,
Which (the burgesses voted by common consent)
Was no more than his due who brought good news from Ghent.

7 DENOUEMENT: GHENT TO AIX

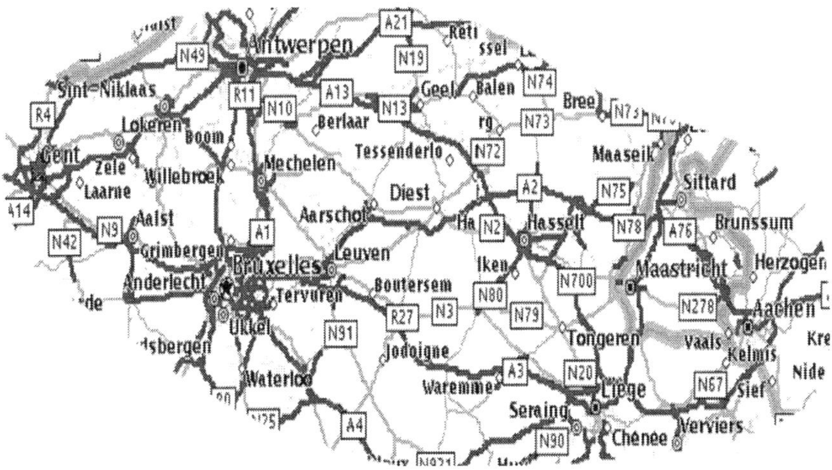

A brief look at the modern map shows a fair distance between Ghent and Aachen in Germany, which was known as Aix La Chappelle in the seventeenth century. Even as the crow flies it is a long distance, about 120 kilometers or more. Travelling as Browning's riders did from Ghent to Lokeren to Boom to Mechelen to Aarschot to Hasselt to Tongeren and then Aachen, would have been even longer. Almost certainly this is a journey that no horses could make in one night and without stopping. It is beyond possibility. Indeed, according to the critics and to Browning himself, there was no such ride, no such horses, no such riders, no such good news and no event in history which this represents. For English school students of a certain generation this wonderful narrative poem with its incredible rhythm may be etched in our memories but all that it is is a story, with rhythm, by Browning, with rhymes. All then that is left at the end of the poem is the memory, the recitation, the feeling engendered by the poem and the performance of it.

Unfortunately, the effect of legal ethics is rather similar. There are no real "ethics", just a set of conduct rules. Sometimes these rules are obeyed and sometimes they are not obeyed. When large commercial firms decide that the conflict of interest rules are unimportant or not for them, they create "Chinese walls" or "cones of silence" without any clear authority or regulatory backing.[7]

For most law firms there is very little policing of misconduct. Across the world, conduct cases against lawyers are very low in number. They tend to rely either on angry clients, or "the other side" to report any misconduct. Where misconduct is reported only small proportions are found to be correct and even in these cases only small numbers of such cases are punished. Where punishment exists it is usually at the lower end of the spectrum rather than at the higher end.[8] Therefore, what does occur really only amounts to a few attempts at conduct policing for show, or "for the books". The conduct rules read well, they are well drafted, idealistic assertions of exhortation to good behaviour, and they feel good to have around. But obedience to such conduct rules does not really occur.

We need something rather different in order to make a difference. We have not sufficiently identified the distinctions between ethical failure and in-

---

[7] Guide to the Professional Conduct of Solicitors, 8th edition, The Law Society, pp. 316 and 322 – Chinese walls being used in far more situations than merged firms.

[8] See R. ABEL, *Why Does the ABA Have Conduct Rules?*, and the ABA SPECIAL COMMITTEE ON EVALUATION OF DISCIPLINARY ENFORCEMENT, 1970, *Problems and Recommendations in Disciplinary Enforcement*, Chicago and A. SHERR, "Legal Ethics in Europe", Chapter 17 in K. ECONOMIDES (ed.)., *Ethical Challenges to Legal Education and Conduct*, Oxford, Hart Publishing, 1998, p. 351.

competence, service complaints, lawyer management and lawyer negligence. Even in this conference we have skated over some of these issues and talked about each as if it were the same as the others.

In order to make our analysis more useful we need to take into account, apart from conduct rules, issues of management, monitoring, negligence actions against professionals, and client service complaints. And we need to reconsider the map of these issues of client lawyer dissatisfaction in ways which will make more of a difference.

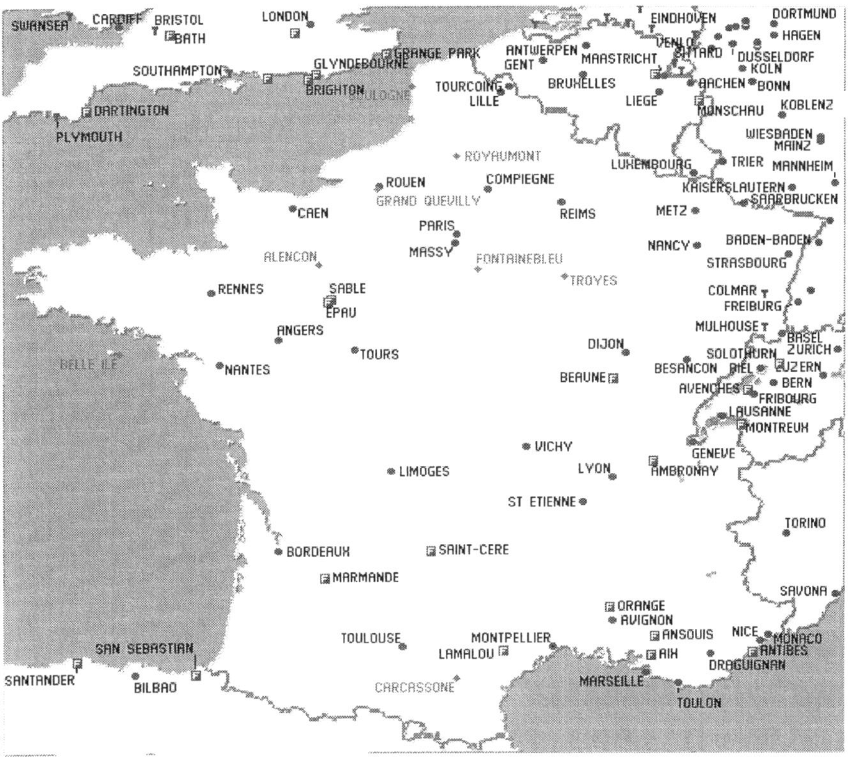

The International Sociological Association for Sociology of the Professions, Subgroup on the Legal Professions will meet again in June 2002. Its meeting takes place not at Aix La Chappelle but at Aix en Provence. We need to take these issues and this analysis further, there. In this way, we may be able in Browning's terms to bring more good news from Ghent to Aix.

THE COMPLAINTS AND DISPUTES HANDLING SCHEME. A PILOT PROJECT IN THE NETHERLANDS

Daan De Snoo, Head of the Legal Practice Department of the Dutch Law Society

The Netherlands Bar association is striving for another means of dispute regulation than has hitherto been usual for the legal profession. This for the first stage, in which correction is still possible, as well as for the next phase, in which third parties must make a decision. This information package will clarify the how and why.

1 COMPLAINTS AND DISPUTES HANDLING SCHEME OF THE LEGAL PROFESSION

1.1 The strength of a complaint

The corporate sector is more and more coming to the realisation that complaints, although unpleasant, are very useful. Consequently, businesses are increasingly spending, and more professionally so, attention to complaints than in the past. And with good reason. Research shows that for every customer that complains, there are 19 customers that do not and that ventilate their dissatisfaction to others. In addition, a structured handling of complaints provides a better insight in product and service, and is thereby a good tool for improving both. The legal profession too can benefit from that.

1.2 Drawbacks of current handling of complaints

As they are generally not able to assess the quality of the content of legal services, clients usually complain about the manner in which the service is provided. Formally speaking, this is only possible through disciplinary proceedings. Many complaints of a practical nature, for example concerning poor (customer) service, faulty services or an unsatisfying price are thus - improperly so- judged by the standards of a norm that is highly sensitive for lawyers: professional misconduct (art. 46 Law on Advocates). This is a long, painful road that frequently introduces unnecessary legal dimensions to the situation and from which the client by no means always benefits. Furthermore, the entrances are very fragmented: President, disciplinary judges, budgetary procedures before the Council of Supervision and damages via the judge.

This cluttered situation is hard to fathom for clients and lawyers alike.

1.3 Back to basics: two new tools

For these reasons, the Bar association wants to bring the handling of complaints back to a level on which they can be processed in a simpler, speedier and more client-orientated manner. Primarily, therefore, within the law firm itself. Another reason for this is: the closer to the source a complaint is handled, the greater the chance of success. For complaints that can, nevertheless, not be resolved, the Bar association is striving for lower-threshold settlement via a disputes scheme. This new regulation, which will be elaborated upon later, will co-exist with and bring disciplinary law back to its authentic role in cases that truly merit this heavy tool. In this new system, the President will retain his important reference function.

1.4 Internal complaints procedure

In the first instance, complaints must be handled in complaint schemes that have been set up by the law firms themselves. The Bar association has been advised by the organisation bureau Nijhuis and Wibbelink on the manner in which best to set such a procedure in order and comply with it. This advice, which has been added to this information package, also illustrates the advantages of such a procedure for the law firm itself. This package further contains an example of an intake form. For complaints are, if unavoidable, at least more easily redressed if that which has been agreed upon with the client has been laid down.

1.5 Dispute scheme for the legal profession

In the case of the internal complaint scheme not leading to a solution, the second tool will come into view: the Disputes Committee for the Legal Profession. As of 1 June 1999, one can (without intervention by the President) go to this Disputes Committee. From that date onward, various law firms in the country have been working with this new regulation in so-called pilot projects. Although the Bar association would like to see a quick adoption of this new forum by the legal profession, the dispute regulation is not compulsory. The client and the lawyer will have to agree upon its applicability beforehand.

The Disputes Committee for the Legal Profession will work under the auspices of the Foundation for Consumer Complaints Boards (SGC), which the Bar association recently joined. This foundation, which is subsidised by the government, was founded in the 1970s with the purpose of handling consumer complaints by the Consumers' Association, the Royal Dutch Touring Club (ANWB) and several branch organisations. Presently, the number of affiliated branch organisations has grown to about thirty, among which are banks, hospitals and public utilities companies. Parties to the co-operation agreement are the SGC, the Consumers' Organisation and the Bar association. Before elucidating the Disputes Committee's method of working, an illustration will be given hereunder of its advantages as well as the sort of cases it will handle.

1.6 What does the Disputes Committee for the Legal Profession do and what can it do?

The Disputes Committee will adjudicate cases concerning the quality of services rendered and financial problems relating to fees or damages claims. Bringing a case before the Disputes Committee can be done not only by a client, but also by a third party that has to carry the costs of the aforementioned fees or damages (the legal assistance- or nonlife insurer) as well as the lawyer himself insofar as the collection of his fees is concerned. A counterclaim is also possible.

If the complaint has no financial interest, the ruling will be limited to declaring that complaint unfounded. In case of the price-quality relationship being at stake, finding that the claim is founded can lead to moderation of the fee, also with collections. After negotiations with the Federation of Insurers, the maximum for a damages claim has been set at DFL 20,000.

1.7 Advantages

The advantage of this form of dispute settlement is, for the client as well as the lawyer, the clarity resulting from bringing under one roof and being able to handle in one instance three sorts of disputes: quality, fees and (limited) damages. Moreover, this forum -due to its being recognised by the government- has an aura of objectiveness, works quickly and in a low-threshold manner and is well equipped in an organisational sense as well as in terms of facilities. Thus, it is able to attract high-quality arbitrators. An added advantage is that the lawyer (via collection) can choose the moment at which he wants to bring up a matter in dispute.

1.8 Arbitration and possible binding advice

The Disputes Committee arbitrates on basis of its own regulations and consists of three arbiters that have been selected depending on the nature of the case as well as one secretary. The chairman is a judge; one member is a lawyer and the other representing the consumers of legal services. One judge alone will handle small-interest cases. In the interest of this arbitration model, the SGC will found a new foundation (the Foundation for Professions and Businesses Complaints Board), the reason being that its own by-laws only allow binding advice. As the SGC considers it a more suitable tool for consumers, only private persons will be able to opt for binding advice rather than arbitration.

The fact that a binding advice does not result in entitlement to enforcement, does not harm the lawyer. Because if any fees remain unpaid, the client is, within four to five weeks, obliged to place a deposit under the SGC. Failure to do so will lead to forfeiture of the client's right to choose so that he will have to follow the arbitration route. Commercial clients cannot choose: for them arbitration is the only possibility.

A disadvantage arising for clients that opt for binding advice, is that no cost award is possible. If the client brings along a lawyer (an infrequent occurrence), he will always have to carry the attendant costs himself, whereas such could be otherwise with arbitration. When legal action comes into view, it is therefore necessary to point out the difference between arbitration and binding advice to the client.

1.9 Costs of procedure

As is customary, the Disputes Committee will charge administration costs to the claimant.

In the case of there being two independent claims, each of both claimants will pay his share. The losing party will reimburse these costs to the other and/or carry his own share therein himself.

In damages claims, the losing party can be sentenced to paying (a part of) the other party's legal assistance costs. This does not occur in disputes concerning fees or in cases without a financial interest.

1.10 Agreeing to the complaints and disputes handling scheme of the legal profession

As said earlier, the scheme is voluntary and its applicability must be agreed upon with the client. On the back of the intake form, a short explanation of the Complaints- and disputes handling scheme of the Legal Profession has been printed. The arbitration clause printed on the front is in keeping with the regulation and has to be uniform within the branch.

The text is as follows:

> *Our law firm is participating in the Complaints- and disputes handling scheme of the Legal Profession. Any disputes that may arise from the realisation and/or the execution of our services, including all disputes concerning*

fees, will be settled according to the Regulation for the Disputes Committee for the Legal Profession. This regulation provides for arbitration, in the understanding that in certain cases the possibility also exists of opting for a ruling by way of binding advice. When we do not succeed in resolving possible complaints about our services with you, then you can present your complaints to the Disputes Committee for the Legal Profession. The applicability of the Complaints- and disputes handling scheme of the Legal Profession will come about by the signing of this form or by signing the confirmation of the order that we will send you which refers to the scheme.

Art. 1020 of the Dutch Civil Procedure Code (Rv) stipulates that an arbitration agreement is proven by means of a written document. It is therefore necessary, to avoid discussion at a later stage, to request the return of a signed copy of the order confirmation: a stamped addressed envelope could render useful services in this respect.

1.11 More information for the client and yourself

It is recommendable to make a brochure for your clients in which you provide a short explanation of the complaint procedure and the disputes scheme. In this packet, you will find a draft for the afore-mentioned as well as an invitation with sign-up slip for a course in Complaint-handling, the participants of which obtain training credits.

If you still have questions about the complaints- and dispute scheme, you can contact the Bar association, Legal Practice department, tel. 070-335 35 73

2 THE LAW FIRM COMPLAINTS REGULATION

2.1 Introduction

The implementation of a complaints regulation is a good step in the direction of quality care within a law firm. Complaints are *the* means with which a law firm can improve the quality of its services. The regulation provides for standardisation of the process of complaint handling. In consequence thereof, this process will be less dependent on the manner in which each lawyer chooses to deal with it. The quality in this field will increase and become more consistent. This is the point of departure of the implementation of quality care.

How can a law firm give shape to a structured handling of complaints?

This chapter will cover the setting up of a complaints regulation within a law firm and the implementation thereof.

2.2 Conditions for a complaints regulation

The following demands will be made of a complaints regulation:

2.2.1 *Low-threshold*

The complaints procedure must make it easy for clients to complain. This means that the law firm is open for criticism, remarks and suggestions. The client gets the feeling that the complaint is welcome information and will be dealt with in a meaningful way by the law firm. A client must be informed at the earliest possible stage about the way in which complaints can be filed, how they are handled and who handles them. This can, for example, already be done during the initial interview. The law firm can also print a brochure about the Law Firm Complaints Regulation and make it standard practice to explain this brochure and provide the client with a copy on the occasion of the initial interview.

The brochure describes how the procedure works (see next paragraph), what the terms are and to whom one must turn.

2.2.2 *Immediate response: quick action aimed at solutions*

The law firm responds immediately to the complaint. It turns out that a quick, serious handling of objective as well as subjective complaints produces the best effect for the client as well as the lawyer.

2.2.3 *Insight*

The client has insight in which way the handling of complaints takes place, who is responsible for this and which paths have to be followed to handle a complaint. Similarly, the client must have insight in the discussion of the content of the complaint. It is of importance that the client knows what to expect from the handling of the complaint. A brochure about how the complaints procedure works can provide for this need.

Such a brochure is also in keeping with the requirement that the law firm should actively provide information about the handling of complaints.

2.2.4 *Standardisation of complaint handling*

An unequivocal approach to dealing with complaints is important for professionalising the handling of complaints. By laying down norms concerning the handling of complaints, there will be clarity for clients and employees. An unequivocal handling of complaints can also reap benefits at a policy level as it provides management information on basis of which the quality of the services can be improved.

2.2.5 *Independent*

It should not make a difference for the client who handles the complaint within the law firm. In addition, the possibility should be guarded against of personal motives or presuppositions about the client playing a role in the handling of the complaint.

2.2.6 *Research after the cause*

The complaint has consequences for the law firm organisation or the work method of the lawyer. It is of importance that the cause of the complaint is sought after so that it can be taken away to prevent further complaints.

For that reason, complaints must be registered and evaluated. In this way, it can be ascertained whether the complaint is incidental or whether one can speak of a certain pattern.

The complaints regulation that will be elucidated in the next paragraph meets these requirements.

2.3 The complaints regulation

The complaints regulation consists of a description of the law firm procedures in force concerning the handling of complaints. Who does what when there are complaints and in what way? Which road must be taken? What is the desired way of responding?

The regulation will also provide directives about the way in which the content of complaints must be "weighed".

The setting down of a complaints regulation is, in effect, nothing other than the making and laying down of agreements concerning the way in which complaints are handled. The content of agreements can vary per law firm. It is a result of the choices that a law firm makes.

In any case, the regulation contains the following elements:

- the objective of the complaints regulation
- the complaints procedure/work method (see flow chart)

2.3.1 *The objective of the complaints regulation*

Firstly, the law firm will lay down, in general terms, the objective of the complaints procedure. In any case, the procedure will have to be aimed at the actual handling of existing complaints of the clients. Furthermore, we strongly recommend that the aim also include the improvement in the course of a certain period of time of the services rendered, as a result of complaints that have arisen.

Hereby it is important that realistic goals are set. Unfeasible goals lead to frustration and, in time, even stagnation. Striving to reduce the number of complaints is a goal that must be avoided. The danger of such an approach, is that complaints will be avoided and seen as unwelcome information. Complaints should, on the contrary, be considered welcome information.

Examples of objectives are:

- the resolving of dissatisfaction or complaints from clients in a more client-orientated manner;
- the standardising of the handling of complaints;
- the preserving of the relationship with the client.

2.3.2 *The complaints procedure*

According to the flow chart below, the complaints procedure looks as follows:

1. Definition of complaint

↓

2. Registration of the complaints form

↓

3. Classification of the complaint

↓ ↓

4.a. Handle complaint yourself | 4.b. To complaints official

↓ ↓

5.a. Reactions and solutions | 5.b. Reactions and solutions

↓ ↓

6.a. Feedback to the client | 6.b. Feedback to the client

↓ ↓

7.a. Refer is case of dissatisfaction | 7.b. Refer in case of dissatisfaction

↓ ↓

8. Discuss internally

↓

9. Analysis of complaint

↓

10. Preventive action

2.3.2.1 Definition of a "complaint"

A definition shall first have to be made of that which the law firm considers to be a complaint. We recommend that the term "complaint" be broadly interpreted so as to encompass the definition "a complaint is any expression of dissatisfaction by a client". In this way, all displays of dissatisfaction, great or small, oral or in written form, will be handled in a standardised, client-orientated manner and registered.

Such a broad interpretation, will put the relationship with the clients in the first place. In this way, the law firm will also be able to collect as much management information as possible to improve the services.

2.3.2.2 Registration of the complaint: complaints form

As a minimum, the following will be registered:

upon receipt of a complaint:

- data on client
- description of service/case
- date of intake
- indication of problems/complaints
- person handling the complaint

upon handling the complaint

- agreements made about action to be taken and feedback to client
- date on which the complaint has been handled

However, for a good overview, we recommend registering all steps to be taken. In this way, it will always be possible to retrieve how far a procedure has been followed and what the state of affairs is. This entails filling in the complaints form at each stage of the process. An example of a registration form has been added as a supplement to this information packet.

2.3.2.3 Classification of the complaint

The complaint will have to be classified. This classification is necessary for two reasons. Firstly, it will depend on the classification whether the complaint will be handled by the lawyer himself or by a complaints official. Secondly, complaints can only be used as management information if there is insight in the nature of the complaints. This insight can only be obtained by means of classification.

The following categories of complaints are possible:

- class I. complaints about the work method of or treatment by the lawyer
- class II. complaints about aspects concerning the legal content of services rendered

- class III. complaints about financial aspects of the services rendered
- class IV. complaints about method of running practice in general

Thereby, it is also possible to make a further categorisation:

- class A written complaints
- class B oral complaints

As mentioned earlier, the classification does not reveal anything about the seriousness of the complaint. He who complains, the client, does not distinguish between the difference categories.

In the interest of the evaluation of the pilot project, the pilot law firms are requested to keep to these categories as much as possible.

2.3.2.4 Handling of complaint

Some complaints, for example those concerning legal content, are best handled as much as possible by a lawyer other than the one concerned. This other lawyer frequently can, as he is less personally involved with the client and the case, more professionally handle the case than the lawyer in question. In addition, complaints officials can be chosen from among persons who already possess the necessary skills. These persons could also receive training in this respect.

The complaints official will not only have to direct his skills to the client, but also to his fellow lawyers or supporting staff. Speaking to colleagues about complaints is not an easy task.

For each class, it can be determined whether the complaint will be referred to the complaints official or that the lawyer in question will handle the complaint himself. Sometimes, it can be recommended that the lawyer in question handle the complaint himself, as referral could go at the expense of the trust-based relationship between the lawyer involved and the client. The choice will also stem from the definition of the complaint (under 1).

The broader the definition of the term "complaint", the less likely it is that the complaints official will be able to deal with all displays of dissatisfaction.

For example, if a lawyer holds an evaluative talk with his client after the conclusion of a case and the client tells him that he is content, but that he thinks it a pity that he was not kept abreast of the developments in the procedure at a certain moment, this would, according to the broad definition we are advocating, constitute a complaint that should be subjected to the complaints procedure. This complaint will then be registered, classified and the client should get a reaction to his display of dissatisfaction. However, in the above-stated case we feel that it is not necessary to call upon a complaints official.

We recommend that all written complaints and those oral complaints in which the client uses the word "complaint" or otherwise displays a, for him, deep sense of dissatisfaction be referred to the complaints official. In addition to on the foregoing, the choice depends on the classification and the definition of the term "complaint". Law firms can make their own choices.

Larger law firms (more than five lawyers) are in the position of being able to appoint one or more lawyers to complaints official. We recommend letting one or more of the law firm's partners act as complaints officials. It can also be useful to replace the complaints official by a complaints committee.

For smaller law firms, it is not always possible to have another lawyer than the lawyer in question handle a complaint, as there are frequently not enough partners. Given the hierarchal relationships within the firm, it is not desirable to allow the handling of complaints to be done by trainees or associates. Moreover, it is also not desirable towards the client. Clients could get the impression of not being taken seriously, if their complaint were not handled by a partner.

For one-man law firms, it is difficult to give shape to calling in an independent complaints official. In such cases, the Bar association proposes to entrust a lawyer in the same district with the handling of complaints. It is also possible that a small group of firms creates a common complaints structure. In addition, it is conceivable that small firms make an appeal to the President or one of the members of the Council of Supervision for the handling of complaints.

At any rate, the fact that no independent complaints official can be called upon within the firm does not mean that a one-man law firm or the only partner of a firm cannot follow the rest of the complaints procedure and give his client a standardised handling of his complaint(s).

Firms with more than one branch offices would be well advised to appoint a complaints official for each office.

If a Law Firm Complaints Committee has been installed, it is advisable to let its members decide together about the reactions to and the solutions of complaints (see 5b).

2.3.2.5 Reactions and solutions

The firm lays down the points of departure that will be used in responding to complaints. For example:

- taking the complaint seriously even if it is unfounded in the eyes of the lawyer;
- inquiring into the cause.

Many complaints are easy to resolve. For that, it is necessary that the person handling the complaints have a certain freedom of action, as the effective handling of complaints requires an immediate response. For that reason, agreements are made internally about that which can and that which cannot be promised to the client.

The measures to be taken for the different categories of complaints are to be described within general frameworks. For example:

- room for financial accommodation;
- criteria for awarding accommodation;
- an apology by the lawyer in question;
- setting right of the complaint and determining the further handling of the case.

2.3.2.6 Feedback to client

At this point, it is important for setting short terms for feedback. It will also be determined who informs the client about this term and in which way this happens.

2.3.2.7 Referral in case of dissatisfaction

If clients are not satisfied about the complaint handling, they will be referred. If the lawyer in question handles the complaint himself, he can refer the client to the complaints official at the firm. If the client is not satisfied with the complaints official's handling of the case, he will be referred to the Disputes Committee for the Legal Profession. The firm will provide clear information to the client about this possibility.

2.3.2.8 Discuss internally

It is important for the quality of the services rendered that the office actually discusses the complaints internally. At this point, it will have to be determined which categories of complaints will be discussed where, in what way and with what regularity (in general terms or in such a way that it becomes clear to whom the complaint is directed) and who will have to be present at this talk.

Considering that all employees determine the quality of the services rendered, we recommend that the talk not be limited to the lawyers. In part, the supporting staff determines the quality of the services rendered. For them too, the reaction of the clients is an important indicator of the quality of their services. Moreover, they are frequently the ones who will have been confronted on the phone with the dissatisfaction.

2.3.2.9 Analysis of the complaints

Here, it will have to be determined in which way, by whom and with which frequency the complaints will be analysed. Prerequisite to the analysis is a good insight in the complaints expressed. In order to gain this insight, the following information is necessary:

- numbers of complaints;
- number per sort of complaints;
- numbers and sort of complaints per lawyer (not in order to censure each other, but, for example, to track down overtaxing);
- solutions;
- degree of satisfaction about the handling of the complaints.

The data will be stored at one point. It is preferable to used an automated system for this. Here, it is important that this system can select on each of above-mentioned sorts of data. In addition, it is helpful to also keep a short description of the complaint. One person should be responsible for correctly storing the information.

On basis of above-mentioned data, an analysis of the complaints can be made. An analysis entails a comparison of pieces of the data in relation to each other, in relation to preceding periods and in relation to possible measures to be taken. It is processing the data. It provides insight into the percentage of most frequent complaints, increases/decreases in relation to the preceding period etc.

It will have to be determined:

- who is responsible for the making of the analysis;
- which insight will minimally be expected;
- with what frequency the analysis takes place.

2.3.2.10 Preventive action: measures to improve

On basis of the analysis made at 9, preventive action can be taken. Here also it is important that it is decided who takes the action and how soon.

A point of attention is also the creation of support within the firm for this preventive action. The taking of preventive action entails the following elements:

2.3.2.10.1 The collection of as many solutions/ideas as possible concerning improvements

This stimulates creativity and gives space for venting unexpected and unorthodox ideas. Up to what extent the solutions can be executed is, at this point, not really relevant. The collection of as many solutions/ideas as possible is best done by more than one person, for example by the complaints committee.

2.3.2.10.2 *The selection of solutions*

In this step, the choice of a solution/measure is central. By comparing and combining, a certain solution can be chosen. The partnership / management of the firm can play in role here.

2.3.2.10.3 *Implementing the chosen solution*

Co-ordination is important here. It will have to be decided who does what when.

2.3.2.10.4 *Evaluating the solution*

In this phase, it will be seen whether the solution / the measure has led to the desired result. Has the problem been solved? Is there any apparent improvement? When the problem is not solved, a new problem has to be defined and the process will have to be followed again.

2.3.3 *Setting up and implementing a complaints regulation: step-by-step plan*

Before all else, the setting up of a complaints regulation requires that the entire management or all members of the partnership support this plan. All members of the partnership must commit themselves to the plan of setting up and implementing a complaints regulation. For this, it is necessary that all partners understand the possible consequences of a complaints procedure for their own practice and for the firm as a whole. If this is not the case, the plan is doomed to fail.

The intention and its consequences will then have to be passed down to all the firm's employees. The importance of implementing a complaints regulation and the priority that this implementation has must be clear to each employee, lawyer and secretary, bookkeeper or receptionist.

As mentioned earlier, the setting up of a complaints procedure not only has a procedural side. A complaints procedure without the right mentality is half the work. If the prevalent mentality in the firm is not one of stimulating and taking the expressing of dissatisfaction seriously, there is a significant chance that the number of written complaints shall be high and the less forceful expressions of dissatisfaction small. In this case, clients will have to cross a high threshold to express their dissatisfaction, so that smaller misunderstandings and other subjects of dissatisfaction will not, or hardly at all, be discussed. These will therefore have a greater chance of becoming serious complaints. This taxes the firm's complaints procedure. Complaints will more quickly become heavy, more quickly end up with the complaints official or the complaints committee and be less easy to solve than in the case of a mentality whereby the firm is open to all expressions of dissatisfaction. Or complaints are not expressed at all and the clients leave the firm.

For that reason, the advocating of a complaint-orientated mentality is an important part of the setting up of a complaints regulation. A focused training of all lawyers or of those handling the complaints can be helpful in this respect.

After that, the regulation has to be laid down.

It is important that each partner and associate knows which steps he must take in the event of expressions of dissatisfaction from a client and in which way he must inform the client about the complaints regulation.

Step by step, the implementing of a complaints procedure looks as follows:

a) Achieving support within partnership / management
b) Disseminating the complaints procedure that is to be set up and the consequences thereof for the work of all employees
c) Gaining insight in the current mentality
d) Promoting the right, complaint-orientated mentality
e) Preparing the content of the regulation
f) Determining the content of the regulation
g) Informing all employees about the regulation
h) Implementing the regulation
i) Evaluating the procedure and guarding its progress

2.3.4 *One can learn from mistakes*

A complaint-friendly culture demands an open and positively critical style of leadership. When executive lawyers within a firm reprimand associates / trainees because of dissatisfaction that their clients express, dissatisfaction and complaints will be smoothed over by employees.

This means that, within the firm, the culture that making mistakes is human and that one can learn especially much from mistakes has to be prevalent. Executives play a main role in creating this culture. By, on the one hand, showing their own mistakes and, on the other hand, not reprimanding their subordinates on their mistakes, they will create such a culture. Only by learning from mistakes, will it be possible to come to a true improvement of the service.

Thereby, the realisation has to be present that some mistakes do not depend on the actions or omissions of one person, but that they can be the result of the internal communication or organisation as a whole.

REBUILDING THE CATHEDRAL? - THE PARTNERSHIP QUESTION AND THE EFFECT OF "MODERNISATION" ON THE PROFESSIONALISM AND ETHICS OF THE ENGLISH BAR

Peter Kunzlik, M.A. (Cantab.), LL.M. (Cantab.), Associate Dean, Nottingham Law School, Nottingham Trent University, Barrister[*]

In 1983 Raymond Cocks noted that "[a]lmost everywhere it seems that the Bar is regarded as some great cathedral which has remained quite untouched by any changes in architectural style since its foundations were first established long ago."[1] He then helped demonstrate how far that perception really was from the historical truth. The "cathedral" of the Bar, like so many actual cathedrals, exhibits not only characteristics attributable to its early origins, but also the accretions of the intervening years.[2] Its foundations have been shaken before and, with the process of "modernisation" of justice upon which the Government embarked in the late 1990s, have been shaken again. Indeed, two years ago I suggested that certain aspects of modernisation challenged the concept of the English Bar as a discrete profession and required fundamental adjustment of its ethical code.[3] Much has happened since then. In this paper I shall argue that, at the level of principle, modernisation has resulted in the abandonment of all but one of the "traditional" ideological foundations of the Bar; and that the surviving foundation, the Bar's concept of itself as a profession of independent sole practitioners, although retained as a matter of principle, has been fatally undermined in practice. I will seek to substantiate this argument by demonstrating how modernisation has provoked a much greater degree of collective organisation of barristers' practices than is consistent with the "sole practitioner" paradigm. Before going further, however, it is perhaps opportune to summarise the key elements of the modernisation process itself before reviewing the effects that they have had to date.

---

* The author would like to thank Ms. Julie Waplington, Research Assistant at the Nottingham Law School, for her help in following press coverage of the various mergers and transfers between, and dissolutions of, chambers that have taken place over the last three years.

1 R. COCKS, *Foundations of the Modern Bar* (Sweet and Maxwell, London, 1983) p. 6.

2 For descriptions of two key periods in the history of the Bar see W.R. PREST, *The Rise of the Barristers - A Social History of the English Bar 1590 - 1640* (Clarendon, Oxford, 1986) and R. COCKS, *o.c.*

3 P. KUNZLIK, "Conditional Fees: The Ethical and Organisational Impact on the Bar" (1999) 62 *Modern Law Review* 850.

1 THE PROFESSIONAL CONTEXT

As is well known, the English legal profession has traditionally been a "split profession" comprising, in reality, two professions; the solicitors and the barristers. Traditionally, each profession had its characteristic monopoly and each enjoyed the privilege of self-regulation. So far as the Bar was concerned, its members had the monopoly over rights of audience before the higher courts; it was regulated by the General Council of the Bar whose "Code of Conduct" contained its rules of professional ethics and etiquette.[4] The Bar's conception of itself as a separate profession was predicated upon a number of specific assumptions, assumptions from which ethical consequences were drawn by the Code of Conduct. These assumptions were fundamental to the Bar's coherence as a profession but, as we shall see, all but one of them have now been revised or discarded in response to the modernisation process. The assumptions to which I refer are as follows. First, that the interests of justice demanded that each barrister should practise as a sole practitioner, albeit that barristers should be permitted to share certain expenses (*e.g.* office accommodation and the services of a clerk) by practising in sets of chambers with other barristers.[5] Second that the Bar was a "referral profession" i.e. that it would not accept instructions directly from (lay) clients but only through the intermediation of the solicitor.[6] Thirdly that, given the Bar's monopoly over higher rights of audience, barristers should be obliged to accept instructions in cases within their field of practice, regardless of their views of the client or his /her prospects of success (subject only to rules as to conflict of interest, to the barrister's availability for the dates in question, and to agreement of a "reasonable" fee) – the so-called "cab-rank"

4 As to the organisation and professionalism of the Bar see especially B. ABEL-SMITH and R. STEVENS, *Lawyers and the Courts* (Heinemann, London, 1967); R.L. ABEL, *The Legal Profession in England and Wales* (Blackwell, Oxford, 1988); R.L. ABEL AND P.S.C. LEWIS (eds.), *Lawyers in Society – An Overview* (University of California Press, Berkeley, 1995) ch. 2, "England and Wales – A Comparison of the Professional Projects of Barristers and Solicitors"; and R. HAZELL, *The Bar on Trial* (Quartet Books, London, 1978).

5 These assumptions are expressed in the current (7th) edition of the Code (as amended) in para. 104 (a)(ii) which provides that the general purpose of the Code is to provide rules requiring, inter alia, barristers in independent practice "to be completely independent and in professional standing as sole practitioners"; and in para. 205 which provides that "[a] practising barrister must not supply legal services to the public through or on behalf of any other person (including a partnership company or other body corporate) except as permitted by par. 502" [which in turn permits certain employed barristers to provide legal services to clients of their employers].

6 For the general rule to this effect see the Code para. 104 (a) (ii) which provides that the general purpose of the Code is to provide rules requiring, inter alia, barristers in independent practice "to act only as consultants instructed by solicitors and other approved persons".

rule.[7] Finally, consistent with its conception of itself as a disinterested liberal profession, and with its understanding of the requirements of justice, the Bar insisted that barristers should have no financial interest of their own in respect of the cases in which they accepted instructions.[8]

2 MODERNISATION

2.1 The modernisation programme

The key elements of the modernisation programme - which has transformed the context within which the Bar works and has shaken central aspects of its professional ideology - are: the reform of civil procedure ("The Woolf Reforms"); [9] the extension of the use of conditional fee agreements ("CFAs") as a means of funding civil litigation, and a corresponding retrenchment of civil legal aid;[10] reform of the funding and organisation of representation in criminal cases;[11] review of the criminal justice system;[12] the abolition of the practising Bar's monopoly over rights of audience in the Higher Courts;[13] and a diminution in the autonomy of the legal professional bodies so far as self-regulation is concerned.[14] The process has been implemented in a gen-

---

7 For the current formulation of the rule see the Code, paras. 601 - 606.

8 The Code, para. 603(e) requires barristers to decline instructions in cases in which there is a conflict of interest and para 3.7 of the Written Standards accompanying the Code continue to state that a barrister should not appear as a barrister "in any matter in which he...has a significant pecuniary interest".

9 The reforms were implemented primarily by the adoption of new Civil Procedure Rules 1999 following *Access to Justice, The Final Report of the Woolf Inquiry to the Lord Chancellor on the Civil Justice System in England and Wales* (London, 1996, HMSO).

10 See P. KUNZLIK, *o.c,* p. 850.

11 Involving the setting up, pursuant to the Access of Justice Act 1999, of a Criminal Defence Service; see P. KUNZLIK, *o.c.*, p. 850.

12 See A Review of the Criminal Courts in England and Wales by the Rt. Hon. Lord Justice Auld, September 2001 (<http://www.criminal-courts-review.org.uk>).

13 The Access to Justice Act 1999, ss 36 - 38, provides that every barrister and solicitor (whether in private practice or whether employed) is to have a right of audience before every court in relation to all proceedings subject to the rules and regulations of the Law Society and Bar Council. Section 41 and Sched. 5, para. 6 of the Act make it easier than hitherto for the Lord Chancellor to authorise new bodies to grant rights of audience since they dispense with the need for him to obtain the approval of the designated judges and the (now defunct) Advisory Committee on Legal Education and Conduct ("ACLEC").

14 Section 41 and Part III of Sched. 5 of the Access to Justice Act 1999 empowered the Lord Chancellor to make orders altering the qualification regulations and/or rules of conduct of the Bar Council (and other authorised bodies) if he considers that they unduly restrict a right of audience or the exercise of such a right. Authorised bodies must thereafter either conform to government policy or risk interference in a central area of their self-regulatory function. See Lord Irvine, HL Deb col. 1111 14 December 1998.

eral climate which has included sustained public denunciations by Government of "fat cat" lawyers, continuing efforts by Government (as the major purchaser of legal services) to drive down lawyer's fees in publicly funded work; the introduction of a less benevolent basis of the taxation for lawyers;[15] the subjection of lawyer's professional practices to scrutiny by the competition authorities;[16] and the abolition of the advocate's traditional immunity from suit.[17]

2.2 Impact upon the Bar's Ideology

The modernisation process has, of course, attacked the most fundamental traditional assumption of all about the Bar. It has abolished the very monopoly which had distinguished barristers from other types of lawyer[18] and which had therefore justified its identity as a *separate* profession. In parallel it has also significantly constrained the extent to which the Bar can be considered to be autonomous in terms of self-regulation.[19]

Modernisation has, however, also challenged each of the specific principles upon which the Bar's ideology was traditionally constructed. In doing so, it

---

15 The Inland Revenue has ceased to tax professionals (including barristers) on the basis of payments received but instead taxes them on the basis of earnings (i.e. work done). For the Bar this was mitigated only by exempting new barristers from the new regime for the first seven years of practice: see "Young Bar exempt from professional tax change" *The Lawyer* 24 March 1998 p. 44. For a profession such as the Bar in which there may be significant time lags between doing work and receiving payment (as to which see main text below) the effect of this may have been significant. The impact will have been felt most severely by barristers doing publicly funded work since the BDO Stoy Hayward, *Report on the 2000 Survey of Barristers' Chambers* (July 2000) indicated that amongst those who owed barristers money "the slowest payer continues to be the Legal Aid Board (now the Community Legal Service)." So under the new rules the State has been taxing practitioners on fees earned in publicly funded work even though the fees have not actually been paid (and may not be paid for a period of years) and even though the delay in payment is caused by the State itself. The potential cash flow problems inherent in such a situation are obvious.

16 The Department for Trade and Industry has accepted the recommendations made in *Competition in Professions: A Report by the Director General of Fair Trading* (OFT 328, March 2001) that legal professional rules should be subject to the application of the Competition Act 1998. This can be done by removing their designation under para. 2 of Sched. 4 of that Act which designation, has by virtue of para. 1 of that schedule, has hitherto excluded such professional rules from the prohibitions in chapter 1 of the Act. See DTI press release "Professions to be subject to competition law" P/2001/141. Cf. *Competition in Professions – The Bar's Consultation Paper in Response to the OFT Report* (July 2001).

17 Arthur J.S. Hall and Co v. Melvyn Keith Simons [2000] 3 W.L.R. 543 (HL). See M. SENEVIRATNE, "The Rise and Fall of Advocates' Immunity" (2001) *Legal Studies* pp. 644 – 662.

18 See n. 13 above.

19 See n. 14 above.

has undermined the coherence of the Bar as a *unified* profession. The concept of the Bar as a "referral only" profession has, for example, already been surrendered as a matter of principle since the Bar has been forced to respond to the threat (and later the reality) of abolition of its monopoly by permitting direct access, albeit that such direct access is only afforded to clients from certain professions recognised by the Bar Council as competent to instruct barristers ("BarDIRECT" clients).[20] Similarly, the "cab-rank" principle, which was for so long central to the Bar's ideology[21] and was fundamental to its justification of itself as a separate profession, has been abolished not only in conditional fee cases[22] (where its application would be inconsistent with the CFA barrister's role as a risk-taker) but also in respect of the acceptance of direct instructions from BarDIRECT clients.[23] The advent of conditional fees has also undermined another central tenet of the Bar's traditional faith, that the barrister must never have a financial interest in the outcome of his/her cases. The CFA lawyer will, after all, only be paid if his/her client wins and then, of course, will be entitled to an enhanced fee.

At the level of principle, therefore, most of the guiding concepts which had provided both the ideological orientation and organisational coherence of the Bar have been surrendered. Only the concept of the barrister as an independent sole practitioner appears to remain in tact. Amid the maelstrom of reform, however, the practising Bar has undergone a significant process of re-structuring and this has involved material changes in the way in which practices are organised. This has itself involved such a degree of collectivisation of practice at the Bar that the "sole practitioner" paradigm has, for much of the Bar at least, become a fiction. This paper will therefore argue that events have overcome the traditional justification for the Bar's ethical rules against barristers' partnership, rules which are, in any event, being subjected to significant attack from within the Bar as well as from without.

3 COMMERCIALISATION AND COLLECTIVISATION OF THE PRACTICE AT THE BAR

The replacement of civil legal aid by conditional fee agreements in many fields of practice required barristers to take risk for reward - to agree to forego their fees if their client's action failed in exchange for an agreed "uplift" in those fees if the action were to succeed. This posed a number of spe-

20 See the Bar Council's Bar Direct and Recognition Regulations (annexed as Annex F to the Code); the Bar Direct Terms of Engagement and the Approved List of Direct Access Bodies.

21 See P. KUNZLIK, *o.c.*, p. 861.

22 The Code, para. 604 (c) and see P. KUNZLIK, *o.c.*, p. 861.

23 The Code, para. 604 (e).

cific challenges to the Bar's ethical code.[24] It also required barristers to reconsider their approach both to risk and to their relationship with their (lay) clients. Furthermore, the practical requirements of CFA practice also militated in favour of greater cooperation between barristers taking CFA cases[25] and so undermined the paradigm of the barrister as a sole practitioner. Furthermore, the whole system of CFA-based litigation depends upon the existence of a market in after-the-event insurance and upon the insurers. This is because the English cost-shifting rules normally mean that a losing party becomes responsible for the payment of his/her opponent's costs. The risk that such a liability might arise was thought likely to inhibit potential litigants from entering into CFAs and thereby to inhibit their access to justice. (If unsuccessful litigants were to face the potentially crippling burden of having to pay the costs of the victorious party, the fact that their CFAs would protect them from having to pay their own lawyers would offer them little comfort). Thus a market has developed in "after-the-event" insurance in which a potential litigant bringing a case on a CFA basis can insure against the risk of having to pay the opposing party's costs if he/she loses. This central role of after-the-event insurance in making a generalised system of CFA-based litigation feasible has enhanced the importance of insurers making them an even more powerful force than hitherto in the litigation (and advocacy) services market.[26] So much so that, in practice, the range of

---

24 See P. KUNZLIK, *o.c.* and the *Report of the Society of Advanced Legal Studies Working Group* (chaired by Richard Southwell QC) *on the Ethical Implications of Conditional Fee Arrangements* (SALS, London, 2000).

25 Practical considerations militate in favour of adopting collective approaches to CFAs. It is, for example, necessary to set up arrangements whereby a number of barristers can have confidence in the quality of their respective risk assessments so as to ensure that if the barrister accepting a CFA brief were to become unavailable, another would be willing to take the case on the basis of the original CFA. The Bar Council has now itself recognised the need for collective organisation in respect of CFAs. See the Bar Council's *Guidance on Conditional Fee Agreements* (February 2001). This contemplates that members of one or more sets of chambers may enter into standing agreements "as a chambers or in groups" (p. 5, para. 4, p. 27 para. 33 et seq.). When such agreements exist the Guidance states that "the agreement of any persons or group required by the procedures [contained in the agreement] should be obtained before a CFA is agreed" (p. 30, para. 26). The need to spread the risk, and the cash flow implications, of CFAs militates in favour of still more fundamental collectivisation of practice, see P. KUNZLIK, *o.c.* This point was also emphasised by the *Report to the General Council of the Bar on the Future Structure of the Bar Following the Government's Proposals for Change in the Delivery of Legal Services* (Biddle, Solicitors, 11 May 1998, "The Biddle Report") which concluded that just because partnership was perceived as incompatible with the Bar's cab-rank rule, that was no reason for eliminating such structures from consideration.

26 For descriptions of the development conditional fee agreements and of the ATE insurance market see Callery v. Gray; Russell and Pal Pak Corrugated Ltd. [2001] EWCA Civ 1117, 17 July 2001. See also Imran Sarwar v. Muhammad Alam [2001] EWCA Civ 1401, 19 September 2001.

potential intermediaries from whom many barristers may compete for work has been significantly narrowed to a smaller number of solicitors approved by the after-the-event insurers or claims management companies, or to the still smaller number of insurers or claims management companies themselves.[27] In responding to the requirements of such purchasers of their services barristers need to operate collectively rather than as sole practitioners, and to operate on the basis of commercial approaches (*e.g.* the discounting of fee rates for volume)[28] which might, not so long ago, have been regarded as unthinkable. Similarly, the need to be able to negotiate block contracts[29] for the conduct of publicly funded work carried out, for example, for the Community Legal Service, or the Crown Prosecution Service and to provide the various quality assurance mechanisms which are required for such work also implies a need for collective organisation.[30]

Perhaps more fundamentally, however, another factor militates in favour of the adoption of collective forms of practice at the Bar and of a more com-

---

27 In Imran Sarwar v. Muhammad Alam [2001] EWCA Civ 1401, 19 September 2001, the Court (at para. 18) described the "ATE Group" as representing 15 after-the-event insurers and that small number does seem to encompass all those active in the market. Claims management companies include companies such as Claims Direct and Accident Group.

28 Barristers have needed to negotiate directly with insurers and claims management companies on a chambers basis, a phenomenon which would surprise few in other walks of commercial life, but which apparently disturbs the Bar Council: see "Bar meeting with Claims Direct sparks Council angst" *The Lawyer* 23 July 2001 p. 4. One set of chambers is currently under investigation by the Bar Council for allegedly making payments to Claims Direct in return for work: see "Bar probes 4 KBW over Claims Direct payments" *The Lawyer* 24 September 2001 p. 1. Paras. 307(d) and (e) of the Code seem apt to prohibit such behaviour. They provide respectively that a barrister must not "give a commission...for any professional purpose whatsoever to...any client or any person entitled to instruct him as an intermediary" and must not "make any payment... to any person for the purpose of procuring professional instructions."

29 For an early example in which the Legal Aid Board awarded its first contract to a set of chambers for direct provision of advice to lay clients see "LAB awards direct contract to 2 Garden court" *The Lawyer* 2 July 1999 p. 9.

30 The Legal Services Commission has, for example, introduced its "Quality Mark" to which several chambers now conform. Quality control systems in themselves militate in favour of collectivisation of practice management since they all rely upon a process of documenting the existence of managed business processes. Where a sole practitioner is delivering a service, it may well be possible to document a managed process in respect of some aspects of the practice *e.g.* meeting standardised response times for responding to correspondence, instructions etc. But if quality control systems are to give any assurance as to the most important aspect of quality, the quality of legal advice given, they cannot exist only at the level of the individual sole practitioner. Some element of oversight, supervision or quality auditing by others becomes essential and that requires some degree at least of collective practice management. The Bar has sought to assist barristers to come to terms with the quality assurance culture by inaugurating its own scheme, the "Bar Mark" scheme.

mercial approach to the barrister's work. This factor is competition. Enhancing competition in the provision of legal services has been the key instrumental policy of successive governments for many years.[31] It is a policy that continues to be applied with vigour and it can safely be asserted that none of the remaining traditional practices of the Bar can be regarded as secure from attack on competition grounds.[32] The abolition by the Access to Justice Act 1999 of the Bar's monopoly over rights of audience in the Higher Courts was, of course, an expression of this policy. It was designed to open up the market for advocacy services in the Higher Courts to "inter brand" competition (i.e. to competition between barristers and solicitors (and others) having "higher rights").[33] The abolition of that monopoly will no doubt have significant effect in due course upon the work available to the Bar.[34] It may well be, however, that sufficient advocacy capacity has not yet been developed by solicitors to threaten the Bar in the short term. The Bar is, however, under much more immediate pressure from other circumstances, namely the impact on the market, and upon "intra brand" competition (i.e. competition between barristers) of the Woolf Reforms of civil procedure. These have resulted in a significant reduction in the volume of litigation.[35] The effect of this has been so severe,[36] that some barristers have undoubtedly been under financial pressure.[37] This seems to have made what until recently was en-

---

31 See P. KUNZLIK, *o.c.*, p. 853-854.

32 See *e.g. Competition in Professions – A Report by the Director General of Fair Trading, o.c.*, sections XIII and XIV.

33 Section 41 and Sched. 5, para. 6 of the Access to Justice Act 1999 authorise the Lord Chancellor to authorise bodies other than the Bar Council and the Law Society to confer higher rights.

34 Many of the City firms have invested significantly in advocacy training for their (usually junior) solicitors. My own law school (formerly as the National Institute of Trial Advocacy (NITA) UK and latterly under its own corporate name) has provided much of this training for several consortia of City firms. For a recent example see "Nottingham lands contract to train solicitor-advocates" *The Lawyer* 11 June 2001. This does not necessarily mean that all the firms funding advocacy training intend to enter the advocacy market but some undoubtedly do intend to do so. Furthermore, the Woolf Reforms, with their emphasis on case management hearings, seem apt to increase the amount of advocacy conducted by solicitors by increasing the need for procedural advocacy in which the solicitor managing the file will be best placed to address the court.

35 *The Judicial Statistics Annual Report 2000* shows, for example, that claims issued in the Queen's Bench Division fell from 72,161 in 1999 to 26,876. See "Court claims plunge post Woolf" *The Lawyer* 30 August 2001 p. 1

36 See *e.g.* "Commercial bar in crisis as work dries up" *The Lawyer* 26 April 1999.

37 Lord Woolf CJ, in his speech to the 2001 Bar Conference (as to which see main text below), has himself expressed concern that although the earnings of a minority of the Bar are "breathtakingly high" the earnings of "the majority of barristers" who are dependent upon publicly funded work are "disturbingly modest:" *The Lawyer* 22 October 2002 p. 39. There can indeed be little doubt that many barristers have become very anxious indeed about their financial security during the last few years. Furthermore, al-

tirely unthinkable for many members of the Bar quite acceptable.[38] Novel approaches to the organisation of practice at the Bar, involving collectivisation of practice, commercialisation, and the professionalisation of practice management have emerged and have led to a significant process of restructuring of the Bar.

4 THE TRADITIONAL PARADIGM FOR THE ORGANISATION OF BARRISTERS' PRACTICES

To understand this process it is first necessary to understand the traditional organisation of a barrister's practice. The barrister would normally practice in Chambers, sharing "chambers expenses" with other members. A senior barrister would be the "Head of Chambers" which would means that, as well as being a figurehead, his/her name would appear on the lease of the Chambers premises (premises which in London at least would traditionally be leased from one of the Inns of Court). Work would be procured and (to

---

though the BDO Stoy Hayward, *Report on the 2001 Survey of Barristers' Chambers* indicates that the gross receipts of the practising Bar rose marginally from £1.3 billion-£1.4 billion in 2000 to £1.5 billion-£1.6 billion in 2001 this finding may need to be approached with caution. The estimate of the Bar's total gross receipts is "based on cash received according to respondents" to this year's questionnaire." Only 46% of chambers responded to the Survey (The Report, p. 5) and the response rate was lower amongst small chambers than larger chambers. It was as low as 28% in respect of chambers having between 1 and 10 members and 30% in respect of those having between 11 and 20 members. The response rate was significantly higher for larger chambers (55% for those with 21-30 members, 58% for those with 31-40 members, 50% for those with 41-50 members and 62% for those with over 50 members. Although the estimate of the Bar's total receipts is said to be based upon the survey responses "and the profile of respondents" it is at least possible that the high percentage of small sets which did not respond are the very sets whose members have experienced or anticipate financial pressure. If so, the estimated figure for the total receipts of the Bar may tend not to reflect the position of barristers in the less successful chambers. It is undoubtedly the case that barristers in some types of chambers have been worse affected by modernisation than others. The BDO Stoy Hayward, *Report on the 2000 Survey of Barristers' Chambers*, for example, reported that in the 2000 survey period although the income of the Bar as a whole was thought to have risen by between 7 % and 8%, the income of criminal law chambers fell by 6.3% and family law chambers by a staggering 24%. Furthermore, although the Bar continued to grow during 2001, the rate of growth is declining. The BDO Stoy Hayward, *Report on the 2001 Survey of Barristers' Chambers* (London, September 2001) indicates that whereas the average annual rate of growth of the practising Bar from 1986 to 1998 was 4.8%, the annual rate of growth diminished to 2.4% in 2000, and further decreased to 2% in 2001. It notes that: "[c]urrent indications are that the rate of growth continues to fall, leading to a levelling out in numbers" (The Report, Summary of Findings, p.1).

38 For a discussion of the need to change organisational and operational practices in order to thrive in the new environment see David LOCK (who was from 1999 - 2001 a minister in the Lord Chancellor's Department) "Wave of change" *Legal Week*, 8 November 2001, p. 20.

the extent that it did not come in for a named barrister), allocated by the clerks. The traditional relationship between the barrister and his/her senior clerk was complex. The clerks would often have few professional qualification, learning the necessary skills "on the job" as junior clerks. Professionally and socially the barrister would regard him/herself as the superior to the clerk[39] and yet would depend absolutely during the early years of practice upon the success and fairness of the clerks in allocating work. The power of the clerks over the success or failure of barristers should still not be underestimated. Traditionally clerks did not, however, proactively advertise or market the services of barristers in their chambers since "touting" was forbidden by the Bar Code. They were, however, well remunerated by receiving a percentage of the fees of every barrister in their chambers. More recently, of course, clerks have generally been remunerated on a fixed salary basis, perhaps with an additional (smaller) percentage incentive payment. Within this context, notwithstanding the power of the clerks and the professional authority of the Head (and other senior members) of Chambers, the individual barrister was a sole practitioner and operated as such. Chambers themselves were structured to reflect this conception so that most important decisions (*e.g.* the admission of a new member of chambers) would have to be put to a vote of all existing members. Typically individual barristers would spend their whole professional lives in the same set of chambers and the number of barristers in a set would be comparatively small.[40] Furthermore, although there was a degree of specialisation of practice, it was common for chambers to include a broad mixture of specialisms. Thus, for example a set might include some criminal practitioners and some civil. Some junior members of chambers might do both types of work practicing, for example in criminal and personal injury work. Some chambers did, of course, develop reputations as specializing in, for example, "commercial" or "chancery" work.

5 SIZE MATTERS

The current position is quite different and a number of trends have already become apparent in the post-modernisation period. First, there has been a clear trend for chambers to try to grow in size.[41] In facing the uncertainties of

39 As indicated by the practice whereby until comparatively recently, clerks always addressed barristers as "Mr, Ms etc" whereas barristers addressed clerks by their first names.

40 The average number of members in a set of chambers in 1986 was just 16: BDO Stoy Hayward, *Report on the 2001 Survey of Barristers' Chambers* (Summary of Findings) *o.c.*, p. 1).

41 Since 1986 the average size of chambers has been 28 members compared to 16 in 1986, an increase of 75% over that period: BDO Stoy Hayward, *Report on the 2001 Survey of Barristers' Chambers*, p. 14. According to the chambers' profiles published in the *Cham-*

the post-modernisation world "big" is seen to be beautiful. There has been an element of "merger mania" at the Bar,[42] with an unprecedented number of actual[43] and attempted[44] mergers between chambers. Of equal significance, however, has been number of barristers "transferring" between Chambers as many sets have sought to grow by "lateral" recruitment of

---

bers Guide to the Legal Profession 2001-2002, 5.26% of sets now have between 1 and 9 members (11sets); 10.52% between 10 and 19 members (22 sets); 22.48% between 20 and 29 members (47 sets); 24.4% between 30 and 39 members (51 sets); 21.53% between 40 and 49 members (45 sets); 8.61% between 50 and 59 members (18 sets); 4.78% between 60 and 69 members (10 sets); 0.96% between 70 and 79 members (2 sets); 0.48% between 80 and 89 members (1 set); 0.48% between 90 and 99 members (1 set); and 0.48% between 100 and 109 members (1 set). The turnover of several sets of chambers, for example, is reportedly as big as that of many a mid-sized firm of solicitors: see for example, "One Essex Court poised to gross £35m this year" *The Lawyer* 29 January 2001.

42 See *e.g.* "Special Report: The Bar - The bigger the better" *The Lawyer* 26 March 2001 p. 30; "Chambers mergers - game set and mismatch" *The Lawyer* 27 March 2000 p. 18; and Generally "Merger mania reaches chambers" *The Lawyer* 6 December 1999 p. 2; "Merge or submerge?" *The Lawyer* 17 February 1998 p. 20.

43 In the period 1998 - 2001 at least 17 mergers have taken place including mergers between: 17 Old Buildings and 10 Old Square; 3 Paper Buildings and Plowden Buildings; 7 Fountain Court and Priory Chambers ("Chambers merge to create super sets" *The Lawyer* 12 May 1998 p. 1); Martin's Building Liverpool and The Corn Exchange ("Liverpool merger creates biggest set in North West" *The Lawyer* 8 December 1998); Manchester House Chambers and Queens Chambers, Manchester ("Manchester sets to merge" The lawyer 11 January 1999); 9 Stone Buildings and 3 Paper Buildings ("Stone Buildings and 3 Paper agree to merge" *The Lawyer* 8 March 1999); 14 Castle Street, Liverpool and 25-27 Castle Street ("Liverpool chambers in merger talks" *The Lawyer* 14 June 1999); 11 Bolt Court and 7 Stone Buildings ("Bolt Court and 7 Stone Buildings merge" *The Lawyer* 11 October 1999); One Hare Court and Serle Court (One Hare Court and Serle Court merge" *The Lawyer* 13 December 1999; 13 Old Square and 7 Stone Buildings ("Leading sets wed in bid to join commercial bar elite" *The Lawyer*); One Paper Building and 2 Crown Office Row ("Chambers merger to create 73-strong set" *The Lawyer* 22 November 1999 p. 1; One Essex Court and 2 Paper Buildings ("One Essex Court and 2 Paper Buildings merge" *The Lawyer* 4 December 2000); 1 New Square and 12 New Square ("New Square sets announce merger" *The Lawyer* 7 August 2000); 9 Park Place and 30 Park Place, Cardiff ("Cardiff sets merge to create regional giant", *The Lawyer* 27 November 2000); 10 Park Square Leeds and 9 Woodhouse Square Leeds ("Special report: the Bar – the bigger the better" *The Lawyer* 26 March 2001 p. 30); 32 Park Place Cardiff and Newport Chambers Cardiff ("Special report: the bar – The bigger the better" *The Lawyer* 26 March 2001 p. 30); and One Raymond Buildings and 5 New Square ("New chambers Hogarth throws down IP gauntlet" *The Lawyer* 2 April 2001 p. 5.

44 For details of the progress of the protracted but ultimately abortive merger negotiations between Monckton Chambers and 4 – 5 Gray's Inn Square see "Monckton opens merger talks with 4 – 5 Gray's Inn" *The Lawyer* 24 January 2000 p. 4; "Monckton and 4 – 5 Gray's Inn set to vote on merger" *The Lawyer* 7 February 2000 p. 5; "Le Clezio and Wells fight for top job" *The Lawyer* 3 April 2000 p. 2; "Search for premises delays sets merger" *The Lawyer* 21 February 2000 p. 5; "Monckton Chambers and 4 – 5 Gray's Inn Square" *The Lawyer* 12 June 2000 p. 3; and "4-5 Gray's Inn calls off merger with Monckton" *The Lawyer* 3 July 2000 p. 4.

individuals (or large groups of individuals) from other chambers.[45] Even some Heads of chambers have resigned in order to join other specialist

---

45 In 1999 the "turnover" rate was 5%, with the result that on average barristers moved chambers every 20 years. In 2000 and 2001 the turnover rate was 7% and barristers moved between chambers on average once every 14 years: BDO Stoy Hayward, *Report on the 2001 Survey of Barristers' Chambers*, p. 16. The number of such transfers over the last three years has been so large that space will not permit them to be documented in full. Nonetheless, the following may give some sense of the frenetic " transfer market" which has existed over the last few years and which would, previously, have been unimaginable at the Bar. See "4 Field Court loses tenant to 199 Strand" *The Lawyer* 17 September 2001 p. 2; "4 Field Court loses five to 4 Essex Court" *The Lawyer* 2 July 2001; "Cardinal blow as Cloisters swells ranks (6 barristers transferring from Cardinal chambers to Cloisters) *The Lawyer* 11 June 2001; "4 Pump Court wins top construction silk" (three barristers joining 4 Pump Court) *The Lawyer* 4 June 2001 p. 4; "5 King's Bench swoops as Mitre Court closes" (16 barristers moving to 5 KBW) *The Lawyer* 28 May 2001 p. 4; "Weatherill moves to Enterprise" (QC transfers between chambers after 25 years in one set) The lawyer 21 May 2001 p. 6; "Old Square hires PI silk" *The Lawyer* 8 January 2001 p. 5; "11 KBW hires 5 Paper Bldgs senior junior" *The Lawyer* 11 December 2000 p. 4; "News in brief - 4 - 5 Gray's Inn Square" (two senior juniors transferred to these chambers) *The Lawyer* 20 November 2000 p. 5; "News in brief - Gerald Godfrey QC" (QC changes chambers) *The Lawyer* 30 October 2000 p. 5; "Matrix raids rival sets for commercial gain" *The Lawyer* 9 October 2000 p. 4; "News in brief - 11 King's Bench Walk" (2 juniors transferring to 11 KBW from 4 - 5 Gray's Inn Square) *The Lawyer* 18 September 2000 p. 3; "One Essex Court loses Aaronson and Conlon" (taxation QC and junior moving to a niche specialist set) *The Lawyer* 18 September 2000 p. 2; "Seven leave 4-5 Gray's Inn in public law exodus" *The Lawyer* 11 September 2000 p. 3; "One Raymond Buildings barrister joins IT boutique" 21 August 20000 p. 2; "Cloisters invests in employment team" *The Lawyer* 14 August 2000 p. 5; "Matrix Swoops to pick up trio" *The Lawyer* 14 August 2000 p. 5; "Isaacs leaves 4-5 Gray's Inn for 3-4 South Square (QC and 2 juniors leaving set after failure of merger talks) *The Lawyer* 7 August 2000 p. 4; "Three leave 4 Paper Buildings for Littleton" *The Lawyer* 31 July 2000 p. 5; "Eleven set to quit One Essex Court" 11 civil practitioners leaving common law i.e. chambers with mixed criminal and civil practice to join civil practitioners in anther chambers whose criminal lawyers had recently split off) *The Lawyer* 31 July 2000 p. 3; "News in brief - 3 Verulam Buildings" (senior banking law junior transferring to a banking law set) *The Lawyer* 31 July 2000 p. 3; "11 King's Bench Walk loses Mehigan to former chambers" (QC transferring back to former chambers after only 4 months) *The Lawyer* 17 July 2000 p. 4; "Doughty Street takes on four Cloisters tenants" *The Lawyer* 17 July 2000 p. 4; "199 Strand boosted by three new tenants" *The Lawyer* 26 June 2000 p. 5; "One Essex Court suffers defection number 5" (3 QCs and 2 juniors having left a leading commercial set) *The Lawyer* 19 June 2000 p. 4; "Matrix takes eight more as it opens for business" (eight new tenants transfer to new human rights specialist chambers) *The Lawyer* 29 May 2000 p. 5; "Fountain Court loses senior practitioner" and "2 Temple Gardens loses its third silk in a month but denies crisis" *The Lawyer* 10 April 2000 p. 2; "Two barristers quit merging Crown team" (a QC and senior junior transferring from a newly merged set) *The Lawyer* 3 April 2000; "Cardinal Chambers boosts criminal team with six barrister appointments" *The Lawyer* 27 March 2000; "Enterprise continues bar hire sprees" (QC and eight other barristers join Enterprise Chambers) *The Lawyer* 26 March 2000 p. 6; "10 - 11 Gray's Inn Square poaches top tenant and moves in downstairs" *The Lawyer* (20 March 2000 p. 2; "News in brief - Temple Gardens" (two QCs leave set) *The Lawyer* 13 March

sets.[46] This has led, not only to the growth in size of the larger Chambers, but also to the dissolution of other sets, many of which were highly reputed chambers of long standing.[47] The net result is that the number of large sets is growing and the number of small sets is falling.[48]

2000 p. 3; "Seven Stone Buildings hires tenant" (set recruited a new tenant from outside for first time in nearly 10 years) *The Lawyer* 6 March 2000; "Eleven Kings Bench Walk takes on QC" (QC moves transfers between chambers after 18 years in one set) *The Lawyer* 6 March 2000 p. 2; "4 Breams Building silk moves to Blackstone Chambers" *The Lawyer* 5 March 20001 p. 4; "Another two silks opt for Wilberforce" (two QCs transfer chambers) *The Lawyer* 28 February 2000 p. 10; "Top silk quits One Essex Court for his former love" and "One King's Bench swoops as sets sink" The lawyer 21 February 2000; "News in brief - Devereux Chambers" (transfer of three barristers) and "News in brief - No. 6 Park Square" (transfer of family law specialist) *The Lawyer* 24 January 2000; "News in brief - King Charles House chambers" (transfer of two barristers) *The Lawyer* 7 February 2000 p. 3; "Fountain Court Chambers nets public law barrister" (QC transfers) *The Lawyer* 17 January 2000; "News in brief - Four Essex Court" (QC and five juniors transfer) and "News in brief - Enterprise Chambers" (junior transfers) both *The Lawyer* 17 January 2000 p. 3; "One Essex Court poaches top silk from 11 King's Bench Walk", "Criminal set hires four barristers" and "Cloisters shaken by loss of two prominent silks to rivals" all *The Lawyer* 17 January 2000 p. 2; "New tenants boost Littleton Chambers" (transfer of two QCs and senior junior) *The Lawyer* 10 January 2000 p. 5; "St. Philip's poaches local QCs" *The Lawyer* 29 November 1999 p.9; "Plowden Buildings hit by departures" (11 barristers leave a se over a six month period) *The Lawyer* 22 November 1999 p. 8; "London set in crisis as tenants quit" (small set losing nearly half its members) *The Lawyer* 15 November 1999 p. 9; "£1m-a-year QC defects to rival set" *The Lawyer* 27 September 1999 p. 1; "Hardwicke signs four new tenants" *The Lawyer* 2 August 1999; "News in brief - 42 Castle Street" (two juniors transfer) *The Lawyer* 2 August 1999 p. 3; "Cloisters gains four new tenants in set shake-up" *The Lawyer* 2 August 1999 p. 4; "Smith leaves Field Court for Essex Court" (junior transfers) *The Lawyer* 26 July 1999; "Kushner, Neaves quit 36 Bedford Row for St. Philip's" (two juniors transfer) *The Lawyer* 26 July 1999 p. 9; "Doughty Street snaps up negligence heavyweight" *The Lawyer* 19 July 1999 p. 9; "Silk quits 39 Essex Street for Brick Court" (QC transfer) *The Lawyer* 5 July 1999 p. 8; "Muller hires nine new tenants" *The Lawyer* 7 June 1999 p. 3; "St. Philip's adds top QC and four juniors to its growing portfolio" *The Lawyer* 24 May 1999 p. 5. See generally, "Top chambers begin tenant poaching spree" *The Lawyer* 29 March 1999 p. 8 and "Set-jumping trend gains impetus as 11 move chambers" *The Lawyer* 18 January 1999 p. 2. In order to be able to recruit valuable tenants speedily some chambers are amending their constitutions to allow executive committees to recruit new tenants without putting them to a vote of all existing members. See "4-5 Gray's Inn retains emergency recruitment" *The Lawyer* 27 November 2000.

46 Perhaps the most high profile case would be that of Michael Beloff QC who left 4 - 5 Gray's Inn Square, where he was Head of Chambers, (after much speculation that he would join Matrix Chambers) to join Blackstone Chambers. See *e.g.* "Beloff steps down to join Booth's new set" *The Lawyer* 17 January 2000 p. 1, "Beloff will join Matrix within a year" *The Lawyer* 1 May 2000 p. 2; "Beloff opts for Blackstone" *The Lawyer* 2 April 2001 p. 1; and "I want doesn't get" *The Lawyer* 2 April 2001 p. 25.

47 The following 10 sets, for example, have been dissolved: 5 Bell Yard "Top Aviation Chambers Disintegrates" (5 Bell Yard) *The Lawyer* 1 September 1998 p. 1 and see *The Lawyer* 23 August 1998 p.2; Westgate Chambers, Newcastle "Newcastle 12 to form "superset"" *The Lawyer* 24 January 2000 p. 10; Queen Elizabeth Buildings (Lindsay Burn)

Size, of course, is not an end in itself. The spur to growth derives from the impact of modernisation. Thus, for example, if chambers need to set up quality control processes, to negotiate block contracts, to employ staff to chase aged debt,[49] to implement risk assessment processes for CFAs (and specifically to accommodate the return of briefs on CFAs), to win contracts for work for insurers[50] and claims management companies, and to comply with social/regulatory policies mandated by the Bar Council,[51] the cost to each practitioner will be less if the total cost is spread over a larger number of individuals. Equally, chambers have responded to the currently ultra competitive state of the market by engaging in advertising and marketing activi-

---

"One King's Bench swoops as sets sink" *The Lawyer* 21 February 2000 and "Chambers see host of movement across UK" *The Lawyer* 14 February 2000 p. 2; King's Chambers, Eastbourne (Regional Bar dissolutions free tenants" *The Lawyer* 3 April 2000 p. 3; 8 Gray's Inn Square (Patrick Soares), 2 Mitre Court Buildings (Roger Gray), Sussex Chambers (Paul Ashweb), New Court Chambers (George Carmen QC), 1 Gray's Inn Square (Baroness Scotland QC); *Legal Week* 27 September 2001, pp. 10, 11; and Barnard's Inn Chambers (Alan Saggerson) "No 1 Serjeant's Inn takes on six as Barnard's Inn dissolves" *The Lawyer* 17 April 2000 p. 5. See generally "Divided We Stand" *Legal Week* 27 September 2001.

48 BDO Stoy Hayward, *Report of the 2001 Survey of Barristers' Chambers*, pp. 2, 14 - 16.

49 We have already seen that the recent change in taxation of barristers exacerbates the Bar's perennial problem of late payment (see note 15 above). It can sometimes take years before a barrister's fee note is paid: BDO Stoy Hayward, *Report on the 2001 Survey of Barristers' Chambers* p. 37. That such a situation has been tolerated so long largely arises from the Bar's traditional ideology, and particularly its view of itself as a referral profession of sole practitioners. Sole practitioners are not best able to assess the credit worthiness of lay clients nor to chase aged debt. The Bar has therefore traditionally sought to avoid this commercial necessity by accepting instructions only through solicitors, by making solicitors (rather than the lay client) responsible for the payment of the barrister's fees, and by seeking to enforce payment by means of a threat of collective boycott of defaulting solicitors: P. KUNZLIK, *o.c.*, p. 876-877. Not surprisingly this approach has permitted the problem of late payment to be endemic since individual barristers are hardly likely to upset their solicitor clients by invoking a collective boycott. Furthermore, an individual barrister will be unlikely to want to upset his/her clerks or others in chambers by pressing a solicitor for payment when the latter (who himself may not have received payment from the lay client) provides a lot of work to the chambers generally. Equally, of course, when the lay client is a monopsony client with regulatory power (such as the government), the concept of collective boycott is risible. Perhaps prompted by the additional strain which the change in taxation basis has imposed, it appears that chambers are increasingly employing dedicated staff to help with chambers accounting and to chase aged debts: BDO Stoy Hayward, *Report of the 2001 Survey of Barristers' Chambers*, p. 37. Such strategies, accompanied by other factors, seem to have been effective in reducing the period of delay in payment somewhat since these periods were shorter in 2001 than 2000 for all types of work except chancery work: *Ibid.*

50 Such as the £6m contract awarded by Fastrack Indemnity to the chambers at 42 Castle Street; *The Lawyer* 11 September 2000 p. 1.

51 See below (main text).

ties[52] to an extent that, only a few years ago, would have been regarded as unnecessary and undesirable. The cost of such activities to each individual can be reduced if spread across a larger number of practitioners. Furthermore a larger number of practitioners advertising collectively may well be able to afford a more sustained, or high impact, marketing campaign than could be afforded by a smaller set. The same can be true of the need to provide sufficient IT systems to enable barristers to exploit on-line research resources and, more crucially still, to meet the expectations of solicitor and lay clients as to electronic communication.

6 PROFESSIONALISATION OF CHAMBERS' ORGANISATION AND MANAGEMENT

Of course, as chambers grow in size,[53] and as they address the administrative demands made upon them by the modernisation process and by their attempts to market their members more effectively, so the need for more sophisticated forms of chambers' organisation and management becomes pressing. Heads of Chambers, as full-time and successful advocates in their own right, cannot devote sufficient time to chambers management to cope with the demands that it now makes upon them. Nor would they necessarily have the required skills and experience. Equally, the background, skills and experience of Senior Clerks do not always qualify them for the task. Not surprisingly, therefore, the trend has developed to appoint "Chambers Directors" or "Chambers Managers," bringing with them experience from other fields,[54] to meet the new need. Nearly a quarter of chambers now give responsibility for day-to-day management to practice managers.[55] In some cases, which would have been anathema to the Bar only twenty years ago, solicitors have been appointed to this role.[56] Other "specialist" management functions have also been recognised and

52 See, *e.g.*, "Chambers' branding is good on paper" *The Lawyer* 27 January 1998 p. 7.

53 The growth in the size of chambers "is having major implications in the way that chambers are managed": BDO Stoy Hayward, *Report of the 2001 Survey of Barristers' Chambers*.

54 Wilberforce Chambers *e.g.* appointed as its first chamber director a former chief executive of an NHS Trust; "Ex NHS trust chief to head Wilberforce" *The Lawyer* 10 March 1998 p. 12. The chief executive of 199 The Strand is the retired head of policy at the Army Training Directorate; "199 Strand overhauls management structure" *The Lawyer* 25 September 2000 p. 2.

55 BDO Stoy Hayward, *Report on the 2001 Survey of Barristers' Chambers*, pp. 2 and 20.

56 *E.g.*, in 2000 Goldsmith Building appointed a former partner in Barlow Lyde and Gilbert as its Chambers Director "Goldmith Building appoints chambers director" *The Lawyer* 3 April 2000 p. 2. Solicitors have also been appointed practice managers at One King's Bench Walk ("King's Bench set names head of chambers and first manager" *The Lawyer* 9 August 1999 p. 2 and at Monckton Chambers ("Watsons director quits to run Monckton Chambers" *The Lawyer* 2 August 1999 p. 7.

functions have also been recognised and appointments made. Thus for example, some sets have appointed commercial directors,[57] marketing directors[58] and IT managers.[59] The recruitment of senior non-legal professionals (or at least non-barrister professionals) to help chambers to formulate and implement their strategies in the face of modernisation must, inevitably, have affected the ideological orientation of the chambers themselves. The thinking of such professionals, whose expertise and experience has been acquired in other, more overtly commercial, walks of life is unlikely to have been constrained by instinctive adherence to the Bar's traditional assumptions. It would hardly be surprising, therefore, if innovative approaches to practice organisation were to emerge. Quite apart from such "managerial" appointments, however, it appears that the Bar may also be awakening (as it recognises the imperative need to improve competitiveness by increasing the efficiency with which barristers use their time) to the need to relieve barristers of work which can properly be transferred to less qualified and less experienced staff. Thus, for example, in 2000, Matrix Chambers became the first to employ paralegals to assist with this sort of work.[60]

Thus a professionalisation of practice management has been under way for a number of years. More fundamentally, however, innovations have also been made in the wider organisational structure of some sets of chambers. These respond to the fact that as chambers grow it becomes essential to delegate decision-making authority in operational matters. Furthermore, as chambers have become bigger they have outgrown much of the traditional accommodation (for example in the Inns of Court) that they have traditionally occupied.[61] In any event, such traditional premises are not always the most flexible or efficient for modern usage (*e.g.* as to "cabling" for the installation and periodic updating of IT systems etc.). Thus big sets of chambers have needed to look to acquire appropriate, and sufficiently large, premises on the open market. In that context, the traditional preference, the renting of the chambers premises, does not always make sense. Some chambers have therefore sought to purchase the freehold of their premises. For a barrister who can afford it, this is in many ways attractive. By selling his/her share in the free-

---

57 *E.g.*, "39 Essex Street gains commercial director and six more tenants" (the new director had previously been partnership secretary at a firm of solicitors) *The Lawyer* 26 July 1999.

58 "Marketing director joins 4 Breams" *The Lawyer* 13 November 2000 p. 4.

59 "Top sets combine IT resources" *The Lawyer* 3 February 1998 p. 3.

60 *The Lawyer* 7 August 2000.

61 The shortage of sufficiently large accommodation within the Inns is quite acute. See "Chambers left in housing crisis as sets find no room at the Inns" *The Lawyer* 7 February 2000. See also "Magic circle sets prepare to expand" *The Lawyer* 24 January 2000 and "Swelling chambers rush for premises" *The Lawyer* 8 February 1999 p. 2. *Cf.* "Lincoln's Inn tempts back top chambers with new premises" *The Lawyer* 22 March 1999 p. 2.

hold upon retirement he/she might well be able to realise a significant capital gain to contribute towards retirement provision. Collectively to purchase the freehold of chamber's premises, however, requires the setting up of a structure that can allow shares in the property to be transferred as barristers join or leave chambers, and which can allow for effective management of the premises and the funding of their maintenance. Such arrangements, therefore, inevitably lead to a greater degree of financial interrelationship between members of chambers than would be the case in a traditional set. Such barristers are not only coming together to share and spread expenses but to manage and exploit a very significant capital asset. Perhaps the most striking example of this approach was the establishment of St. Philip's Chambers in Birmingham. The chambers arose from a merger between Nos. 2 and 7 Fountain Court. The new chambers, however, was quite different. It set up a public limited company (St. Philip's Holdings plc) to own the freehold of its premises and each of its barristers was required to purchase 1,000 shares giving each a single vote. St Philip's Holdings owns St. Philip's Chambers Ltd. which has a board of 14 people comprising the Head of Chambers, representatives from each practice group and the Chief Executive. The Chief Executive is assisted by two chief clerks, an IT manager, a head of finance and an operations manager. He is advised by an advisory committee comprising one of the clerks and representatives from each practice group. The adoption of a corporate structure for the provision of premises and support systems for barristers is, obviously, novel in itself. So far as fee earning is concerned, the practice of members of the chambers is organised into "practice groups" which are "led" by their own "heads". This novel form of organisation has clearly brought a number of benefits to the chambers as evidenced by substantial increases in turnover in the second and third year of the new chamber's operation.[62] St. Philip's is not the only set to have adopted a corporate form for at least some of its operation.[63] Nor is it the only set in which the members of chambers have collaborated to purchase and manage their freehold premises.[64]

---

62 See generally, "Ahead of the Game" *The Lawyer* 4 June 2001. According to the Chambers Guide to the Legal Profession 2001-2002, St. Philip's Chambers, is now the second biggest set in England and Wales, with 91 members. Only 5 Fountain Court (with 107 members) is bigger.

63 *E.g.*, 10-11 Gray's Inn Square reportedly operates within the structure of a limited company which controls financial and administrative management of the chambers; "Muller hires nine new tenants" *The Lawyer* 7 June 1999 p. 3. The BDO Stoy Hayward, *Report on the 2001Survey of Barristers' Chambers*, p. 21 further describes the use by chambers of structures involving service companies and (for tax purposes) trade protection associations.

64 Details of such arrangements have confidentially been provided to the author by members of two other sets of chambers.

For the future, the recent instability of sets of chambers (as evidenced by the splits from, transfers between, and extinction of chambers) also provides an incentive for tighter forms of collective organisation. Recent events have shown that the traditional relationship between members of chambers (based upon the lease of their premises and upon a comparatively loose "chambers constitution") can leave chambers exposed to considerable risk. When, for example, a split occurs a set is likely to experience a significant reduction in turnover so that the financial assumptions on the basis of which it planned its operations (*e.g.* its commitment to premises and staff) may be completely undermined.[65] This risk really arises because of the comparative ease with which barristers can (as a "sole practitioners") resign from chambers, even on comparatively short notice. If chambers learn the lessons of the last few years they will seek to tighten up their constitutions to try to prevent this risk by making it more difficult for barristers to withdraw without chambers' consent, further tying the individual practitioner into the chambers as a joint enterprise.

7 THE GROWTH OF SPECIALIST CHAMBERS OR "PRACTICE GROUPS"

The trend toward growth has been accompanied by an equally marked trend towards the further development of specialist chambers and of specialist practice "groups" within other chambers.[66] Without doubt, this trend has in part been informed by a growing awareness of the importance of the right marketing profile and the need to be able to stay on the "list of approved chambers" of large repeat clients[67] by assuring such clients of strength-in-depth within the specialism and of transactional efficiency. It has

---

65 See for example "Cloisters left £3m down after split" *The Lawyer* 26 June 2000.

66 Chambers market themselves by reference to their specialist groups or the specialist nature of their practices as a whole. Examples are easily gleaned from chambers" brochures, web sites and advertisements. Thus, for example, 40 King Street, Manchester markets itself as providing advocacy and advisory services "through three main practice groups" (planning, environment and public law; chancery and commercial and common law. See *The Lawyer* 17 March 1998 p. 4; Monckton Chambers advertises that it specialises in Competition Law, European Law, Commercial Litigation and Judicial Review; *The Lawyer* 7 April 1998 p. 4; Furnival Chambers advertises specialist skills in Criminal Law and Asset Forfeiture and in connection with Money Laundering; see *The Lawyer* 19 April 1999 p. 26; Matrix Chambers and Blackstone Chambers are two examples of sets which proclaim their specialised experience in human rights and public law; see *The Lawyer* 15 November 1999 p. 24.

67 Failure to do so can be catastrophic; see *e.g.* "Livelihoods on the line as CPS wields axe," *The Lawyer* 24 November 1998 p. 17, which recounted the impact on a number of sets of the Crown Prosecution Service's decision to reduce the number of sets on its preferred list. See also "Eleven sets axed in CPS panel cull" *The Lawyer* 17 November 1998 p. 14.

further been encouraged by the legal industry press[68] and the legal directories[69] which frequently publish "awards,"[70] "league tables," "profiles"[71] and features on the specialist bar,[72] based upon perceived excellence or success in particular specialisms. The urge to specialise is, in part however, also a specific consequence of some of the factors leading to collectivisation of practice. If, for example, a particular set of chambers comprises some barristers doing publicly funded and CFA work and some barristers doing exclusively privately funded work, the potential for tension between the two groups is obvious. The publicly funded/CFA funded practitioners will want the chambers to invest in the procedures necessary to engage in such work. The privately funded practitioners, however, will have no personal interest in the chambers incurring such expenses. Resolution of the tension will in all likelihood require revision of the chambers' constitution treating the two groups differentially[73] and, once that has been done, the coherence of the chambers as a single set may already be undermined. Furthermore, the process of revising the constitution around such issues may itself prove divisive and tend to encourage the breaking away from chambers of groups of dissatisfied practitioners sharing the same specialism and, therefore, the same interests.

Finally, it is probably not too far-fetched to suppose that the development of large sets focusing on particular specialisms is also thought important for another powerful, though perhaps not consciously articulated, reason. It tends to insulate practitioners within such chambers from competition from "new entrants." As a small number of large specialist chambers develop the reputation as "the" chambers in a particular field, so it becomes more difficult for new practitioners in that field, who are not members of those chambers, to be regarded as credible by instructing solicitors or lay clients. At one

---

68 *E.g. The Lawyer, Legal Business, Legal Week.*

69 *The Legal 500, Chambers Directory* etc.

70 *E.g.* "The lawyer Awards" for "Chambers of the Year", "Barrister of the Year" etc. See *The Lawyer* 3 July 2000 p. 26.

71 *E.g.* The profiles of 3-4 South Square as the "clear leader in insolvency work" and of "the best of the rest" as identified in *The Lawyer*'s feature on insolvency (*The Lawyer* 20 November 2000 p. 33).

72 *E.g.* The Specialist Commercial Bar feature in *The Lawyer* 24 May 1999 p. 27; "Focus-professional negligence bar" *The Lawyer* 17 March 1998 p. 15; "Focus – chancery bar" *The Lawyer* 17 February 1998 p. 13; and the employment bar feature *The Lawyer* 13 November 2000 p. 31.

73 The case of St. John's Chambers in Bristol is a good illustration. This set implemented differential financial arrangements as between its civil and criminal law practitioners. Criminal practitioners reportedly pay less to the cost of running chambers than do civil practitioners but on the basis that they have been moved into a separate building and operate there on a "hot-desking" basis to reduce overheads. See "St. John's streams set contributions" *The Lawyer* 20 November 2000.

level, the assumption becomes that anyone who is any good in the field in question would be a member of one of the established specialist chambers/groups. At another level, a solicitor would be unlikely to be criticised by his/her peers for instructing someone in one of the established specialist sets but might feel that he or she is taking a risk by going elsewhere. In such circumstances, by controlling entry to the specialist set, the incumbent practitioners (or their clerks) can to some extent at least control entry to that specialism, especially if the incumbent sets' capacity to fund marketing and advertising activity were such as to present an additional barrier to entry to the potential new entrant.

Whatever its underlying causes, the trend towards the building of specialist chambers and "practice groups" is clear and has fuelled the "transfer market" in barristers moving from one set to another. It has also led to the "splitting up" of some sets along specialism lines.[74] In some cases it may also be having an impact upon the autonomy of individual barristers in carrying out their work, since it has prompted the establishment of specialist practice groups (as we have already seen in the case of St. Philip's Chambers) which are sometimes even described as being "headed" (or, in the characteristic language of the Anglo Saxon legal industry "headed up") by senior individuals.[75] The process is, of course, opaque and one must therefore be wary about assuming that the use of such language has implications beyond the marketing function. On the other hand, it may tend to suggest at least awareness that to develop a "group practice" may require a degree of leadership well beyond that which a senior barrister would previously have been expected to make to the development of practices other than his/her own. Conversely, it may equally imply that the more junior member of the "group" may be expected to accept more direction in the development of his/her practice than would previously have been the case.

---

74 Cloisters chambers, for example, split between its criminal and civil practitioners, with the criminal law practitioners leaving the chambers; see "Cloisters splits after crisis meeting" *The Lawyer* 12 June 2000 p. 1 (which also reported a similar "split" at 8 King's Bench Walk). Similarly, 4 Brick Court decided to split so as to specialise exclusively on family law; see "4 Brick Court splits for family focus" *The Lawyer* 12 July 1999. Ten criminal law practitioners left St. Mary's Chambers, Nottingham to join another local set after failure of merger talks between them; "St. Mary's loses criminal team to rival set" *The Lawyer* 9 August 1999 p. 6.

75 Examples are easily gleaned from chambers" brochures, web sites and advertisements. 5 Fountain Court, for example have announced that a particular QC has been "appointed Head of its Planning and Environmental Practice Group" of ten or so barristers; see *The Lawyer* 21 April 1998 p. 4.

8 THE RULE AGAINST BARRISTERS' PARTNERSHIPS

All of these trends indicate that in reality the conception of the barrister as an independent undertaking or sole practitioner no longer holds true, at least as a universal phenomenon. Barristers are now compelled to organise vital elements of their businesses (marketing, back office administration, asset management and, as we shall see, regulatory compliance) on a collective basis and are organising their business structures - so far as they are permitted - accordingly. They are still not permitted, of course, to pursue the option of partnership. This remains prohibited by the Bar's Code.[76]

Traditionally this prohibition was based upon two rationales[77] namely (i) the contention that partnership is inconsistent with the cab-rank rule since (it is claimed that) a barrister in partnership might be persuaded not to accept instructions out of deference to the interests of the partnership as a whole; and (ii) the contention that access to justice (or more accurately access to advocacy services) will be inhibited by partnerships since a client would not be able to instruct a barrister in partnership to act for him/her in a given case if another barrister in the same firm were to be acting for an opposing party.[78] These rationales were always rather suspect, if only because the cab-rank rule seems more likely to have served the interests of the Bar than the interests of the public;[79] and the "access to advocacy" argument, whilst suiting barristers, paid scant attention to whether it was desirable from the consumer's (the litigant's) point of view to have barristers from the same chambers acting on both sides of a case. Furthermore, the modernisation process itself, and the fact that the Bar has had to respond to it by adjusting its own ideology, have further undermined these rationales. The cab-rank rule was the reverse of the coin of monopoly since barristers could hardly assert a monopoly and then decline to exercise it.[80] The passing of the Bar's monopoly however, reduces the cab-rank rule to merely vestigial importance. Furthermore in the face of modernisation the cab-rank rule has quickly been cast aside in areas where it has become inconsistent with the Bar's commercial interests, namely in respect of CFAs and BarDIRECT clients. The need to ensure observance of the rule, therefore, can hardly be so imperative as to justify denying barristers the ability to form partnerships with each other in

76 See n. 5 above.

77 See P. KUNZLIK, *o.c.*, p. 873.

78 Ibid.

79 The extent to which the cab-rank rule was ever generally observed in the past is itself doubtful: See P. KUNZLIK, *o.c.* The rule was easily evaded by engaging in argument as to what would, or would not, be a reasonable fee (the argument being conducted on the barrister's behalf by his/her clerk.

80 *Ibid.*

order to accommodate the challenges of modernisation. This is especially so since, given the extent to which barristers market themselves collectively, the risk that a barrister in partnership might be prevailed upon to refuse to accept instructions from a particular client because of pressure from his partners is no greater than the current risk that an individual barrister (or his/her clerk) might decline to act for a particular client because of fears that to do so may adversely affect the general chambers' profile. Furthermore, if it is thought satisfactory that barristers in the same set of chambers should be able to appear on both sides of a case even though many aspects of their practices are likely to be carried out on a collective basis, why should the imposition of "Chinese walls" within a partnership of barristers not equally permit that to happen.[81]

Perhaps instinctively, even the Bar itself seems to be recognising that the traditional rationales for the rule against partnership have lost much of their force. In opposing partnership, therefore, the Bar has alighted upon a third rationale, the "independence" of the barrister and the supposed link between the independence of the barrister and the independence of the judiciary: "independence" was therefore the theme of the Bar's Annual Conference in 2001. The theme was further elaborated by one of the most influential supporters of the rule against barristers' partnership, the Lord Chief Justice, Lord Woolf. His speech to the Conference affirmed that

> *"I believe that partnership is inconsistent with the independence of the Bar and is against the public interest."*[82]

Any assessment of the cogency of the "independence" rationale vitally depends upon the meaning of that term. Unfortunately, however, Lord Woolf endowed it with a compendium of different, unacknowledged, meanings. The result was that his argument, whilst rhetorically powerful, does not withstand close analysis. Thus, His Lordship explained that

> *"What I mean by independence is being your own master. Dependent to [sic.] no-one. I mean being responsible to yourself, the courts and the client for the work you do."*

---

81 Chinese walls do, of course, face criticisms of their own. But are they really any worse than the prospect that barristers from the same chambers should act on both sides of the same case?

82 Lord Woolf's speech to the Bar Conference 2001, printed in full in "Independent mind", *The Lawyer*, 22 October 2001. Lord Woolf did not explain this assertion other than by reference to *Competition in Professions – The Bar's Consultation Paper in Response to the OFT Report* (July 2001 which he endorsed as "an extremely impressive document" and which, in his view, "effectively countered" the OFT's case favouring partnership between barristers.

This passage used the term "independence" in a very specific way. To be independent is "be your own master" - to be self-employed. Without further explanation, however, Lord Woolf equated "being your own master" with accountability, with "being responsible" to the courts and the client. This, however, implies a *non sequitur* since whether a lawyer is responsible to the courts and the client has nothing to do with the mode of organisation of his/her practice. Litigators or solicitor advocates who are partners in law firms are, of course, just as responsible to the courts and to clients as barristers even though they are not sole practitioners. One cannot, therefore, invest the status of being a sole practitioner with any ethical value simply on the basis of responsibility to court and client.

Having sought to link the concept of the barrister as a sole practitioner with the concept of the advocate's accountability to the court and client, Lord Woolf then linked it to the functioning of the United Kingdom's unwritten constitution and to the independence of the judiciary, thus elevating the "sole practitioner" rule to the level of constitutional principle. He asserted the importance of

> *"the central role that the independence of the Bar plays in our unwritten constitutional framework….the role it shares with the judiciary in our adversarial system of upholding the rule of law…. the role it plays in ensuring that our judiciary is independent."*

In elaborating this point His Lordship went so far as to argue that the "outstanding" quality of the English judiciary is referable

> *"to the fact that the majority of our judges are recruited directly from our independent Bar. You cannot sever the quality of our judiciary from the quality of the Bar"*

Furthermore since, in Lord Woolf's view, barristers are independent

> *"[t]he result is that on appointment as a judge , they [sic] will start off with the advantage that being independent is already their second nature."*

The difficulty with this approach is that in these respects Lord Woolf was appealing, without explicitly acknowledging it, to concepts of independence which are entirely different from his own definition. The independence of the judiciary is a personal and institutional independence from the government, vested interest and other inadmissible external influences. It has nothing whatsoever to do with the question whether the judge, during his/her previous professional career had been employed or self-employed. Equally, in these passages, Lord Woolf implicitly and subtly moved from talking about the independent practice of the barrister to talking about the concept of the "independence of the Bar" which is an entirely different thing; and which relates, in particular, to the independence of the Bar as an institution from regulatory or other control by the executive, vested interest or other inadmissible influences. The effect was subliminally to equate the independence of the Bar with the concept of the barrister as a sole practitioner; another implicit *non sequitur*. Furthermore, if Lord Woolf was seeking to imply that barristers have an independence of mind, not vouchsafed to lawyers working in partnership (and which arises because barristers are sole practitioners), he signally failed to substantiate the point. There is, in fact, no evidence to suggest that lawyers working in partnership lack independence of mind and I doubt whether anyone who has significant experience of dealing with law firm partners could suppose for a minute that that was the case. More generally, of course, before one could possibly draw a linkage between the independence of the judiciary and the status of barristers as sole practitioners, one would surely have to explain how countries like the United States, where trial lawyers do practise in partnership, nonetheless manage to have robustly independent advocates and a robustly independent judiciary. The experience of partnership does not seem to have inhibited the independence of mind of the American judges, so why would it do so in England and Wales?

Finally, the independence of some sections of the "independent" Bar is itself rather questionable. Those sections of the Bar which have to rely upon the state as a monopsony funder of certain types of litigation are absolutely dependent upon the state and state agencies. Criminal law barristers who practice exclusively or substantially as prosecutors are, for example, dependent upon the Crown Prosecution Service for their livelihoods. It is, in this regard, interesting to note that whilst Lord Woolf expressed concern about

> *"...the majority of barristers who are competent and hard working but dependent upon publicly funded work, whose earnings are disturbingly modest [and who] must feel battered [by modernisation]"*

he did not also consider the possible effect of such financial dependence upon the "independence" of the Bar or the independence of mind of individual barristers which he was eulogising. It is at least possible that lawyers in partnership, who are not as directly financially dependent upon the state as publicly funded "sole practitioner" barristers, may be more, rather than less, independent of mind than those whose livelihoods depend upon continued instruction by a specific state agency.

For all these reasons, the argument that the sole practitioner principle is imperative in the public interest because it underlies the independence of the Bar and the judiciary simply does not withstand critical scrutiny. Although one can understand why the Bar should seek to emphasis the one remaining organisational trait which continues to differentiate barristers from solicitors (the sole practitioner barrister as opposed to the firm of solicitors), the suggestion that this has public interest implications is simply not plausible. Furthermore, since the principle itself denies barristers the freedom to choose from a more complete range of structures within which to conduct their practices, pressure is already growing from some senior members of the Bar itself for partnership to be permitted.[83] Pressure is also mounting from outside the Bar, with the Office of Fair Trading ("OFT") seeing the rule against partnership as constituting an indirect restriction on entry to the profession.[84] Furthermore, in the OFT's view

> *"the requirement that only sole practitioners can supply barristers' services is anomalous in the context of professional services and beyond.... Moreover, the sole practitioner requirement might also have the effect of deterring some people from a career as a barrister who would be at least as able professionally as those who become barristers, but who do not have the financial resources to fall back on if their flow of business were to fall off, or who are quite reasonably averse to such financial risk. Lifting of the restriction could therefore help broaden access to and diversity in the profession."*[85]

9 REGULATORY POLICY AS A SPUR TO, AND RECOGNITION OF, COLLECTISATION OF PRACTICE

The Bar Council's continued reluctance to contemplate permitting partnership between barristers seems almost perverse when considered in light of its own regulatory strategy. This strategy has involved a number of elements which are inconsistent with the concept of the barrister as a sole practitioner. First, in seeking to respond to changing expectations as to the social responsibility of the Bar, the Bar Council has introduced a small but important number of policies which impose collective obligations on members of chambers by requiring the adoption and implementation of policies and procedures on a chambers-wide basis.[86] Secondly, the Bar Council has rec-

83 See "Top silks call for partnership rights" and Andrew Arden QC "The case for Partnership" *The Lawyer* 6 December 1999 pp. 1 and 31. The then Vice Chairman of the Bar (Jonathan Hirst QC) responded in traditional vein in "Partnership offers no benefits" *The Lawyer* 13 December 1999 p. 29. For Arden's rejoinder see his letter to the editor, *The Lawyer* 10 January 2000. A delegation of barristers recently lobbied the Lord Chancellor's Department (the "LCD") seeking abolition of the rule against barristers" partnerships, citing the need to be able to increase efficiency by allowing senior practitioners to delegate appropriate work to junior colleagues, and the benefits that such an arrangement would have in facilitating investment in IT and other assets. The LCD's position was apparently that although the department had no objection to barristers" partnerships it was a matter for the Bar itself rather than for government to determine whether the rule should be abolished.

84 *Competition in Professions*, *o.c.*, p. 14.

85 *Ibid.*, p. 15.

86 *E.g.*, most importantly, the Bar Council's Equality Code. This requires the adoption and application of chambers policies and procedures to prevent discrimination on grounds

ognised that, from a "consumer" perspective, the efficiency of a barrister's practice (and therefore several aspects of the quality of service to clients) depends in part upon the efficiency of collective chambers management and has therefore provided extensive guidance in that regard.[87] Thirdly, the Bar Council has sought to ensure compliance by individuals with a number of their own professional obligations by imposing parallel "oversight" obligations upon the Head of Chambers (representing the chambers collectively).[88] This latter approach is, of course, entirely inconsistent with the concept of the practising barrister as an "atomistic" independent sole practitioner. The imposition of such "oversight" obligations implies a recognition of the reality that the business of a barrister is increasingly part of a collective enter-

---

of race, gender, nationality, citizenship and sexual orientation. This, for example, prohibits chambers from allowing any individual to make certain decisions as to pupillage. Thus, if a barrister wishes to take a pupil, he/she would be required by the Equality Code to submit selection of the pupil to a collective process. Reportedly, the scope of the policy will shortly be extended to outlaw "ageism." See also the Bar Council's resolution requiring chambers (from 31 December 2002) to provide funding for the non-practising period of pupillage (on a compulsory basis, failure being punishable as a breach of the Code). Thus, if an individual member of chambers were to agree to take a pupil, his/her fellow members of chambers would be required to contribute towards payment of the pupil or, at least, to ensure that the pupil master/mistress makes the compulsory payment. Details of the resolution and its implications can be found in the Bar Council's Education and Training Committee's Report Funding Pupillage – Consultation on Waiver (March 2001). Other important practical requirements requiring management at chambers level are, of course, imposed by the general law. see in particular, registration under the Data Protection Act 1998.

87 We have already seen that the Bar Council's Guidance on Conditional Fee Agreements advises that where chambers have entered into standing agreements as to CFAs, an individual barrister in those chambers should obtain the agreement of others (the persons or groups whose consent is required under the standing agreement) before entering into a CFA. So much for the autonomous "sole practitioner" barrister. See also the Bar Council's Practice Management Guidelines, which relate not only to the management of the individual practices of each sole practitioner but to the efficient administration of chambers as a whole. Other requirements, *e.g.* as to procedures to be followed in respect of BarDIRECT clients impose record-keeping requirements which also necessitate the putting into place of chambers procedures. See the BarDIRECT Rules and Recognition Regulations r. 10 (Annexe F to the Code).

88 Thus, for example, para. 404.2 of the Code requires Heads to take all reasonable steps to ensure, inter alia, that (i) chambers are administered competently and efficiently and are properly staffed; (ii) the affairs of the chambers are conducted in a manner which is fair and equitable for all barristers and pupils; (iii) proper arrangements are made for dealing with pupils and pupillage; (iv) all barristers practising from his/her Chambers are members of, and have effected insurance with, the Bar Mutual Indemnity Fund; (v) that all barristers practising in the chambers keep proper records; (vi) all employees and staff are competent to carry out their duties, do so in a correct and efficient manner, and are aware of the provisions of the Code; (vii) that fee notes are sent expeditiously to clients and that in the event of non-payment within a reasonable time, are pursued efficiently.

prise. It also requires that the Head of Chambers (representing the collective) should have a degree of control over the activities of individual tenants. This being the case the Bar Council cannot credibly argue that the "sole practitioner" model remains ethically imperative as the only acceptable model for practising at the Bar.

10 POSITIVE REASONS FOR PERMITTING PARTNERSHIP

By permitting partnerships the Bar Council would be giving barristers greater organisational freedom with which to respond to the challenging and dynamic environment that modernisation has created. I do not argue that partnership should be the only organisational model open to barristers, nor that partnership as an option is a "cure all" which will solve all of the problems of the practising Bar. It would, however, allow barristers to compete amongst themselves (and with others), on the basis of a wider range of organisational structures as well as on the basis of individual and collective reputation. To confine and prescribe the organisational strategies to which barristers may have recourse in struggling to come to terms with the post-modernisation environment can only inhibit the very diversity and innovation in the delivery of advocacy services which the modernisation process has sought to bring about.

We have seen that many of the principles that have hitherto provided the ideological foundations of the "cathedral" of the Bar have already crumbled. If the structure is to be re-built and to have a future beyond the present generation it will need to be based upon a more solid foundation than that provided by the "sole practitioner" principle which is, as I have tried to demonstrate, amongst the last, outmoded, vestiges of a disintegrated professionalism. The Bar's continuing insistence upon the principle as a corner stone of its structure inhibits its ability to find new rationales and models for its continued existence, and to renew its ideology and its ethical code against the needs of the present rather than the past. For that reason above all it does the Bar itself little service.

THE CHALLENGE OF INTERPROFESSIONALISATION AND INTERNATIONALISATION FOR THE PROFESSIONAL BODIES

Koen Geens, Professor by Special Appointment, Catholic University of Leuven, Advocate of the Brussels Bar

It is not even possible to think about the regulation of the liberal professions without confronting their essentially corporate nature. This is a perfectly normal fact of life, a natural expression of their sociological essence.

Professional people who build up a certain amount of experience and a certain reputation over a period of many years inevitably began organising themselves into fraternal learned societies or professional associations of an unionised character. The loneliness of the solo practitioner, who practises his profession in the company of - at the most - a few young people and a handful of administrative staff, arouses in him a perfectly natural desire to become part of a wider organisation that will give him an opportunity to exchange experiences as well as offer him a measure of security within society.

Such a grouping naturally becomes the fountainhead of a set of common rules that its members wish to maintain regarding the treatment of their clientele, and provides the basis of support for unionised action. Later still the group asks the legislator for leave to organise itself as a professional body under quasi-public law, so as to obtain a limited degree of self-regulation.

It is an interesting exercise to test these age-old processes of professionalisation against certain recent developments within the professions. In recent years these developments have certainly been spectacular. Both in breadth and in depth we can discern a fundamental difference between the service provision of, say, the 60s and the 80s and that of more recent times.

When considered in terms of depth, the most striking thing is that professionals are increasingly asking themselves the questions that should be asked by the clients themselves.

Initially this phenomenon could be conceived of as "integral care". The service provider takes the problem with which the client confronts him, makes it entirely his own, and solves it completely without maintaining the aloofness that was so typical in days gone by.

In the next stage of this deepening process the professional identifies the client's problem himself and then solves it. This may be the result of a pre-existing client relationship that allows the professional to draw the client's attention to the existence of a particular problem. Increasingly, however, we can conclude that professionals are daring to draw the attention of <u>potential</u>

clients to problems that they might face, and are then offering a potential solution to those problems.

The fact that service provision is becoming broader as well as deeper is, if possible, even more obvious. The trend on the continent of Europe over the past 30 years - one that originated in the Anglo-Saxon world - has been one of scaling-up, increased specialisation and multidisciplinarity.

These three steps can be clearly distinguished.

Scaling-up is usually a matter of the resources one requires to be able to practise one's profession properly. The more difficult it is to acquire these resources alone the bigger the structures that are required, and so the "one-man office" gradually becomes a rarity.

Specialisation is a second factor that points towards increased cooperation and larger structures. The steady expansion of professional knowledge makes it impossible for any one person to continue to be a master of the whole of that body of knowledge.

Finally, there is the need for complementarity and interdisciplinarity: instead of having to tell the client to go and see the practitioner of another profession, people want to be able to offer the service themselves, "in house". In this formula, the client is assisted by a multidisciplinary entity that presents itself to him - through its organisation and its name - in the form of a unit.

Besides this expansion in both the depth and breadth of services via larger structures, we can also note the increasing internationalisation of service provision. The more the clientele consists of global players located in different countries - even, sometimes, in different continents - the more attractive is such an international dimension for those service providers whose ambition it is to assist their clients worldwide.

In this way there arise interprofessional networks that bear the same name in all countries, and which spread the Gospel across frontiers as a sort of franchise of a (usually) Anglo-Saxon methodology. Within the Economic Unions, freedom of establishment and free movement of services provide the legislative foundation for this apparently irreversible trend.

It goes without saying that these developments must inevitably have a profound effect on a corporate phenomenon that, traditionally, was both unidisciplinary and national. Traditionally, a professional body represented a specific profession in a specific country. That is still the case, of course, but it is obvious that the relationship of the individual practitioner to this professional body has changed radically as a result of the complete transformation of his working environment.

The need that the individual professional feels to be supported by a group - a need previously met by his professional body - is now usually met by the professional and interprofessional network of which the practitioner forms a part. These networks have their own professional and ethical standards, their own working parties, their own in-service training manuals, their own jealously-guarded collective know-how. For these networks the professional body is no longer essential. As oligopolists they are, after all, powerful enough to protect themselves against unfair competition, unsportsmanlike governmental interventions and so on. For these networks the professional body is just another fact of life, an organisation in which they must, it is true, be represented as effectively as possible, but which is not regarded as something that is essential for survival.

Conversely, the professional body no longer has the weapons that it used to have to be able to combat ethical transgressions or to keep professionals on the straight and narrow. It is precisely this process of broadening, deepening and internationalising that we referred to above that is responsible for this.

The concept of a service provider who does not wait for the client to ask a question but instead makes the client's problem entirely his own, or even draws the client's attention to a potential problem, is only slowly permeating the highest levels of the professional bodies, not least because these are full of people who grew up with the concept of the "aloof professional".

The question of how a professional body should react to this "new" form of behaviour - one of active involvement - is not one with an obvious answer. As is certainly the case, the improvement in quality that active involvement brings also carries with it the risk of too strong an involvement - even of complicity. As long as this relationship remains within the statutory limits it is, in my opinion, nothing more than an agreeable stylistic difference that should certainly not be too strongly discouraged. Distance fosters objectivity, whereas involvement inspires loyalty. The professional who combines these two qualities to an optimum extent will achieve a rare and enviable professional balance.

The question of whether the professional bodies can continue to resist the active canvassing of clients can be answered immediately. However much the requirements of good taste and respect for one's professional colleagues may point in the opposite direction, it is obvious that the right to the free expression of opinion in its commercial aspect and the horizontal right of free competition will sooner or later permeate all Western countries, to the extent that they will simply disregard any of the ethical arguments in favour of a continued ban on (direct or indirect) advertising.

The corollary to this inevitable toleration of advertising and other forms of canvassing cannot be anything other than a serious competition and antitrust policy. The use of advertising-style canvassing methods will, after all, give the large structures a higher market profile. Agreements aimed at achieving mutual harmonisation of their market behaviour as well as the merger and joint venture agreements into which they enter must form the subject of close study by the competition authorities.

The "classical" professional bodies are even more powerless, if that is possible, against the phenomenon of scaling-up, specialisation, interdisciplinarity and internationalisation.

Scaling-up makes the individual practitioner less accountable to his professional body: the professional error becomes an anonymous "system fault", something that was unavoidable, and which certainly cannot be attributed to an insufficient grounding in the subject matter, since the practitioner is highly specialised.

Interdisciplinarity makes it more difficult to exercise preventive supervision due to the multitude of different competences and authorisations, and painfully exposes the divergences in repressive disciplinary policy between different professional bodies. We do not even have any agreement between the different professional bodies regarding the *principle,* let alone the arrangements, for interprofessional cooperation. This is leading to a situation in which the greatest legal uncertainty prevails: to take an example, if the practitioners of profession X are allowed to cooperate in an organised manner with the practitioners of profession Y (under certain conditions of course), then nothing could be less true than the reverse situation, because the professional bodies of X and Y have formulated different opinions. Even between individual professionals who are allowed to collaborate interprofessionally by their respective professional bodies, unfortunate situations can arise: for one professional a certain course of conduct can be sanctioned with a mere reprimand, whereas for the other the identical behaviour can lead to being struck off the list or disbarring.

On the face of it, only an interprofessional body or, at least, a very close collaboration between the existing bodies can effectively solve this problem. At the moment there is no sign of such a solution in sight. Of course, such a prospect of greater cooperation between different professional bodies or - if we are talking about closely related professions - even a merger between them, is viewed with mixed feelings: a loss of autonomy and self-determination would be counterbalanced by an increase in cohesion.

If the professional bodies do not themselves rapidly come up with formulas for merger or cooperation then we cannot exclude the possibility that governments themselves will have to organise an interprofessional dialogue. Although understandable, this would have an unfortunate impact on the claims for self-regulation and autonomy that the professional bodies would like to assert.

It should nonetheless be remarked that limited legislative action could be necessary from time to time. Recent disputes have shown that purely professional regulations and interprofessional agreements do not automatically pass the test of the competition legislation. So in Belgium, for example, the legal ban on collaboration between professionals in different branches of medicine (dentists, pharmacists, doctors)[1] is much more firmly rooted than similar disciplinary prohibitions or regulations in other professions.

Even more challenging is the international dimension of the modern professional world. A source of challenge and of the expansion of human horizons, nothing throws national customs and national ethical practices into relief quite like international contact. In itself this experience is salutary, but it also involves a considerable risk.

Ethical rules are, of course, no more than but also no less than the incidental translation in time and space of a set of universal principles, such as loyalty to the client, a sense of responsibility towards society, and reliability. Deducting ethical rules from these principles is certainly not a matter of rectilinear and perfectly logical deduction. On the other hand every profession needs, in its contacts with society, a set of rules of conduct that is as unequivocal as possible.

The internationalisation of professional life, with its secondary aspects of free movement of services and freedom of establishment - either through the creation of branches or through the establishment of subsidiaries - is bringing confusion to this necessary unequivocality. The not entirely accidental consequence of this development among professional practitioners in some of the larger international structures is that they are sometimes more influenced by the international agreements within their own offices than they are by the national rules of their immediate environments. It seems to me that this problem could be remedied by the national professional bodies concluding agreements regarding the harmonisation of codes of conduct. These rules will have to be "found" more and more within the international context or we will end up in a state of relative anarchy.

It goes without saying that the structures required to keep this process of harmonisation on the straight and narrow already partially exist, for example through the consultations required to allow cross-border service provision. Even so, it should be pointed out that these consultations often aimed more at the creation of choice-of-law rules rather than anything else. Regarding the free movement of services, for example, it is a normal choice-of-law

---

1 Royal Decree No. 78 on the practice of medicine of November 1969.

rule that the place where the service is provided determines the applicable ethical rules, at least insofar as these rules relate to the performance of the service itself. Sometimes conflicts between ethical rules have to be decided by making a clear choice: the confidentiality of the correspondence from advocates from different European Member States, for example, is a question that could well be settled differently in the two countries concerned and which, in a cross-border context, can only be resolved by a uniform international rule - something that, incidentally, was achieved in article 5.3 of the CCBE (Council of the Bars and Law Societies of the European Community) Code of Conduct of 12 October 1989.

In spite of the existing official and unofficial structures, this does seem to be an urgent matter for more international consultation. If this does not take place, then there is a threat of a "competition of regulations" in due course between the different States, something that would have a deleterious effect. Professionals whose services are of an international character could quite easily establish themselves where their services would be the least hindered by ethical impediments. If proximity and accessibility to the client are important considerations then, partly thanks to modern communications, the intellectual mobility of professionals and clients should not in the least be underestimated.

There is only one - *bad* - alternative to such an international approach, and that is the prevailing belief. The national professional bodies of each country are being reproached with the argument that they should not behave as if the country for which they are responsible was an island. But, meanwhile, the rules of *the* island par excellence, partially nourished by the expansive North American continent, are being spread across Europe and, indeed, across the whole of the modern capitalist world.

* *

*

The professions and their various professional bodies and institutes are having to contend with new challenges that are shaking them to their very foundations.

International globalization, increasing competitiveness and the necessary interdisciplinarity are three tendencies to which an adequate response - in other words a response at the right level of regulation and cooperation - must be made if the professional bodies want to safeguard their own future and that of the principles onto which the free choice of profession is grafted.

If this is not done then the pressure exercised by the "bottom line" will prevail over the optimum service dosage and the socially responsible level of service quality. If professionals become slaves of the burdens they have to haul around in order to keep things running, to become a partner, to remain a partner, to get a bonus or even just to survive, then there is a chance that ethics and quality will decline.

Of course, economic theory holds that the right price/quality relationship emerges in a situation of perfect competition. The reason why the professions must be regulated, however, lies precisely in the fact that a situation even of quasi-perfect competition is totally unachievable. To use a term from engineering, there is a lot of "noise" in the competition within the professional sector: the market is insufficiently transparent - in other words, the aleatory character of the service means that clients have insufficient power to evaluate the price-quality relationship for themselves - while on the other hand the negative aspects of the service cannot be sufficiently internalised, *e.g.* poor service has too many potential external effects on third parties and on society as a whole to remain unregulated.

If interdisciplinarity, extreme competitiveness and international globalization result in a situation in which services regulated for normal circumstances will *de facto* escape regulation and discipline, then this is an extremely dangerous situation that will jeopardise the very independence of the service itself.

A professional is an entrepreneur, certainly, but he is an entrepreneur who must be able to say "No" to a client who asks him to do the impossible, the unreasonable or the unethical, as well as to the government authority that wants to force him to choose the easiest or the cheapest route. That is something that must always remain the case.

ETHICS, PROFESSIONAL CONDUCT AND PRACTICE RULES IN THE CROSS BORDER PRACTICE. THE LEGAL PROFESSION AT CROSS-ROADS

Carl Bevernage, Partner of Loyens, Former Head of the Brussels Bar

1 BY WAY OF INTRODUCTION

This document focuses on a number of aspects of the practice of law in the framework of a regulated profession in Europe and in the USA. Most comments would not be different if they concerned Commonwealth countries, Middle- and South America, some countries in Africa and in Asia.

The practice of law harks back to very ancient times and the position of legal scholars, of lawyers has not changed that much over thousands of years.

Only since the mid fifties has the phenomenon of group practice emerged. The globalization of commerce and industry has prompted the creation of cross boundary forms of co-operation and mergers between law firms, leading to self-styled global players with up to 2.000 lawyers or more, including four to five hundred partners. Except for so-called niche firms, most firms that want to cater to the needs of big business cannot survive if they do not "employ" at last a few hundred lawyers. Yet, even in the USA more than half the number of active lawyers are sole practitioners or very small firms with no more than a dozen lawyers. This is also the case in Europe.

Notwithstanding this enormous diversity and differences in economic and financial underpinning of the practice of law, all lawyers concerned spontaneously refer to themselves as members of a liberal regulated profession.

2 THE PRACTICE OF LAW BY A REGULATED LIBERAL PROFESSION

2.1 The legal profession is regulated in many different ways and on many different - often local - levels.

Probably for the reason that lawyers used to exercise their profession mainly as litigators before the courts of their own jurisdiction, has the regulatory framework remained very fragmented, certainly in Europe.

Even if the basic status and rules are laid down in national legislation, most rules and regulations that affect the daily life of lawyers are determined at the local level; i.e. by the local Bar Council.

In some jurisdictions independent lawyers must by law register with a local Bar; in other countries or localities the adherence to a professional body is free. In the USA, the American Bar association does not have by law regulatory power. Yet the model rules of conduct of the ABA have quasi-legal force due to the size of the ABA and its de facto monopoly as a representative body of the profession.

The same is true for the Law Society of England and Wales.

2.2 Sometimes the regulatory powers are delegated to a "competent authority", including the profession itself.

In Belgium, France and other "Latin" countries, the legislator has entrusted the Bar Council (national and/or local) with enforceable regulatory powers, including admission to the profession, training and discipline.

In other countries such as the Netherlands and the United States the court system handles disciplinary problems, including disbarment.

2.3 Legal practice encompasses advice, assistance, representation and defence of individuals as well as (legal) entities in non-contentious matters and in litigation.

Whereas traditionally the exercise of the legal profession was inconceivable without litigation as the core practice providing for the bulk of the income, and "pré-emptive" advice came only second, the roles appear to have been largely reversed. Lawyers are consulted, certainly by corporate clients and institutions, on the legal intricacies of the conduct of business. Writing opinions, drafting sophisticated contracts, conducting complex negotiations, structuring deals, and so on, have become the core business for an ever increasing number of lawyers.

During the booming last years of the past 20th century the mega firms took the distinction a step forward by separating there very lucrative "transactional work" from the traditional "advisory work" and "litigation". "Premium work" is now distinguished from "compliance work", "core practice" from "ancillary work".

In some instances one may wonder whether the lawyer has become an entrepreneur of legal business rather than an advisor and defender.

2.4 The legal profession is the only body of practitioners that must facilitate the access to justice and uphold the rule of law.

Notwithstanding these growing mercantile tendencies, lawyers must still operate within the boundaries of the law. In any advice and assistance they provide, they must uphold the rule of law. They cannot recommend or implement illegal solutions nor violate the law.

The fact that in Europe lawyers will be held to denounce to the authorities money laundering schemes of clients, is in keeping with these principles. In their work lawyers must foster the access to justice and ultimately see to it that "justice is done" to their client in case of dispute.

2.5 Pro bono work is part of the professional duties of a lawyer.

The legal profession, together with the medical profession, is probably the only fee-earning body that must in certain circumstances lend its assistance free of charge.

In the United States all major law firms advertise their dedication to pro bono work. This may be linked to the tradition of community and charitable services in a nation with less state aid than in Europe, but it is nevertheless a remarkable phenomenon.

2.6 Fees are freely determined but are also subject to checks and balances.

The practice of law is "liberal" , also in the sense that the "market" determines the level of fees. The cap is generally the margin of unpaid and unrecovered fees.

Clients, who disagree with the amount of fees that are charged, have recourse before the regulatory bodies in most jurisdictions.

The financial importance of the bigger deals on which lawyers are called to advice and provide assistance is such that fee levels - whether charged on an hourly basis or linked - post factum - to the result of the operation have risen considerably. Yet the fee income of lawyers cannot rival with the fees and income charged by investment bankers and financial advisors. Still, in the major capitals of the Western World, the professional income of partners and associates belongs to the top tier of regular - no speculative - income. At the same time, many lawyers who work for private non-wealthy clients earn only a modest income.

2.7 Lawyers are subject to disciplinary control and must assume professional liability for the quality of their work.

Like almost any other regulated liberal profession, lawyers can be disciplined for violations of ethics and professional conduct.

They carry mandatory professional indemnity insurance.

These two very important "restrictions" constitute major safeguards for the clients and public at large.

2.8 Access to the profession is subject to strict rules of qualification and training.

Access to the practice of law as member of a professional regulated profession, is subject to strict rules of qualification (contents en length of university level law studies) and, in most jurisdictions, to mandatory training and follow-up education as well.

There are differences however in training requirements and these have in some cases hampered the freedom of (foreign) establishment. The dispute as to whether a graduate of a law school is a "*produit fini*" or whether the training certificate of the Bar (or the Bar admission test) or a stage, confers this quality, has never been entirely settled.

3 RULES OF ETHICS - PROFESSIONAL CONDUCT - PRACTICE RULES

3.1 Rules of ethics and of professional conduct concern the moral dimension of the law practice

Generally "deontology" is defined in that rather narrow sense and is deemed to encompass:

- independence
- integrity
- loyalty to the client
- professional secrecy

The independence is the corner stone of the profession. A lawyer cannot advise and not defend a client in court if he/she is not totally independent from the court, the authorities, the client and any form of external pressure. The lawyer is the "first judge" of the case or the matter that is entrusted to him. His advice and assistance cannot be tainted by any undue influence. In certain jurisdictions the prohibition for practising lawyers to work in a subordinate capacity, to belong to an MDP or to be in-house counsel, is inspired by this rule.

Even if a lawyer is in almost all jurisdictions an "officer of the court" ("*un auxiliaire de la justice*") and may even be called upon to sit as a substitute judge, he/she is not subject to the authority of the court or of the Minister of Justice.

In Belgium every lawyer takes the oath that he will not defend a cause that he/she in "honour and conscience" knows not to be a "just cause". In other words, a lawyer may not engage in litigation or defend a client, nor advice his/her client in matters that are unjust.

The independence is so characteristic that in most dictatorial regimes lawyers are deprived from this privilege and cannot function as an independent profession.

The integrity is a facet of the former requirement: a lawyer may be intellectually independent, he will however not serve the interests of the client and of the community at large as he should, if he/she does not have the personal probity and integrity that make him/her immune from any moral reproach. This may concern the conduct of his professional activities and even his personal lifestyle.

Loyalty to the client is essential in order not to betray the trust that the client places in his counsel. This requirement is not at odds with the obligation of independence. Only a truly independent lawyer can serve the objective interests of his client in the best possible way.

The answer to tricky questions of conflicts of interest must be analysed in that context. The fact that in partnerships "Chinese walls" are erected to allow the partnership to handle divergent interests in advisory work may lead to the erosion of client loyalty.

Of course the conflict should concern interests handled by one and the same lawyer or partnership. Clients should not try to prevent their counsel from advising and representing "economic competitors" in matters where there is no actual conflicting interest at stake.

Clients should also refrain from creating artificial conflicts by seeking preliminary advice with a plurality of lawyers ("shopping around") for the purpose of "eliminating opposing counsel".

Professional secrecy tops it all. Without professional secrecy the independence is at risk, the interests of the clients cannot be properly defended, the trust of the client can be betrayed. Whether professional secrecy is absolute and may be waived by the client, or "disregarded" by counsel in order to prevent that a crime will be committed is a hotly debated issue that is not resolved in the same way in every jurisdiction.

Of course professional secrecy cannot be used as pretext to violate the law.

Professional secrecy is limited to defence and advice and cannot extend to ancillary tasks of a lawyer, such as quasi-commercial "fiduciary activities" that are allowed in certain jurisdictions.

For a very long time it was held that a lawyer could not disclose the matters he/she has been consulted on. Of course once a dispute or a transactional matter is in the public domain, it will be automatically known that a lawyer is handling a given assignment.

It remains doubtful whether lawyers can advertise in brochures or otherwise the cases that they have handled in order to attract new business, even in jurisdictions that allow advertising.

The professional secrets cannot be shared with non-lawyers other than staff. This basic rule is a brake on the further grip of MDPs on the profession.

3.2 Practice rules define the relationship with clients, colleagues, courts, etc.

These rules are historically determined. Any change to the rules does not necessarily affect the fundamentals of the profession. They comprise for example:

- confidentiality of correspondence
- scope of practice
- forms of partnership
- fee arrangements with clients
- collaboration with other regulated professions

The *confidentiality of correspondence* is dealt with differently in various jurisdictions. In certain countries like in Belgium all correspondence between counsel and client and between opposing counsel is confidential unless stated differently. In Germany and many other countries the rule is the opposite: only when expressly marked as such, is correspondence confidential. The latter rule has been adopted in the Code of Conduct of the Council of the Bars and Law Societies of Europe (CCBE) for cross-border correspondence. The issue of "legal privilege" is a very important one, as any violation of confidentiality may also lead to the betrayal of professional secrecy.

The *scope of practice* of the legal profession is not cast in stone. In some countries (Switzerland, Luxembourg, the United Kingdom) lawyers are allowed to provide ancillary services in financial and corporate matters. In the United Kingdom, solicitors may carry out quasi-notarial work and engage in lucrative conveyance work (real estate transactions). The "fiduciary" practice in countries with a favourable tax status may expose lawyers to serious vulnerability.

The *forms of partnership* are very diverse. Some are incorporated others not, some have the legal format of commercial entities. In France a limited participation in the capital by non-lawyers is possible. Some jurisdictions submit the deeds of partnership to the prior authorisation of the Bar, impose mandatory arbitration in case of dispute, with or without involvement of the Bar. The rights and obligations of partners (total equality or not) may differ and do create problems in cross-border mergers. London and American led absorption of law firms in other countries appear to impose on the foreign partners and associates (economic) obligations that are alien to local Bar traditions. They often deprive the partners of basic equal treatment and protection under local law. The possibilities for third-party participation, directly or indirectly, of non-lawyers, such as in MDPs can pose threat to the independence of the profession.

The *fee arrangements* and for example the prohibition of "no cure no pay" arrangements or "pactum de quota litis" in many jurisdictions attest to the diversity of concepts in this field. The so-called ambulance chasing is frowned upon but tolerated in the USA and even elsewhere.

Charging huge fees as a percentage of punitive damages awards poses serious problems to the independence of lawyers who practice these methods of remuneration.

Charging excessive fees constitutes a violation of professional ethics in many jurisdictions and can be sanctioned.

The *collaboration with other regulated liberal professions*, or the permissibility of *MDPs* has been in the forefront of the preoccupation over the last decade.

MDPs have been hotly debated and rejected as a formula by the ABA. In Europe, except for some quasi multi-disciplinary practice with for example notaries and tax consultants with a law degree, the Bar authorities have rejected direct forms of co-operation with auditors and accountants. The authorities have been forced however to accept indirect forms of co-operation where MDPs have concluded with certain law firms composed of former in-house counsel of the Big 5 de facto referral arrangements. The outcome of the court case before the European Court of Justice in Luxembourg between the Dutch National Bar Council and two of the Big 5 audit firms will either frustrate the ambitions of the Big 5, or on the contrary, seriously affect the (economic) independence of the law profession.

Some have argued that the magnitude of the differences in practice rules between certain jurisdictions is such that cross-border mergers of for example solicitor firms and continental firms amount to actual MDPs and should not be treated differently.

4 THE GEOGRAPHICAL SCOPE OF PRACTICE

Some practices are confined within local or national boundaries.

In many instances the services are rendered across jurisdictional borders:

- from the point of origin by telephone, mail, fax, electronic communication
- during meetings outside the home jurisdiction
- by way of permanent establishment in a host jurisdiction.

These cross-border services may comprise the practice of domestic law, of the law of the host jurisdiction, of a third country, of private or public international law, of "common cross-border law", *e.g.* European Community Law.

The cross-border practice may involve lawyers admitted to practice in more than one jurisdiction, or a plurality of practitioners admitted in only one jurisdiction.

In today's world the importance of "electronic" and "teleconferencing" lawyering should not be underestimated. Advice and assistance in transactional work are often given without reference to specific national legislation. The know-how consists very much the modus operandi rather than in the interpretation and application of substantive law of a given jurisdiction.

In complex matters involving many different jurisdictions there are of course series of opinions regarding specific legal issues and they are usually dealt with separately by lawyers who are qualified under that particular law.

The caution applied by the law firms who handle these matters is in the first place inspired by issues of professional liability and not so much by questions relating to local qualification. In many cross-border deals it is difficult to determine the "governing jurisdiction". Parties resort to a choice of (US or English) law and arbitration, but such a choice could not possibly mean that only lawyers qualified to practice the law of these countries may give advice and provide assistance in these transactions.

5 VARIOUS ISSUES IN A CROSS-BORDER PRACTICE

5.1 Legal qualifications (education and training)

As already mentioned in the previous section, it is hard to reconcile the obligation of local qualification (local or locally accepted law degree and access to the local profession) with the needs of cross-border legal expertise. In the European Union the three key Directives on Services (1977), Recognition of Diplomas of Higher Learning (1988) and the Establishment Directive (1998) have largely solved this particular problem.

Under the first Directive lawyers may appear before all the courts of the EU, unless access is also restricted to local lawyers, to plead a case. This is a largely symbolic measure given the language constraints. The Diploma Directive is intended to facilitate the obtention of a law degree in another European country without having to recommence the law studies from scratch. The impact of this Directive is rather limited not only because of the language restrictions but also because the Establishment Directive has introduced a system of integration in the local Bar, possibly under home title, without requirement to possess the local law degree. There is no need either to co-operate with lawyers of the host jurisdiction.

The "established" lawyers come under the jurisdiction of the host Bar without loosing the possible better protection of the Bar of origin.

The European Union has gone much farther in this respect than for example USA where lawyers admitted to practice in one State may generally not argue a case in another State nor provide services in that State or become established without passing the local Bar examination.

It remains to be seen whether the liberal European regime will be exported to other countries and regions under the GATS drive for the liberalisation of legal services.

5.2 (Mutual) recognition

The further liberalisation can indeed be fostered by mutual recognition agreements concerning adequate qualification obtained in the other jurisdiction. The risk that this facility will lead to the exclusion of lawyers who are qualified to practice in countries with dissimilar systems of legal education, training, standards and discipline.

It would therefore appear that the issue of comparable levels of education and admission to practice as well as of the maintenance of standards must be tackled and resolved first of all.

5.3 Home/Host jurisdiction regulation and discipline

Combined or cumulative application of professional regulations and shared discipline are nice on paper. These solutions do not work if there can be divergent interpretations of dual rules and/or different degrees of severity in the sanctions that can be administered if more than one authority is competent to entertain complaints.

The solution will thus have to be that the rules apply of the primary country of establishment and that a single competent body applies sanctions for violations of these rules with effect in every jurisdiction where the delinquent lawyer has a practice.

It must be granted that this solution is not an ideal one if the infringement is committed by a lawyer in concert with other lawyers (partners) who may be governed by different rules and subject to different discipline.

5.4 Differences in scope of practice

These differences can lead to unfair competition. In an ever more unified or globalized world of practice, law firms or lawyers who may provide more than just legal services, either on their own, or in a multidisciplinary framework may have a competitive advantage over their colleagues who are subject to certain restrictions.

The legal profession will have to take a close look at the advantages and drawbacks of maintaining a sharp focus on the actual practice of law.

It would be most ironic to abandon this focus, now that accountants and auditors as well as other advisors seeks to expand their domain and seek to privilege the practice of law.

5.5 Differences in actual practice rules

The most blatant example of these differences has been for a long time the conflicting attitudes of the Bars towards the practice of "self-promotion" and advertising by their members. This has inevitably led to uneven playing fields. In most jurisdictions the ban on advertising and promotion has now been lifted, leading to sharper competition and higher overhead costs. It remains to be seen if advertising simply increases the notoriety of a lawyer and law firm or whether it brings in new clients and better assignments.

In some jurisdictions there is still a restriction on the number of trainees per partner and this can hamper the growth of law firms.

6 INTERNATIONAL REGULATIONS AND GUIDELINES

6.1 Local "overseas" practice rules

In addition to being subject to the rules of the host country, lawyers who practice elsewhere, remain subject to the rules and discipline of the Bar of origin. The Law Society of England and Wales has a comprehensive set of "overseas practice" rules. Interestingly, although these rules are not "alien" to the practice rules of other jurisdictions, certainly, elsewhere in Europe, they have been issued without prior consultation with the other Bar authorities, probably also due to the lack of an overarching professional body with regulatory powers.

They may lead to the application of "double deontology".

6.2 CCBE Code of Conduct

The enormous merit of the Code of Conduct of the CCBE, adopted by the 18 national delegations representing the Bars and Law Societies of the European Union and the European Economic Area on November 28, 1998, is simply that it exists notwithstanding many differences in the local codes of conduct and practice rules. In certain countries like Belgium, the CCBE Code of Conduct has been enacted by the national Bar council, whereas in The Netherlands where the courts administer disciplinary procedures, the Code of Conduct would have been without actual impact had it not been promulgated by law.

The Code of Conduct lends pre-eminence to the host jurisdiction. Striking features in the Code are the prohibition of the "Pactum de Quota Litis", the emphasis on the importance of the relations with the clients (including professional secrecy, the handling of client funds and professional indemnity insurance) and the public at large, on the independence, the relations of lawyers with the courts, etc.

Although the Code sets forth principles rather than detailed regulations, it contains guidelines that are clearly spelled out and not difficult to apply or enforce. The weakness may be that the Code does not handle issues related to cross-border practice of law firms.

6.3 IBA Code of Ethics

The IBA has issued more than 20 years ago a summary 28 article Code of Ethics that does not specifically address aspects of cross border practice. The IBA has been working on the concept of the Foreign legal practitioner (FLP) and will revisit the Code of Ethics in order to come to grips with the deontology of the "wandering practitioner". It may take some time before we see any results. Moreover, the IBA does not have any regulatory power over its members and non-members alike.

6.4 General Agreement on Trade in Services (GATS)

Within the World Trade Organisation the liberalisation of tradable services is being pursued vigorously. This also includes professional services. The focus is primarily on common qualifications, standards and licensing. Some progress has been made for the auditors and accountants and it may take another decade before the legal profession is tackled head on. The fact that the practice of law is conducted in the framework of a regulated profession, that lawyers are "officers of the court", but that law can also be practised as a salaried function outside the "Bar", may impede for a long time a uniform regulation of the profession on a worldwide scale.

7 AD FUTURUM

7.1 Deregulate?

The absence of regulations governing the cross-border legal practice, which is something different from a uniform code of ethics covering all lawyers irrespective of the jurisdiction of origin or that in which the services are performed, is so conspicuous that there can be no need at this stage to deregulate.

7.2 Regulate at a cross-border level

If local regulations are too divergent or conflicting, or too difficult to apply and enforce in cross-border transactions, can the self-regulating "instinct" of the profession be trusted as an alternative? The argument in favour is that international legal practice has expanded considerably over the past decades without apparently any known significant incident of lawyer misconduct that has brought the profession in disrepute.

On the other hand, is it really conceivable that while lawyer conduct is strictly regulated, monitored and sanctioned at the local level - generally affecting smaller law practices - lawyers working in large firms and in many jurisdictions would be able "to do it their" way. This would sooner or later lead to the creation of a dual profession: of local barristers and international solicitors.

Therefore rules and regulations, or at least guidelines governing cross-border practice will have to emerge eventually.

7.3 Geopolitical and geographical differences?

Most developments in "big lawyer business" are situated in the Western Hemisphere and in Australia. Western law firms are also present in a few Asian countries. Whereas there have been attempts to strengthen the position of the traditional legal practice in emerging countries and countries that have shed the communist systems, it would be unwise to create a new schism between the "commercial" firms in the West and more classic forms of legal advice and assistance elsewhere.

7.4 "Commercial" legal services versus the legal assistance by a regulated profession

The same reasons as mentioned above can be invoked in order to combat the growing tendency to operate a distinction between a so-called "commercial" Bar and what some may refer to as an "ethical" side of the profession. The latter being more geared towards the needs of the public at large and working with lesser means and eventually less know-how.

The ABA has warned that the high cost of legal studies in the USA, which compels students to contract huge loans and to secure reimbursement by seeking employment with top commercial firms only, is eroding the basis of the profession. Public service, the courts, the public prosecutor's offices can no longer attract the best legal minds and this will eventually harm the proper administration of justice.

7.5 Benign neglect?

Should we really worry about the ethical dimension of our legal profession? The phenomenal growth of the number of practitioners, the ever expanding field in which we can render services to our clients has occurred in spite of certain outdated practice rules that were more centred on the protection of privileges, the restriction of competition than on serving the needs of the clients.

True as this may be, it must also be said that especially the needs of business and corporations have been taken better care of than before.

It is, on the other hand, not so certain that the individual citizen whose rights are in jeopardy receives today better and swifter help at an affordable cost.

The conclusion must therefore be that practice rules may evolve without much steering but that ethics should remain the corner stone of our profession.

THE ROLES OF ELITE LAW FIRMS IN THE GLOBAL ECONOMY[1]

John Flood, Professor of Law and Sociology, University of Westminster

1 INTRODUCTION

Financial services have become increasingly concentrated within the global economy. Banks, intergovernmental organizations, professional service firms are located in the major financial centres of the world, especially New York and London. Sassen writes, "Global cities...are sites for...the production of financial innovations and the making of markets, both central to the internationalisation and expansion of the financial industry" (1991: 5). The industry seeks homeostasis, that is, equilibrium "amidst the variations of outer shock and change" (McLuhan 1964: 98). And this is the crux of how the quintessential global activity works, namely, capital markets. The creation of the documentation of capital markets encapsulates and represents the essence of homeostasis and tries to divert randomness and chaos to the darkness that lies beyond the logic of the agreement drafted by the lawyers. Agreements, mezzanine financing documents, and so forth, reach their apotheosis when their normative structures are inscribed in either New York state law or English law, or both. Since the major financial institutions are based in these two jurisdictions, their clout usually ensures that there is no deviation from the juridical norm. Thus the global is deeply embedded in the local.

2 GLOBALIZATION

Globalization is an "essentially contested concept" (Gallie 1955), in that its meaning is always in dispute. There are, according to Held et al. (1999), three perspectives of globalization currently subsisting, namely, hyperglobalization, global scepticism, and transformationalism. The first is a transmutation—McKinsey (consultants) and McDonalds (hamburgers) as exemplars of world domination. Globalization hauls down the barriers between nation states, which themselves become irrelevant; economic activity and cultural identity merge into a multiplex melting pot and global capitalism emerges triumphant (Ohmae 1991, 1995; Ritzer 1996). This process is progressive, unilinear and inexorable. Global scepticism argues against this position, countering the hyperbole of globalization with statistics demonstrating the failure of global economic integration, suggesting at best a move towards regionalization has occurred and that globalization is a myth (Hirst and

---

1 Parts of this chapter have previously appeared in M. LIKOSKY (ed.), *Transnational Legal Processes: Globalization and Power Disparities*. London: Butterworths, 2001.

Thompson 1996). Whereas hyperglobalization postulates that its progressive agenda will lead to radical change for the benefit of all, north and south, scepticism sees internationalisation accentuating the differences between north and south. The third perspective of globalization, transformationalism, recognizes the contingency of action and the historicity of structure as enabling and constraining globalization (Giddens 1990). While transformationalism accepts great change is taking place in the economy, politics and culture, the degree to which it is happening is yet unknown and the redistribution of resources in the world is still unequal with some getting richer and some areas becoming marginalized (Held et al. 1999: 8). The nation state is able to continue claims to power and authority but they are limited more and more by the emergence of stronger supranational forms of governance, such as the European Union and the World Trade Organization. Ultimately, the destination of globalization—if one exists—is unknown. Whichever perspective is chosen, each represents a threat to homeostasis and each can be shown to function within very loose normative structures.

Globalization is not entirely anarchic but nor is it tightly rule-bound. The law of globalization is almost a new *lex mercatoria* only partially dependent on state authority for its legitimacy or its disputing systems (Dezalay and Garth 1996; Teubner 1997). Global law is derived from a number of sources, among the most popular is contract—private ordering—the drafting of agreements. Contract is able to enmesh states as parties to an agreement without the protection of sovereign immunity. Contract can transcend national boundaries more easily than international law is capable of doing. It is at the level of private ordering that difference is resolved into a document that circumvents the contingencies of jurisdictional conflict. Private ordering emerges away from the centre, as Teubner argues, "*...global law will grow mainly from the social peripheries, not from the political centres of nation-states and international institutions*" (1997: 7).[2] Global law is a *malleable law* made by professionals during the construction of deals.[3] Without this malleability, global law could hardly come into being: it would be brittle and weak, under constant disputation. Yet malleable law is remarkably successful in constituting the global legal order.[4]

---

2 Note that social periphery here needs to be interpreted broadly, since the major international financial institutions are hardly peripheral.

3 In some cases this is referred to as soft law, which it isn't as it depends on New York and English law for its legitimation. Soft law operates in contexts where there is no governing law. see *e.g.*, FLOOD and SKORDAKI (1997) where soft law operates in international insolvency.

4 The rule of law is usually held up as the defining element of civilised society. Under malleable law, however, the rule of law often has a harsher, more rugged character. The following anecdote demonstrates. During the closing of a major deal of an acquisition of

In the next part one aspect of private ordering is displayed. Capital markets is one of the fastest growing forms of financial activity in the world, but it can only be understood against the background of its possible failure in insolvency and its combined localized and globalized character.[5]

3 CAPITAL MARKETS

At the end of 1999, the managing directors (the former partners) of Goldman Sachs received remuneration packages to the order of about $10 million each (Garfield 1999: 13). Most of it was reward for being the top financial adviser and underwriter in the world, being in the biggest deals such as advising Vodafone in its takeover of Mannesman, producing a telecommunications company worth £225 billion (Gow 2000: 32). Capital markets work is high value service with enormous premiums for those who do it.

The fifty years following World War II constituted a key expansion period for global capital. Foreign direct investment grew, the Eurodollar market increased global capital liquidity, and immense political change issued in a wave of privatisations as states sloughed off their possessions—state industries, utilities and service providers. The market rather than the state was to reign (Gamble 1994). In the 1980s "Big Bang" in the UK enabled the global banks, especially those in the US, to establish investment banks free from constricting regulation. For the American banks, the Glass-Steagall Act had corseted their activities by preventing the simultaneous engagement of commercial and investment banking (Finch et al. 2000). Stock broking changed as brokers and jobbers merged and the stock exchange rules were relaxed outlawing cartels. Although the recession of the late 1980s and early 1990s constrained growth for some time, as shown by the rise in insolvency statistics, global investment rose inexorably, as demonstrated by the increases in foreign direct investment flows (FDI) (Held et al 1999: 249). In the last 15 years of the 20th century, the progress of the economy has altered in that boom and slump can co-exist in different parts of the world. Thus at the end of the century while the US was economically triumphant, the Asian tigers were limping in a field of thorns. In order to recapture their ferocity,

---

a company by another, the documentation was continuously being changed and redrafted. The directors of the selling company came to their lawyers' office in the City of London expecting to sign the documents, close the deal and depart celebrating their new riches. On arrival they were placed in a conference room and told they would have to wait while the last few wrinkles were ironed out. Seventy-two hours later they were released from their confinement when the documents were finally agreed between the lawyers. The lawyers couldn't let the directors leave the office because they knew they wouldn't return, so they held them until they could sign. There was nothing the directors could do but comply. They were under the force of the rule of law.

5 SANTOS (1995: 275) calls this type "globalized localism" and "localized globalism".

the Asian economies have begun to produce their own big bangs (Kinami 1998; Mannix 2000). One other feature of this period ought to be mentioned and that is the growth in regulatory institutions in the global economy. The most assertive has been the Securities and Exchange Commission (SEC), which now appears to be seeking the role of global regulator. During the 1980s the SEC was dealing with various insider trading scandals, including the savings and loans industry and the manipulation of the junk bond market (high yield debt) created by Michael Milken and which subsequently crashed in 1989 causing the downfall of Drexel Burnham Lambert a year later (Stewart 1991).[6] During the 1990s the junk bond, now high-yield debt market recovered and was legitimised (Sheldon and Abbondante 1991). The global economy, with the success of the GATT Uruguay Round, has now a transnational watchdog and dispute arbiter in the World Trade Organization.

In other ways, the SEC has begun to reduce the barriers to American markets for foreign investors by easing its disclosure requirements (Kamman and Covello 1999). Taking regulatory manoeuvres into account during the economic activity of the last 50 years, capital markets work has boomed. For example, "the six largest mergers/acquisitions in 1998 totalled over $300 billion and were funded by a combination of equity and debt issues" (Hodgart 1999: 6). Hodgart also notes that "the six largest auto manufacturers [in 1999] are reported as having a "strategic acquisitions war chest" totalling in excess of $100 billion" (*id.*)

Capital markets work involves gaining access to finance in markets throughout the world. This may be through issues of stock, bonds, securitization of debt or loans,[7] depositary receipt programmes, initial public offerings (IPOs), or privatisations. The last 20 years have shown bankers' and lawyers' ingenuity in developing new forms of financing and means of packaging them. Demands for creativity have risen as the equities market globalized and diverse jurisdictions' requirements had to be coordinated in strategic ways. If we compare debt markets with equities markets the difference becomes apparent: trading in debt markets requires less research and availability of information, relies on high quality borrowers with less concem about the underlying credit, and therefore was able to intemationalise more rapidly; whereas information deficits are greater in equities markets where borrowers are a more diverse group than in debt

6 DREXEL BURNHAM LAMBERT, and MILKEN, underwrote 60 per cent of the junk bond market in the second half of the 1980s (SHELDON and ABBONDANTE 1999: 16).

7 For example, see LEWIS' (1989: 97 *passim*) description in *Liar's Poker* of the creation of the mortgage bond market by Salomon Brothers.

markets and concepts such as pre-emption rights predominate in some jurisdictions and not others (Neate 1987: 8-15).

The best way to illuminate capital markets work is through case studies of capital markets work in action over the previous two decades. We are fortunate to have records that illustrate the practice. The first is the privatisation of British Gas during the Thatcher premiership.

3.1 British Gas (1986)[8]

The British Gas privatisation followed that of British Telecom (BT) by two years. BT had been problematic because the value of half of it was £4 billion, "... some seven times bigger than any previous UK issue and some four times bigger than any issue attempted anywhere in the world. It represented approximately the amount which the big UK investment institutions, the pension funds and insurance companies had put into the equity market over a two-year period" (Clementi 1987: 58-59). The British Gas privatisation was to be bigger than BT's. Three constituencies were identified for the issue: the UK institutions, the UK retail market, and the overseas market. The first two required substantial educational investment to create a widespread market: seminars, roadshows and extensive mailshots. This pre-issue publicity was to have deleterious consequences for the US market since it conflicted with US regulatory norms. The overseas market was further split between the US, Canada, Europe and Japan. Each had a local investment syndicate to nurse the deal to fruition, which would sell only in their territories (Clementi 1987: 64).[9]

One of the crucial cultural differences between the UK and US practice revolved around the purpose of the prospectus. Within the UK it is seen as a sales document while in the US it is regarded as a liability document. Therefore American lawyers influence greatly the content of the prospectus to ensure it is risk averse, even pessimistic (Joyce 1987: 78).[10] In the UK merchant bankers keen on marketing the offering shape the prospectus to reflect their interests rather than those of the lawyers. Because the UK was to be the key market for the offering the English lawyers wanted the UK prospectus to be the "base" prospectus with "wraparounds" for the other jurisdictions. While easy to accomplish throughout Europe, the US, Canada and Japan were difficult to accommodate in this pattern. The statutory

---

8 Source of case: NEATE (1987: 56).

9 The allocations to the three sectors were 40% to UK institutions, 40% to the UK public, and 20% to overseas investors (CLEMENTI 1987: 60).

10 In the US strict liability is imposed on the issuing company for statements in its prospectus.

requirements of the American system, especially the SEC, threatened to uncouple the. American prospectus from the UK base. However, the cardinal rule for the issuers and lawyers was that the same message about British Gas should be disseminated everywhere. Thus all drafts of the US, Canadian and Japanese prospectuses had to be checked against the UK base document. Slaughter and May, as UK government lawyers, devoted many associates' hours to the task (Henderson 1987: 70).

Timing was problematic. The offer and underwriting had to be synchronised, but again the jurisdictions imposed different schedules. Under the UK timetable, December 8, 1986, was the crucial date when the UK underwriting agreement became effective, with all underwriting agreements being signed and the price fixed on November 21, 1986. The overseas' underwriters usually signed agreements only a few days before the effective date; thus, they were being asked to commit to exposure far earlier than normal. Still there were obstacles insofar as the SEC would not have necessarily declared the registration statement effective, nor would the Canadian authorities sanctioned the statement. Whereas in the US the regulatory material was handled by a single agency, the SEC, in Canada securities regulation was the task of the individual provinces' securities commissions, even though the US lawyers attempted to argue that Canada should not be perceived as an independent market, but merely a subset of the US one, which nettled the Canadians. Eventually the US and Canadian lawyers formed a "North American" group to coordinate the offer, but the Americans would often forget to insert the work "North" (Ross 1987: 84). To obviate the need to deal with all 10 provinces individually, the commissions agreed to the Ontario Securities Commission being the lead regulator for the issue. Both US and Canadian lawyers had to persuade their regulators to grant various exemptions—for advertising and disclosure—to enable the offer to proceed in synchrony. For example, under US due diligence the lawyers have to examine all legal documents, including oil and gas purchase contracts. The British Gas management were horrified by the request. No one ever looked at their contracts. Ultimately, a Sullivan and Cromwell partner was allowed to read them in a locked room for a day (Henderson 1987: 81). The SEC insisted that the Financial Times and the Economist carry no publicity for the British Gas offer in their US issues, a demand that would be impossible to enforce with the advent of the internet. As the due date came all sides had signed various conditions that would manage the failure of the issue if it flopped. The conditions also financially benefited the North Americans and Japanese because of their longer underwriting exposure. The British government's fiscal actions almost damaged the offer when it imposed a tax on American Depositary Receipts (the form the shares would take in the US). Despite the underwriters' argument that the government should pay themselves, the tax was passed on to US investors.

Twelve years on when Deutsche Telekom was being privatized similar problems came up. In Germany the issue was advertised, which was still against SEC rules. The lawyers managed to find a sympathetic hearing at the SEC who gave them a "no-action relief": One of the lawyers concerned noted, "The SEC was extremely cooperative. They were keen to see the issue happen, as part of their campaign to encourage foreign issuers" (*International Financial Law Review* 1997: 19). There were also difficulties in coordinating the time frames in multiple jurisdictions and for how long the underwriters would have to be exposed. Since this was a major privatisation for Germany, its regulatory structure had to be revised to take account of the new corporate structure. The revisions of the regulatory schemes were coterminous with the preparations for the privatisation, and it was not until the issue was almost due to occur that the rules were finalized. Thus the regulatory framework was a constant moving target for the lawyers.

Following the "Velvet Revolution" in Eastern Europe in the late 1980s and early 1990s, the pace of privatizations picked up. As the countries of the region, with the assistance of the European Bank for Reconstruction and Development (EBRD), attempted to rejoin the free market system, many state industries were put up for sale, including breweries, automobile manufacturers, utilities, and telecoms. The EBRD believed, "a standard view among academics and policy makers in the early days of the transition process was that faster privatisation would automatically lead to faster restructuring of enterprises. Several years into the transition, the relationship between privatisation and restructuring has proved to be more complex" (EBRD 1995: 128). The next case demonstrates the complexity of investing in an emerging market.

3.2 Sakhalin II, Russia (1998)

Sakhalin is an island in Arctic Russia with the Piltun-Astokhskoye oil and gas field lying offshore, which may contain as much as the North Sea reserves. This project is Russia's first offshore oil and gas project with an estimated cost of $9 billion. It is also the first project commissioned under Russia's Power Sharing Agreement law (PSA) of 1996. The legal advisers were Freshfields, for the lenders, and Coudert Brothers, acting as international counsel for the project company. They faced a number of challenges in negotiating the deal, including coping with multiple layers of national and local regulations along with strict environmental laws. As the first offshore project, it had *to develop local laws* as it progressed. A PSA is a direct agreement between the government and investors on a tax regime that the government guarantees to apply to the project for its entire duration. This enables investors to plan costs more accurately and provides security.

A challenge for Sakhalin II was that only 70% of the necessary legislation was in place to support the PSA. Furthermore, the long-term nature of the project means that the project company will have to negotiate contracts to cope with different groups of lenders over time. This may mean lenders submitting documentation to prevent the project company from borrowing in the future. Although this was avoided in the first stage of Sakhalin, the project has raised the issue and may use such documentation in its second stage. Finally, the deal was completed in spring amidst a deteriorating Russian economy and falling oil prices. The project company, Sakhalin Energy Investment Company, was sponsored by Mitsui, Marathon, Shell, and Mitsubishi. The lenders were the European Bank for Reconstruction and Development, Overseas Private Investment Corporation (US), and the Export-Import Bank of Japan. The first stage of Sakhalin was funded by sponsor equity of $385 million. A further $348 million in debt was to be raised. The project is in jeopardy because of the Russian financial crisis (IFLR 1999: 23).

The final case shows how complex the problems can be with cross-border mergers and restructurings.

3.3 Alstom (1998)[11]

In 1998 the largest non-privatization IPO was a French company, Alstom, amounting to $3.7 billion. Alstom was owned equally by GEC of the UK and Alcatel of France. It had over 400 subsidiaries in over 60 jurisdictions and was registered as a Netherlands NV. Among the advisers the global coordinators were Goldman Sachs and Credit Suisse First Boston, and their advisers were Davis Polk 8 Wardwell and Stibbe Simont Monahan Duhot 8 Giroux, a "large" (but in reality quite small) French law firm. Acting as counsel to the issuer were Shearman and Sterling and Lovell White Durrant. And finally counsel to the selling stockholders were Freshfields and Gide Loyrette Nouel, another "large" French law firm. Before the IPO launched the company's in-house counsel had to take charge of reorganizing the company and its various subsidiaries from a Dutch company into a French one. This involved numerous government authorizations, adding to the already complicated and logistically challenging nature of the deal. Preparation for the IPO ran in parallel to the reorganization and involved French, English, US, and international tranches, consisting of a primary offering of shares sold by Alstom and a secondary offering by Alstom's

---

11 Source of case: IFLR (1999:10).

parents. The shares were listed in Paris, London, and New York and were subject to full regulatory review simultaneously by the SEC in the US, the London Stock Exchange in the UK, and the COB in France.

The offering involved the isssuance of American Depositary Receipts, listed in New York, and the first ever UK Depositary Receipts, listed in London. Lovell White Durrant structured the UKDRs and advised Alstom on its employee share offering, which covered some 35 jurisdictions and ran as part of the public offering. Davis Polk and Wardwell led the due diligence, ensuring that the company's diverse material assets and subsidiaries were intact and included in the deal, or at least making sure that fall-back plans were in place if the reorganization was not completed by the time of the IPO. The firm also advised on the core disclosure document, the adequacy of the disclosure and the underwriting agreement itself.

Just one month before the closing of the IPO, Alstom acquired Cegelec, an electrical contracting and process control business owned by Alcatel which was itself a quarter of the size of the combined issuer. All the work which had been to demonstrate what the group would look like after the reorganization was redone taking into account the new business. After five months' work the deal was priced to go.

4 ELITES AND CAPITAL MARKETS

The numbers of active players in capital markets are relatively small. Seven investment banks dominate global capital markets, and of those seven only three comprise the top tier. I referred earlier to the bonuses awarded at Goldman Sachs, which is probably the most successful investment bank in the world measured in volume and size of deals. Hodgart (1999: 6) noted, "three investment banks dominated the global adviser market in 1998, handling $2.23 billion of deals, with the next three banks handling $1.18 billion. Within the US the three leading firms (the same as world wide) handled $1.2 billion. compared with the next three banks with $690 million."

By 1999 the big three investment banks, Goldman Sachs, Morgan Stanley Dean Witter, and Merrill Lynch, had "each advised on more than "$l trillion in world-wide mergers and acquisitions..." (Deogun 2000: 13). The value of the deals also indicates the rewards to the investment banks and others who participate in capital markets work. What is clear about this sector is that the critically decisive players are few in number and their networks are densely structured encouraging repeat-player patterns of activity. Ferguson (1997: 33) spells out the connections:

A small band of major banks call the shots on the big-ticket equities issues. These are the people to impress for law firms looking to develop market share on these deals. Unfortunately for the pretenders, the banks sit comfortably alongside a similarly small band of law firms. On Wall Street, relationships extend beyond even the eldest partners, and banks and forms share a lineage steeped in the history of New York's development as a financial centre. Some of these old-school ties are part of Wall Street folk law [*sic*]: Goldman Sachs and Sullivan and Cromwell, Morgan Stanley and Davis Polk and Wardwell.

For example, the relationship between Morgan Stanley and Davis Polk goes back 110 years (Forster 1997: 37).

In all we are distinguishing around 12 law firms in New York and London that dominate the global capital markets field. They work with each other repeatedly and have adapted to each others' cultural norms. Indeed, they probably do not work with many other firms at all, since they represent the top tier on both sides of the Atlantic. They are the aristocracy of the legal profession.

Capital markets work requires lawyers who understand the intricacies of both US and UK markets and law. For example, I took the January 1997 issue of *International Financial* Law Review which contained details of the 11 biggest capital markets deals in 1996. The firm with the most deals was Sullivan and Cromwell and it was followed by Shearman and Sterling, both blue-chip, Wall Street law firms. On the English side Linklaters and Clifford Chance were the highest ranking firms. On all scores the US law firms do best. Between the US firms there is not a great deal of variation. For example, Cleary Gottlieb has the biggest total value, while Shearman and Sterling has the most deals, and Sullivan and Cromwell has the highest average value per deal. The "magic circle" of firms competes within itself.

The importance of the US capital markets cannot be exaggerated here, which ties in American law firms and investment banks. No other market has such huge resources. This is rendered visible by the high numbers of venture capitalists and hedge funds. Even though London is a major market in its own right, because of obstacles like the Glass-Steagall Act it has been a productive home for many investment banks. But UK capital markets are not as large as the US, hence the hegemony of US institutions in the field.

Cultural differences intrude in styles of working between American and English lawyers. The quest for disclosure in due diligence is quite different. US lawyers think in terms of the litigation potential of disclosure: has the verification process been conducted to the standard expected by a trial judge? This is usually Rule 10b-5 under the Exchange Act 1934, which an investment bank will request of the lawyers. But as one Skadden Arps attorney opined, "It is negative assurance that nothing has come to our attention that indicates that there are misleading statements or omissions in the disclosure document" (Forster 1996: 20). In the British Gas privatisation the Shearman and Sterling lawyer distinguished the difference in disclosure under the American and British regimes:

One of the conflicts in the Gas offering ...that caused me the most sleepless hours was the contrast between the US system of due diligence ...and the UK system of verification. Now I do not really pretend to understand verification, but it seems to involve taking each sentence of the prospectus and finding someone, either in the government of the company, whose initials can be put next to it. The US system is much more haphazard and less carefully structured but takes a different slant. Under US practice, lawyers for all parties attempt to look at every legal document that can be found to back up the statements in the prospectus (Joyce 1987: 81)

These stylistic differences have motivated the English law firms to create US practices that can compete on equal terms with US firms, although the English firms may not be hiring sufficient numbers of US attorneys as one US lawyer commented that just because a big American name joins a UK firm, he still "needs to go and hire 20 people to convince US underwriters that they can do the due diligence" (Forster 1996: 21). Another US lawyer also noted that UK firms "have hired some excellent lawyers but the firms as a whole lack some of the resources that we bring to the task and for example some of the sophisticated US tax knowledge for tax disclosure. Also there is the long history and knowledge of how disclosure issues have handled in the past" (Forster 1996: 21). This is where we rejoin Santos' "globalized localisms" and "localized globalizms" mentioned earlier. In order to succeed in the capital markets field law firms must have multijurisdictional skills in sufficient strength that are accepted as both strong global players and good local players. The investment banks will seek out local expertise as well as global reach.

The key to succeeding in the field is to achieve the capacity to be the global coordinator for a deal. This, in effect, means being the adviser to the lead bank in the deal. So, even though some UK law firms may involve themselves in a large number of deals, they will not be the global coordinator. Instead, they will most likely be a form of local counsel or lead firm for one of the other entities involved in the deal. Only in 1999 did a UK law firm, Linklaters, for the first time advise an underwriter, Merrill Lynch, on an SEC-registered offering (Mannix 1999: 9). The advantage lies therefore with the American law firms, because of their historical ties with the banks, their long involvement and expertise in capital markets work, and the dominance of US capital markets as sources of funding. In other words, the market is structured through longstanding social and economic ties (Granovetter 1985), which generate high levels of trust (cf. Baker 1990).

These firms do not have to advertise, they already constitute an index of quality of service (Podolny 1993). It is therefore feasible for elite, capital markets, US firms such as Cravath Swaine, Davis Polk, and Sullivan and Cromwell to establish London offices that offer only New York law for capital markets work, instead of becoming multinational practices with local capacity; they get ample numbers of UK and European clients eager for access to US capital markets (Lee 1997: 31). The corollary being that UK firms cannot depend solely on UK law. As a Chicago lawyer put it, "Clients are increasingly indifferent to what the governing law of a capital markets transaction is" (*id.*).

5 CONCLUSION

Capital markets work is symbolic of the globalization of finance and professional services. In this respect, the transformationalist view of globalization is the most appropriate in that institutions are changing and there is a clamour to be encompassed by these changes. We cannot talk of total globalization, nor can we deny the process is occurring. But we can question its limits or reach.

Those endowed with social, cultural and economic capital to carry out capital markets work exist in a rarefied atmosphere inhabited by only a few. The rush to embrace capitalism by the former communist regimes, European and Asian, is matched by the eagerness of the caudillo countries. All want access to the wealthiest market of all, the United States. The Securities and Exchange Commission has altered its disclosure rules for registration to enable greater entry to American capital markets by foreigners.

It is clear that individual jurisdictions remain legitimate sources of state norms, and we have not yet arrived at the hyperglobalizers' utopia nor are we in the sceptics' dystopia, but these, in many cases are being overridden by malleable law created through contract and agreements that usually owes its "allegiance" to either New York state law or English law. Local law is in the process of becoming subsumed under highly competitive systems of law that market themselves aggressively. The result is that local law declines in importance in spite of whatever changes it may introduce to modernize itself. The Anglo-American axis is too powerful to defeat in the capital markets field. It dominates the transnational institutions such as the IMF and WTO; the prime investment banks are based in the US, and the lawyers are either in New York or London. Local bar associations, for example, are powerless to regulate this activity, as it often does not involve local lawyers. But what we are beginning to see is the rise of the transnational bar association, which has a direct interest in pursuing these matters, either as a matter of ethical concern or because the elites who populate these bar associations wish to consumate their paramountcy. The combination of institutional global reach, normative creativity and pluralism, and professional service flexibility and responsiveness to market changes appears impregnable.

6 REFERENCES

BAKER, W.E. (1990) `Market Networks and Corporate Behavior," *American Journal of Sociology* vol. 96, 589.

BANK OF NEW YORK. (1999) "How to Issue and Trade Depositary Receipts," in *US Capital Markets Report*. London: Euromoney.

CLEMENTI, D. (1987) "World-Wide Public Offerings of Securities: British Gas," in NEATE, F. (ed) *The Developing Global Securities Market*. London: Graham and Trotman.

DEOGUN, N. (2000) "Top 3 Firms for Deals Set $1 Trillion Mark," *Wall Street Journal Europe* 13, 23 (January 3).

DEZALAY, Y. and GARTH, B. (1996) Dealing in Virtue: International Commercial Arbitration and the Construction of a Transnational Legal Order. Chicago: University of Chicago Press.

DIGNAN, C. (1999a). "Are UK Firms Ready for Global Banking?" *The Lawyer Online* <http://www.thelawyer.co.uk/TLglobalbank.html>

EBRD. (1995) Transition Report 1995: Investment and Enterprise Development. London: EBRD.

FERGUSON; N. (1997) "What the Client Demands," International Financial *Law Review* 33-35 (December).

FINCH, S., MACDONALD, G. and WALKER, J. (2000) "Replacing the Depression's Final Legacy," *International Financial Law Review* 9 (February). "

FLOOD, J. (forthcoming) "The Vultures Fly East: The Creation and Globalization of the Distressed Debt Market," in NELKEN, D. (ed).

Forster, R. (1996) `International Equities Survey: Davis Polk and Wardwell Leads the World's Equity Advisers," *International Financial Law Review* 17-25 (September).

FORSTER, R. (1997) "New York Firms Seek the World's Business," *International Financial Law Review* 36-39 (December).

FRYDMAN, R. and RAPACYNZSKI, A. (1994) *Privatisation Eastern Europe: Is the State Withering Away?* Oxford: Oxford University Press.

GALLIE, W.B. (1955) "Essentially Contested Concepts", *Proceedings of the Aristotelian Society* 56, 167-198.

GAMBLE, A. (1994) *The Free Economy and the Strong State*, 2nd ed., Basingstoke: Macmillan.

GARFIELD, A. (1999) "High-flying Goldman Sees Wage Bill Double to $8.7bn," *Independent* 13 (December 22).

GIDDENS, A. (1990) *The Consequences of Modernity*. Cambridge: Polity Press.

GOW, D. (2000) "Now Vodafone Wants Net Alliances," *Guardian* 32 (February 5).

GRANOVETTER, M. (1985) "Economic Action and Social Structure: The Problem of Embeddedness," *American Journal of Sociology*, vol. 91, *481*.

HELD, D., MCGREW, A., GOLDBLATT, D. and PERRATON, J. *(1999) Global Transformations: Politics, Economics and Culture*. Cambridge: Polity Press.

HENDERSON, G. (1987) "World-Wide Public Offerings of Securities: British Gas," in NEATE, F. (ed) *The Developing Global Securities Market*. London: Graham and Trotman.

HIRST, P. and THOMPSON, G. (1996) Globalization in Question: The International Economy and the Possibilities of Governance. Cambridge: Polity Press.

HODGART, A. (1999) "Introduction", *IFLR Review of the Year: Capital Markets Forum* 1999 6. London: Euromoney.

INTERNATIONAL FINANCIAL LAW REVIEW. (1999) "International Equities Team of the Year (Eastern Europe)", *IFLR Review of the Year: Capital Markets Forum 1999*. London: Euromoney.

INTERNATIONAL FINANCIAL LAW REVIEW. (1997) "Deals of the Year: Blockbusters Boost Final Months of Record Year," *International Financial Law Review 18* (January).

INTERNATIONAL FINANCIAL LAW REVIEW. (1999) "Cutting Edge: Milbank Tweed Leads on First US-Style LBO in Post-Recession Asia," *International Financial Law Review* 6 (December).

JOYCE, T. (1987) "World-Wide Public Offerings of Securities: British Gas," in NEATE, F. (ed) *The Developing Global Securities Market*. London: Graham and Trotman.

KAMMAN, E. and COVELLO, A. (1999) "New SEC Disclosure Rules for Non-US Companies," in US *Capital Markets Report*. London: Euromoney.

KINAMI, N. (1998) *The Japanese Big Bang*. London: Freshfields.

LEE, P. (1997) "Country Survey: US Firms Embrace English Law Capability," *International Financial Law Review* 30-32 (April).

LEWIS, M. (1989) *Liar's Poker*. London: Coronet Books.

LUKES, S. (1974) *Power: A Radical View*. London: Macmillan.

MANNIX, R. (1999) "European Equity Clients Favour One-Stop Shops," *International Financial Law Review* 9-13 (October).

MANNIX, R. (2000) `Foreign Investors Snap Up Korean Bargains," *International Financial Law Review* 28-33 (February).

MCLUHAN, M. (1964) "Roads and Paper Route", in *Understanding Media: The Extensions of Man*. London: Routledge.

NEATE, F. (ed) (1987) "World-Wide Public Offerings of Securities: British Gas," in *The Developing Global Securities Market*. London: Graham and Trotman.

OHMAE, K. (1991). *The Borderless World*. London: Fontana.

OHMAE, K. (1995). *The End of the Nation State*. New York: The Free Press.

PODOLNY, J.M. (1993) "A Status-based Model of Market Competition", 98 *American Journal of Sociology*, vol. 98, 829.

REUTERS. (2000) "US Calls for World Bank Reform," <http://www.altavista.co.uk/content/reu_news_article jsp?category=businessandid=0>

RITZER, G. (1996) "The McDonaldization Thesis: Is Expansion Inevitable?" *International Sociology*, vol. 11, 291.

ROSS, D. (1987) "World-Wide Public Offerings of Securities: British Gas," in NEATE, F. (ed) *The Developing Global Securities Market. London:* Graham and Trotman.

SANTOS, BOAVENTURA DE S. (1995) Toward a New Common Sense: Law, Science and Politics in the Paradigmatic Transition. New York: Routledge.

SASSEN, S. (1991) *The Global City: New York, London, Tokyo*. Princeton: Princeton University Press.

SHELDON, C. and ABBONDANTE, T. (1999) "Great Expectations: HighYield Debt in European Leveraged Acquisition Finance," in US *Capital Markets Report* London: Euromoney.

STEWART, J.B. (1991) *Den of Thieves*. New York: Simon and Schuster.

TAYLOR, J. (1996) "New Laws, New Lawyers and the EBRD", *International Business Lawyer*, vol. 24, 98.

TEUBNER, G. (1997) ""Global Bukowina": Legal Pluralism in the World Society", in TEUBNER, G. (ed) *Global Law Without A State*. Aldershot: Dartmouth.

"THROUGH A GLASS DARKLY": REFLECTING ON THE PROSPECTS FOR LEGAL ETHICS EDUCATION

Julian Webb, Professor of Law, University of Westminster

My title for this paper draws of course on a famous passage in the Christian New Testament: St Paul's First Letter to the Corinthians,[1] which I chose for the very simple reason that, as a phrase, it seemed to sum up the sense of uncertainty that we face in both defining and teaching a legal ethics at the start of the 21st century. In fact, if one researches the context,[2] there is, perhaps, some analogy too between the Corinthians search for moral authority and our re-emerging concern with ethics at the end of the second Millennium; but I do not intend to labour that point here, nor will I suggest that we will find our answers in some kind of Pauline conversion!

What I will do, however, is try to identify some of the issues around teaching legal ethics that have emerged from debates in the Common Law world.[3] By so doing I hope this paper will offer a basis for further reflection on the problems and possibilities we are likely to encounter in teaching ethics to the future legal professions in Europe.

1 THE CONTEXT

Over the last decade legal ethics has become one of the most widely written about issues in legal education. Aside from a growing number of academic books and articles there has been a string of reports from the USA, Canada, New Zealand, Australia, England and Wales, and most recently, of all, Hong Kong.[4]

---

1 Specifically 1 CORINTHIANS 13, v.12.

2 1 Corinthians as a whole offers an exposition of significant elements of early (Christian) theology and ethics to the Corinthian Christians who were themselves a morally divided community located in a bustling, multi-cultural metropolis, dominated by the demands of trade and the pursuit of wealth.

3 I have deliberately focused most of my attention beyond the USA, where there is a much more established tradition of legal ethics teaching, in order to offer a more "Commonwealth" perspective on current developments. That said, the American literature inevitably tends to permeate much of the writing in this field, including many of the sources cited below.

4 See sequentially R. MACCRATE, Legal Education and Professional Development - An Educational Continuum. Report of the Task Force on Law Schools and the Profession: Narrowing the Gap (Chicago, American Bar association, 1992) hereafter "MACCRATE REPORT"; W. BRENT COTTER, Professional Responsibility Instruction in Canada: A Coordinated Curriculum for Legal Education (Quebec, Conceptcom, 1992) hereafter "COTTER REPORT"; W. BRENT COTTER and C. ROPER, Report on a project on Education and Training in Legal Ethics and Professional Responsibility for the Council of Legal Educa-

The reasons for this spate of activity are manifold. Undoubtedly, much of the initiative has come from the professions themselves, reflecting their concern (albeit perhaps a fairly strategic and sometimes market-driven one) at the marginal role professional ethics has formally played in legal education.[5] Some pressure has come from within the academy also, derived from both "liberal"[6] and "critical"[7] legal theory and from the burgeoning clinical education movement.[8] But this is probably not the whole story. More generally we might point to the extent to which the growing concern with ethics reflects increasing social, even global, complexity and disorder, which creates new ethical problems for our societies, or at least adds new twists to old problems.[9] Legal ethicists have also identified the ethical turn in legal scholarship as a feature both of a wider regulatory response to declining standards in public life, as well as being a specific intellectual reaction to the social and moral crisis over foundational beliefs in the late modern age, a crisis expressed as a growing dissatisfaction with the positivist tradition of legal scholarship, and its tendency to separate the study of law from its

tion and the New Zealand Law Society (Wellington, New Zealand Council of Legal Education, 1996), hereafter "COTTER-ROPER REPORT"; LORD CHANCELLOR'S ADVISORY COMMITTEE ON LEGAL EDUCATION AND CONDUCT, First Report on Legal Education and Training (London, ACLEC, 1996), hereafter "ACLEC REPORT"; AUSTRALIAN LAW REFORM COMMISSION, Review of the Adversarial System of Litigation: Rethinking Legal Education and Training, Issues Paper 21 (Canberra, AGPS, 1997); P. REDMOND AND C. ROPER, Legal Education and Training in Hong Kong: Preliminary Review (Hong Kong, Steering Committee on the Review of Legal Education and Training in Hong Kong, 2001), hereafter "REDMOND-ROPER REPORT".

5 See *e.g.*, COTTER REPORT, para. 1-1; ACLEC REPORT, para.1.19-1.20; the COTTER-ROPER REPORT in New Zealand was itself in large part commissioned as a response to professional concerns at the growing level of defalcations by lawyers – D. WEBB, "Ethics as a Compulsory Element of Qualifying Law Degrees: Some Modest Expectations" [2001] *Legal Ethics*, forthcoming.

6 Particularly in its "idealist" version, in which legal theory conceives of legal discourse as a species of moral discourse – see R. BROWNSWORD, "Ethics in Legal Education: High Roads and Low Roads, Mazes and Motorways" (1999) 33 *Law Teacher* 269 at 270-1; also cp. R. BROWNSWORD, "Law Schools for Lawyers, Citizens and People" in F. COWNIE (ed.) *The Law School: Global Issues, Local Questions* (Aldershot, Dartmouth Publ., 1999) and J. WEBB, "Ethics for Lawyers or Ethics for Citizens? New Directions for Legal Education" (1998) 25 *Journal of Law and Society* 134.

7 C. DOUZINAS "Justice, Judgment and the Ethics of Alterity" in K. ECONOMIDES (ed.) *Ethical Challenges to Legal Education and Conduct* (Oxford, Hart Publishing, 1998); D. NICOLSON, "Truth, Reason and Justice: Epistemology and Politics in Evidence Discourse" (1994) 57 *Modern Law Review* 726.

8 J. WEBB, "Inventing the Good: A Prospectus for Clinical Education and the Teaching of Legal Ethics in England and Wales" (1996) 30 *Law Teacher* 270; A. EVANS, "The Values Priority in Quality Legal Education: Developing a Values/Skills Link Through Clinical Experience" (1998) 32 *Law Teacher* 274.

9 Z. BAUMAN, *Postmodern Ethics* (Oxford, Blackwell, 1993), p. 1.

normative foundations.[10] Nevertheless, as a subject in its own right, legal ethics remains a marginal feature of legal education and scholarship in most Common Law jurisdictions outside of the United States.[11]

While I share many of these critics' concerns about the absence of an ethical dimension to the study of law and lawyering, and would wish to see ethics teaching made a greater part of the law curriculum, my aim in this paper is not to set out any kind of blueprint for the delivery of an education in legal ethics.[12] More modestly I intend to identify a set of what can mostly be described as boundary questions,[13] which nevertheless show how these wider uncertainties may impact on our capacity to deliver an ethical legal education.

2 WHICH ETHICS?

The first issue we need to address is essentially: where do we start? In large part this will depend on the intellectual mission we in the law schools set for ourselves: there are numerous intellectual justifications for teaching legal ethics, and both the point at which we commence the endeavour, and the degree to which we expect ethics to pervade legal education and training will depend on the path that we have chosen.[14]

In addressing this, the key questions it seems to me are, firstly, how far one seeks to integrate the applied legal ethics with an underlying moral philosophy, and secondly, what kind of legal ethics we intend to focus on.

---

10 See K. ECONOMIDES, "Introduction" in ECONOMIDES (ed.), *supra*; D. MORGAN, "Doctoring Legal Ethics: Studies in Irony" in R. CRANSTON (ed.) *Legal Ethics and Professional Responsibility* (Oxford, Clarendon Press, 1995); D. NICOLSON and J. WEBB "Taking Lawyers' Ethics Seriously" (1999) 6(1) *International Journal Legal Profession* 109 at 110-11.

11 See for example H. ARTHURS, "Why Canadian Law Schools Don't Teach Legal Ethics", and A. GOLDSMITH and G. POWLES, "Lawyers Behaving Badly. Where Now in Legal Education for Acting Responsibly in Australia" both in ECONOMIDES (ed.) *supra*; A BOON and J. LEVIN, *The Ethics and Conduct of Lawyers in England and Wales*, (Oxford, Hart Publishing, 1999), pp.152-63. Within the US, too, there are those who argue that ethics is widely undervalued in the curriculum, see *e.g.*, D. LUBAN and M. MILLERMAN, "Good Judgment: Ethics Teaching in Dark Times" (1995) 9 *Georgetown Journal Legal Ethics* 31 at 37-8.

12 Though I have set out some suggestions elsewhere, particularly as regards undergraduate education: see J. WEBB, "Inventing the Good" and "Ethics for Lawyers and Ethics for Citizens" both *supra*; also "Developing Ethical Lawyers: Can Legal Education Enhance Access to Justice?" (1999) 33 *Law Teacher* 284.

13 I am therefore disregarding for the moment a number of significant resource questions concerning who teaches what and how, with what resources: see further the COTTER REPORT, *supra*, ARTHURS, *supra*, pp.109-12 and GOLDSMITH and POWLES, *supra*, pp.131-4.

14 See *e.g.*, BROWNSWORD, "Ethics in Legal Education", *supra*.

Philosophical debates about ethics tend to operate in one of two forms.[15] These forms may be thought of as "normative" or "substantive" ethics on the one hand, and "meta-ethics" on the other. Normative ethics involves "first-order" questions about the contents of ethical theories, and the principles that different traditions have developed to prioritise norms and resolve ethical dilemmas. Meta-ethics, by contrast, is concerned with the underlying issues of ontology and epistemology which ground normative ethical theories. Its focus is thus on the underlying justifications for the different answers theory offers to Socrates' question "how should we live?" Both meta-ethics and normative ethics can be made relevant to the study of legal ethics, both as regards the subject's more purely theoretical and applied (professional) zones. Meta-ethical justifications can be used to inform and justify decisions about the appropriate normative approach, and perhaps even the content of normative theories. Normative ethics, even more directly has an impact on the applied terrain, since applied ethics is largely an exercise in resolving domain-specific problems by the development and application of general theory to that applied terrain.

Normatively, the fit with professional legal "ethics" *per se* is not good. The codes of conduct that have emerged from the Common Law professions tend to assume a fairly crude deontological - duty-based – ethics. Even if we ignore those countervailing philosophical traditions which cast doubt either on the validity of codes in general or of detailed disciplinary codes in particular, the codes of conduct in general are not good examples of deontology. There is often an absence of clear moral principle and even rational structure;[16] rules are frequently ambiguous and open-textured, underlying principles sometimes conflict without there being any clear secondary rules to offer guidance as to the priority that is to be given to conflicting principles.

In this context, moral philosophy can provide both useful critical insights into alternative ways of doing legal ethics, and a language with which to categorise and critique, but at the same time, it does not offer a simple set of "right" answers, and, if delivered in an overly simplified form, it can give students the impression that all ethics can be reduced to a version of easy-going relativism which means that a moral justification can be found for pretty much any course of action. This of course misses the point that the philosophy first and foremost gives us a mechanism for moral reasoning, so

---

15 These distinction are introduced and developed in D. NICOLSON and J. WEBB, *Professional Legal Ethics: Critical Interrogations* (Oxford, Oxford University Press, 1999), ch.2.

16 For a critique of the form and focus of the Anglo-Welsh codes, see D. NICOLSON, "Mapping Professional Legal Ethics: The Form and Focus of the Codes" [1998] *Legal Ethics* 51; also NICOLSON and WEBB, *supra*, pp.100-111.

that we can respond with decisions that are, by some (usually) external standard, rational and coherent.[17]

Secondly, even if we say our focus is essentially on the applied terrain of legal ethics, we must ask ourselves what this means. Legal ethics has at least three conceivable dimensions:

There is the *macro-ethics* of the legal system itself. I have defined this elsewhere as "the system ethics... that functions at the institutional interface of law and society and explains the values underpinning legal processes and structures."[18] It includes therefore those principles of justice and due process implicit in the concept of law itself - what Fuller describes as the "inner morality of law".[19] The terrain of professional legal ethics, arguably must nest within this macro terrain, but as a field of study it can be distinguished in two variant forms -

The first of these variants can be called a *meso-ethics.* It focuses on the institutional norms and functions of professional and regulatory bodies. It is thus a kind of intermediate ethics between the ethical principles and values which shape the legal system *qua* system and those which shape the activities of individual lawyers.

It is of course the latter, the ethical roles and responsibilities of individual lawyers that comprises our final, *micro-ethical* layer, and which tends to be the dominant focus of most discrete courses on legal ethics at present.

I will come back to this distinction and some of its implications later in this paper.

3 WHOSE ETHICS?

As the title of this volume conveys, we - the lawyers of the 21st century - are functioning in a transitional environment. The national legal professions are becoming increasingly fragmented, not just because of the continuing, formal, distinctions between, say, barristers and solicitors, or notaries and attorneys (or their equivalent),[20] but because new forms of lawyering (*e.g.* mediation/mediation advocacy) are emerging, alternative forms of legal practice are operating on a larger scale (*e.g.* the expanding role of in-house lawyers) and because, in the terrain of private practice, differences between the

---

17 Cp. D. CANDEE and B. PUKA, "An Analytical Approach to Resolving Problems in Medical Ethics" (1984) 2 *Journal of Medical Ethics* 61.

18 "Ethics for Lawyers or Ethics for Citizens?" *supra,* p.136.

19 L. FULLER, *The Morality of Law* (New Haven (Conn.), Yale University Press, 1969).

20 Indeed some of the formal distinctions may actually be disappearing either as a result of inter- and intra-professional turf wars or because of legislation attacking perceived restrictive practices.

clients that different lawyers serve, and the rewards they obtain for those services are becoming increasingly polarized. The rise of transnational legal practice and the globalization of corporate legal services, particularly as delivered by the mega-law firms, are also part of this process of change.

As our notion of legal practice changes, so too might our notion of legal ethics. Specific codes (or sub-codes) of conduct are being created for in-house lawyers, lawyer-mediators, for lawyers acting in or before new dispute resolution *fora,* such as the WTO's dispute resolution mechanism and the international war crimes tribunals, and for lawyers engaged in cross-border practice. This explosion of ethical content and contexts does more than simply beg the question as to what emphasis we should place in legal education on these alternative local, or sometimes global, ethics relative to national ethical standards. More fundamentally, if we start from the reasonable premise, advanced by Andy Boon and John Flood,[21] that ethical understanding is in large part culturally constructed, these current tendencies, which threaten simultaneously to localize and universalise different aspects of legal culture, raise important questions about our ability to teach a legal ethics which is culturally informed. In short it may become even harder to move meaningfully beyond the formal rules. But, at the same time, the pressure of change on the formal rules themselves, reflecting the growing complexity of national and international lawyering, may be such that these rules become increasingly geared to principles that represent irreducible "lowest common denominator" norms, rather than something more extensive, or more aspirational.[22]

4 WHAT OBJECTIVES: PROFESSIONAL COMPETENCE AND/OR PERSONAL DEVELOPMENT?

In thinking about the objectives of ethics teaching, much of course depends on our initial focus as regards the balance between the macro, meso or micro terrains, and whether our primary focus is on ethics as a matter of either "academic" or "vocational" study. Nevertheless, if we take legal education as a continuing process, as logically we might if we are to ensure that ethics

---

21 "Globalization of Professional Ethics? The Significance of Lawyers' International Codes of Conduct" [1999] *Legal Ethics* 30 at 50-56.

22 A distinction is often drawn in the literature between disciplinary and aspirational codes, the former imposing enforceable minimum regulatory standards, the latter seeking to create a "best practice" culture. The interesting problem with *supra*-national codes may be that they can perform neither disciplinary nor aspirational functions that effectively, since they must be of sufficient generality to avoid major conflicts of double deontology between local and *supra*-national standards, and sufficiently achievable to garner widespread support from national Bar associations.

is taken sufficiently seriously, it seems reasonable to suggest that the following objectives might all lay claim to a place in the curriculum.[23]

Objective	Stage
To develop students understanding of the nature of the legal process and of the lawyer's role within it	Academic
To introduce students to a range of ethical principles which underpin legal ethics	Academic
To introduce students to the professional standards expected of a competent practitioner	Vocational (only?)
To enable students to engage in applied ethical reasoning	Academic
To enable students to identify their ethical responsibilities as they arise in (common) professional contexts	Vocational
To enable students to develop their attitudes and values as regards the legal system and the professional responsibilities of lawyers	Academic Vocational
To foster in students a commitment to the rule of law, and to justice, fairness and high ethical standards.	Academic Vocational

This kind of listing exercise usefully enables us to focus on two key boundary problems.

The first of these concerns the role and positioning of the division between academic and vocational (and perhaps also continuing education - though for simplicity's sake I have left the latter out of the equation in this paper[24]). First, I think it is notable that, when we look at where these objectives are perhaps best met, the balance falls in favour of the academic stage. This is significant not least because it runs counter to existing practice in some jurisdictions, such as England and Wales, Scotland and some Australian states where the bulk of ethics education (such as it is) takes place at the vocational stage. The case for developing an integrated ethics education across these stages is a strong one.[25] An integrated programme has intellectual integrity, it emphasizes the pervasive and developmental nature of ethics from its

---

23 See COTTER-ROPER REPORT, pp. 21ff; REDMOND-ROPER REPORT, pp. 72-6; BAR COUNCIL, *Bar Vocational Course: Course Specification Guidelines* (London, Bar Council, 2001); S. BURNS, "Teaching Legal Ethics" (1993) 4 *Legal Education Review* 141; A. PATERSON, "Legal Ethics: Its Nature and Place in the Curriculum" in CRANSTON (ed.), *supra*; D. WEBB, *supra*.

24 Though *cf.* the COTTER-ROPER REPORT at pp.21 and 42-48 for some suggestions as to the role of Continuing Legal Education (CLE) in legal ethics education.

25 An integrated approach is implicit in the ACLEC REPORT. It is discussed in greater detail in both the COTTER REPORT, ch. 3 and the COTTER-ROPER REPORT, pp. 12-14. See also Lord Justice POTTER, "Ethics in Legal Education" (1999) 33 *Law Teacher* 298 at 299.

academic foundations to its professional applications and perhaps offers more opportunity to inculcate in students a deeper and more lasting commitment to ethical standards and values - in other words it offers a more aspirational outcome than simply trying to limit breaches of conduct rules. Nevertheless integration of this order may prove to be a counsel of perfection. Even in a small jurisdiction like New Zealand, where an integrated approach was introduced at the start of the 2000 academic year, there is anecdotal evidence that the universities have adopted different emphasise, particularly as regards the balance between studying underlying principle and studying the detailed rules of professional conduct, and that this is generating some difficulties of delivery at the vocational stage.

The second issue is the extent to which we move beyond a concern with professional competence, to embrace a more developmental agenda which seeks to enhance the individual moral development of students and/or foster an individual commitment to certain professional values. I have argued elsewhere that we must make a set of choices about the goals, values and learning processes of our courses.[26] As a consequence of these choices, courses may be characterized as more or less instrumental or developmental in approach. Instrumental courses, I suggest, reflect the more conventional rule-centred paradigm that characterizes much traditional law teaching. Ethics and conduct thus become another part of the substantive law curriculum, and can be learned in the same way. By contrast, development courses recognize that ethics is different, and that, for ethics courses to make any possible difference to attitudes and behaviour, they must seek to shape both how students think and how they act in situations of ethical difficulty or conflict.[27]

It follows, then, that an instrumental approach is more likely to adopt goals which focus on "learning the rules" of professional conduct; that, if it addresses values at all, it will treat them relatively uncritically as the values reflected in the standard conception of the lawyer's role, and, in terms of delivery, may appear more amenable to passive, or tutor-centred approaches to teaching and learning. Conversely, the more developmental the approach, the more it will emphasise the normative, personalized and active process of learning ethics. This last point also leads me to my final question concerning the role of values in legal ethics education.

---

26 J. WEBB, "Conduct, Ethics and Experience in Vocational Legal Education: Opportunities Missed" in ECONOMIDES (ed.), *supra*; see also "Developing Ethical Lawyers" *supra*.

27 Rest thus characterises moral development as a process requiring the capacity to recognise moral dilemmas, reason our way to a solution, and act on that solution. He proposes that an effective ethics education needs to engage with all of these elements: see J. REST "Introduction" in J. REST and D. NARVAEZ (eds) *Moral Development in the Professions: Psychology and Applied Ethics* (Hillsdale, NJ: Lawrence Erlbaum Associates, 1994).

5 THE PLACE OF VALUES

It seems to me that the question of values is one that must be raised, precisely because it is one of the most fundamental issues we face in seeking to develop through education some notion of an ethical professionalism.

Let me begin with a simple definition. Philosophically speaking "values" can be defined broadly as those desires and wants which are intrinsically good (though whether they are intrinsically good because of some universal or culturally-specific standard is not an issue I will explore; rather I will assume that some degree of value pluralism[28] is acceptable for the purpose of this analysis). Values are clearly important within an essentially normative terrain like law, but they are also problematic, not least because, certainly in England and Wales, there seems to have been relatively little cogent discussion of the nature and scope of fundamental legal values.[29]

In terms of professional ethics, professionalism itself is a deeply value-laden notion, as the literature on the sociology of professions has recognised for many years.[30] Moreover, not only are lawyers, like it or not, the purveyors of a set of professional values and principles, they are also, like it or not, implicated in the value choices of their clients. We are professional decision-makers, and much professional decision-making involves choices (whether our own or our clients) that are value-based. This has implications for both theory and pedagogy, and here I will limit myself to three preliminary observations.

As regards theory, I suggest we still need to do much more work to develop a conceptually or philosophically grounded understanding of the values of the legal profession, and of individual lawyers. This kind of theory construction is patently a task for the academics. At the same time, the practical and individual implications of such work for practitioners can also be viewed as a proper concern of both academic and professional training.[31]

---

28 See further J. SKORUPSKI, "Value Pluralism" in D. ARCHARD (ed.), *Philosophy and Pluralism* (Cambridge, Cambridge University Press, 1996); J. KEKES, *The Morality of Pluralism* (Princeton, NJ, Princeton University Press, 1993).

29 But see K. ECONOMIDES e.a., *Fundamental Values* (Oxford, Hart Publishing, 2001), J. TASIOULAS (ed.) *Law, Values and Social Practices* (Aldershot, Dartmouth, 1997); also K. ECONOMIDES and J. WEBB "Editorial: Do Law Schools Care About Law Students and Legal Values?" [2000] *Legal Ethics* 1, notably at pp. 4-9 for a brief overview of recent literature and some identification of the issues. See also the MACCRATE REPORT for a possible formulation of legal professional values.

30 See *e.g.*, E. DURKHEIM, *Professional Ethics and Civic Morals*, (London, Routledge, 1992); A PATERSON, "Professionalism and the Market for Legal Services" (1996) 3(2) *International Journal of the Legal Profession* 137.

31 A similar argument is developed in the COTTER-ROPER REPORT, pp.27-8.

As regards pedagogy, I have two observations. The notion of commitment, which I earlier identified as a potential objective of ethics teaching, is seen by some teachers as problematic. It smacks of indoctrination. My response to that starts from the position that a value-free ethics is a contradiction in terms. If we teach ethics we are implicated in the teaching of values, whether we like it or not. However, commitment, to be sure, implies something more than a mere recognition that legal ethics has certain basic values, and here we might well ask (assuming we could be clearer about what these core values are!) whether it should be for the academy to support uncritically the values of a particular notion of either macro or professional ethics. In reality, I suspect there are certain legal values which would command, within a modern liberal-democratic society, near universal consensus, but whether that is an assumption we should impose on our students remains a moot point. My own preferred position is that my role is not to develop in students a commitment to certain specific values. Rather I would like them to recognize that values are important in the study and practice of law, and that thinking about one's own values, and the values of the legal system, goes to the heart of any meaningful notion of professionalism. In essence, I want them to commit to *a way of thinking about ethics* that will enable them to question their own value systems and the accepted (ethical) wisdom of the profession.

My second point in some ways follows from the first. There is much in contemporary legal education that breeds conformity and an adherence to orthodoxy. The adoption of a rule-based (or at least rule-described) paradigm discourages students from critiquing the normative basis of the law. The kind of textbook problems we set for assessments also ensures that students are not exposed to the messiness - and especially the ethical complexity - of much real-world decision-making. In practice legal decision-making is often about, in John Flood's well-known phrase, the "management of uncertainty",[32] and yet undue reliance by educational institutions on orthodoxy, and students' understandable desire to conform with that orthodoxy, serves only to close down the possibility of uncertainty as an important theme of legal education. We should, I suggest, be doing more to educate for uncertainty, and a more integrated and pervasive approach to ethics would serve an important function in that process.

32 J. FLOOD, "Doing Business: The Management of Uncertainty in Lawyers' Work" (1991) 25 *Law and Society Review* 41

6 CONCLUSIONS

These boundary questions emphasise the extent to which, as ethics teachers we are looking through a glass darkly, with little idea as yet of what could lie on the other side. Our vision is obscured both by significant gaps in our conceptual and pedagogic frameworks for teaching the subject, and by the continuing transitional state of professional practice.

The academic legal profession must play its part in shedding new light on legal ethics by making it a less marginal activity. More research and scholarship are needed to help us (re-)conceptualise the subject and understand it empirically. Continuing experimentation with and proper evaluation of alternative pedagogies is also essential if we are to claim that the legal academy is taking ethics seriously.

CONCLUDING NOTES

Koen Raes, Professor of Applied Ethics, Ghent University and Bart Claessens, Research Assistant of the Fund for Scientific Research – Flanders

1. Should the current ethical framework within which lawyers provide their professional services be adapted to the transformations which the legal profession has been (and still is) undergoing in the new economy?[1] This was the central question the contributors were asked to answer from various viewpoints. These involved the perspective of individual lawyers, law firms, bar associations (and other governing bodies) as well as educators and academics.

The objective of these final notes is to draw tentative conclusions from the contributors' viewpoints and suggest some lines along which these findings could be analysed at greater length. We will do this by raising the following questions:

- What constitutes the legal profession's ethical framework?
- Who elaborates this framework?
- Who sanctions possible infringements upon this framework?
- Who is (or which activities are) governed by this framework?

2. The conference proceedings suggest that the ethical framework for the legal profession consists of three components. The first component encompasses the ethical values crystallized in the notion of professional legal ethics. The relevance of considerations related to business ethics and the so-called "ethical economy" are probably less evident in this context but it is arguable that they have to be integrated in this framework too. Such contextual approach (which includes many other aspects which fall outside the scope of these proceedings) is essential in order to understand its scope and dynamic.[2]

---

1 See, for a more exhaustive analysis of the impact of the legal economy on law, legal institutions and the legal profession, H.W. ARTHURS and R. KREKLEWICH, "Law, legal institutions, and the legal profession in the new economy", 34 *Osgoode Hall Law Journal* 1996, 1-60.

2 D. NICOLSON and J. WEBB, *Professional Legal Ethics: Critical Interrogations*, Oxford, Oxford University Press, 2000, 8. See also D.B. WILKINS, "Legal Realism for Lawyers", 104 *Harvard Law Review* 1990-91, 468-524; W.H. SIMON, *The practice of justice: a theory of lawyers' ethics*, Cambridge (MA), Harvard University Press, 1998, 264 p.; A.C. HUTCHINSON, *Legal Ethics and Profesional Responsibility*, Toronto (Ont.), Irwin Law, 1999, 34.

2.1. Professional legal ethics is a phrase with various meanings and dimensions.[3] These concluding remarks are not the place to analyse these aspects in detail.[4] Suffice it to emphasize only a few.

First, professional legal ethics is not a study of the black-letter rules in the codes of conduct which govern professional behaviour. It is principally concerned with the moral dimensions of lawyering.[5] This broader framework of values allows us to understand and, if necessary, question the sources, coherence and enactment of the rules of professional conduct.[6] It follows that only this approach to professional legal ethics allows to evaluate the legitimacy of a possible new ethical framework for lawyers.[7] We might not have had time to explore at greater length the legitimacy of all options which have been advanced during this conference but it stands to reason that this legitimacy can only be claimed if this new ethical framework (continues to) promote(s) trust in the legal profession.[8] Trust is arguably advanced by certain core values, *i.a.* competence, independence, integrity, etc.[9], the interpretation of which can vary according to the nature of the professional services which are rendered by lawyers.[10] More importantly, ethics are a manifestation "not merely of virtues but of virtues set in the context of a defining 'good'".[11] This good consists arguably of lawyers' commitment to the pursuit of substantive and procedural justice.[12]

---

3 *Cf.* Webb's analysis based on the questions 'which ethics' (p. 241) and 'whose ethics' (p. 243). See also, A. BOON and J. LEVIN, *The Ethics and Conduct of Lawyers in England and Wales*, Oxford, Hart, 1999, 7-9.

4 See, for a more thorough and critical analysis of professional legal ethics, D. NICOLSON and J. WEBB, *o.c.* See, on professional ethics in general, also D. KOEHN, *The ground of professional ethics*, London, Routledge, 1994, 224 p.

5 *Cf.* Webb's perception (p. 248) that "value-free legal ethics is a contradiction in terms".

6 A purely positivist approach to legal ethics entails several limitations. See A. SHERR, "Legal Ethics in Europe", in K. ECONOMIDES (ed.), *Ethical Challenges to Legal Education and Conduct*, Oxford, Hart, 1998, (341) 345; A. BOON and J. LEVIN, *o.c.*, 7-9.

7 A. BOON and J. LEVIN, *o.c.*, p. 9.

8 A. BOON and J. LEVIN, *o.c.*, p. 9. *Cf.* D. NICOLSON and J. WEBB, *o.c.*, p. 280-281.

9 See for a different approach of these core values, *i.a.*, R. CRANSTON, "Legal ethics and professional responsibility", in R. CRANSTON (ed.), *Legal ethics and professional responsibility*, Oxford, Clarendon Press, 1995, (1) 6 [who distinguishes secrecy, diligence and fidelity].

10 *Cf.* the notion of value pluralism in Webb's contribution (p. 247). See also A.C. HUTCHINSON, "Legal ethics for a fragmented society: between professional and personal", 5 *International Journal of the Legal Profession*, 1998, (175) 185 [who argues that the traditional concepts and practices of honesty, confidentiality, trust, etc. remain most pertinent, but they are given meaning and bite as the context varies]

11 A. BOON and J. LEVIN, *o.c.*, p. 22.

12 A. BOON and J. LEVIN, *o.c.*, p. 24. See, for the distinction between both forms of justice, Sherr's contribution (p. 158).

These observations are reflected in various ways in the conference proceedings. The delivery of legal services through the internet raises a variety of ethical and legal questions (*cf.* Ford's presentation).[13] Whilst some are not (entirely) new but appear to be more imminent because of this new medium (*e.g.* conflicts of interest), others require an innovative analysis. Especially the so-called shift from a full-service model to a consumer's driven unbundled model where the client selects the legal assistance according this his own needs (and means) appears to be promising as it effaces some of the inefficiencies of the traditional model of legal services delivery but, at the same time, it could become controversial because of perceptions that it leads to unethical conduct and/or increased incidence of malpractice.[14] Whilst the *audite et alteram partem* principle is a cornerstone of litigation, separate talks between the mediator and each of the parties - or the "caucus" as they are called by Wackie Eysten and Bosnak (p. 23) - can be a tool to facilitate a solution in a mediation process.[15] It appears from Van Eeckhoutte's contribution (p. 30) that it will be difficult to maintain the independence argument with regard to the individual position of lawyers within firms in those countries (*i.a.* Belgium and Italy, as Gerard explained) where they are still deemed to be self-employed.[16] Admittedly, the notion of subordination which characterises a labour contract is distinct from the intellectual independence, moral autonomy and professional responsibility which are required from a lawyers. The vital discussion regarding the admissibility of MDPs should be based on the justifiability of the (core) ethical values of the legal profession in the 21st century (*cf.* Fish's approach, p. 89) and not narrowed down to the interpretation of possibly equivocal or contradicting rules and regulations.[17] The prior approach is undoubtedly adopted by the Court of Justice in the

---

13 See R. SUSSKIND, *Transforming the practice of law. Essays on Technology, Justice and the Legal Marketplace*, Oxford, Oxford University Press, 80 [who refers to the legal paradigm as the "the currently accepted view of the world and to the prevailing mindset and accepted background assumptions in particular"]; Id., *The future of the law*, 2nd ed., Oxford, Oxford University Press, 1998, 376 p. See the extensive ABA website on e-lawyering at <http://www.e-lawyering.org>.

14 W. HORNSBY, "Improving the delivery of affordable legal services through the internet: a blueprint for the shift to a digital paradigm", <http://www.elawyering.org/what/improving.asp>, visited 14 November 2001; C.J. LANCTOT, "Attorney-client relationships in cyberspace: the peril and the promise", 49 *Duke Law Journal* 1999, (147) 253.

15 Wackie Eysten and Bosnak rightly specify that it is important that the mediator maintains a perfect balance between the parties.

16 The fact that this discussion is not solved yet might be related to the impact of another aspect of professional ethics - the ethical economy - upon which we will touch later.

17 See, on the distinction between mere regulation and core ethics, *i.a.* A. CRAWLEY and C. BRAMALL, "Professional rules, codes and principles affecting solicitors (or what has professional regulation to do with ethics?)", in R. CRANSTON (ed.), *o.c.*, (99) 105-108.

Court of Justice in the long-awaited judgement in the Nova-case (whereas, at the time of the conference, only the opinion of advocate-general Léger was known) which was rendered on 19 February 2002. The Court first ruled, as expected[18], that lawyers are undertakings because they carry on an economic activity and subsequently that bar associations are associations of undertakings (and not public authorities).[19] It concluded that it was reasonable for the Dutch bar association to ban MDPs with accountants because those measures, despite the effects restrictive of competition that are inherent therein, were necessary to ensure the proper practice of the legal profession.[20]

Second, Webb's distinction between the macro-, meso-, and micro-level in legal ethics (p. 242) has proven to be essential to properly understand the forces which can drive legal ethics.[21] It will be interesting to explore the interaction between these levels or dimensions and their respective roles in shaping the ethical boundaries of legal practice in the future.

2.2. Business ethics might appear to be an anathema when discussing ethics and the legal profession as lawyering is considered to be a professional activity and *not* a business or commercial activity.[22] It is no surprise that earlier allegations that the ethics of business is overtaking the traditional ethics of lawyers, have been vigorously challenged.[23] However, lack of commercial aspects could lead to financial weakness and a greater temptation to behave unprofessionally.[24] It should also be reminded that successful businesses, too, are expected to adopt wider social responsibilities.[25] We should therefore enter into a debate about the kinds of business strategies that are compatible with an ethical professionalism (knowing that both types of ethics can be perceived as forms of applied or professional ethics).[26] The development of clearer practice and higher expectations with regard to cli-

---

18 Prior to the decision in the Nova-case, Lamon rightly argued from a legal theory viewpoint that lawyers should be regarded as undertakings (p. 6).

19 Court of Justice, 19 February 2002, Wouters e.a. / NOVA, C-309/99, par. 47-48 (lawyers are undertakings) and par. 64 (bar associations are associations of undertakings).

20 *Id.*, par. 110.

21 D. MORGAN, "Doctoring legal ethics: studies in irony", in R. CRANSTON (ed.), *o.c.*, (203) 212; D. NICOLSON and J. WEBB, *o.c.*, p. 5 (n. 35).

22 It is not out intention to enter into the [overworked] distinction between profession and business (or commerce) which has dominated public discussion of late.

23 A. BOON and J. LEVIN, *o.c.*, p. 14.

24 P. LEVY, "IBA council debate: commercialism versus professionalism - do lawyers still want to be a profession?", *International Legal Practioner*, September 2000, (76) 80 [referring to the viewpoint of Ward Bower]

25 D. NICOLSON and J. WEBB, *o.c.*, p. 289. *Cf.* the bottom-line of business ethics: people, planet, profit.

26 D. NICOLSON and J. WEBB, *o.c.*, p. 289.

ent care (*cf.* Sherr's contribution) might be one of the areas where both disciplines meet.[27]

2.3. The third component of this framework is – what Arthurs defines as – the "ethical economy". This notion encompasses "the social, political, economic and cultural forces, inside and outside the profession, which help to define which conduct will be treated as deviant or unethical and to identify who will be sanctioned for engaging in such conduct".[28] The growing impact of European and/or national competition rules (*cf.* Lamon's presentation) will undoubtedly shape the contours of this component.[29] The financial implications of the discussions about the social position of lawyers in law firms might be perceived as such economical component (*cf.* Van Eeckhoutte's paper). Practice management systems (*cf.* Pickup's address), too, are likely to affect the rights and obligations of lawyers.[30] We would suggest that even code – *i.e.*, the open and malleable architecture of cyberspace – affects the extent to which ethical concerns regarding the provision of online services can be governed as well.[31]

3. Globalization has been one of the key themes throughout the last decennium.[32] Ethical considerations surrounding the globalization of legal practice (reflected in the contributions of Flood and Bevernage) have been the focus of our attention and have entailed a reorientation of our research on the legal profession.[33] Both the strengths and weaknesses of international codes of conduct have been highlighted.[34] It should be reminded, however,

---

27 D. NICOLSON and J. WEBB, *o.c.*, p. 289.

28 A. ARTHURS, "The dead parrot: does professional self-regulation exhibit vital signs?", 33 *Alberta Law Review* 1995, (800) 804.

29 We already referred to the judgement in the Nova-case. Please note that the Belgian Competition Council ruled on 8 January 2002 that national competition law applies to lawyers (*cf.* Lamon's presentation, p. 16, n. 42). It was also brought to our attention that the Dutch Competition Council ruled on 21 February 2002 that the prohibition on 'no cure no pay' and 'quota pars litis' infringes upon Dutch competion law.

30 See K. THIERGART, Haftungsrechtliche Auswirkungen von Qualitätsmanagementsystemen aus anwaltlicher Sicht, Bonn, Deutsche Anwaltverlag, 2001, 311 p.

31 See on code, L. LESSIG, *Code and other Laws of Cyberspace*, New York, Basis Books, 1999, 297 p.

32 K. ECONOMIDES and J. WEBB, "Codification of professional duties: the global and the local", 2 *Legal Ethics* 1999, 1-4.

33 See B. GARTH, "Comparative law and the legal profession: notes toward a reorientation of research", in J.J. BARCELO III and R.C. CRAMTON (eds.), *Lawyers' practice & ideals: a comparative view*, The Hague, Kluwer Law International, 1999, 227-240.

34 See *i.a.* J. TOULMIN, "A worldwide common code of professional ethics", in M.C. DALY and R.J. GOEBEL (eds.), *Rights, liability, and ethics in international legal practice*, Transnational Juris Publications, Irvington-on-Hudson (NY), 1995, 207-218. Cp. H.W. Arthurs, "A global code of legal ethics for the transnational legal field", 1 *Legal Ethics* 1998, (59) 69 [who argues that a global code of legal ethics is likely to be no more effective in regu-

that the legal profession is also highly stratified as well as functionally and hierarchically diversified.[35] Substantial progress in adequately governing legal practice could be made by tailoring regulation to particular lawyering contexts to increase the likelihood that all segments of society can benefit from a competent and independent legal profession.[36] It should reflect on a variety of rules which can be either immutable (rules that cannot be changed) or default rules (that cannot be changed contractually). Law firms have to take their own responsibility. This might include institutional regulation by in-house ethics advisors.[37] They should also be involved in the drafting of new rules. Law firms should indeed by encouraged to adopt their own codes of professional responsibility to fill gaps in the framework. Law firm codes could opt out of default rules in bar association codes or opt into rules on topics not adequately addressed by the bar.[38] Hence, the ethical project of professions should be *participatory*, should promote the ethical autonomy of their members and their members' clients.[39].

4. The self-regulatory powers of the legal profession include the power to control the professional activities of lawyers and impose sanctions if rules are infringed. This control often lacks transparancy. We therefore welcome initiatives such as the Dutch pilot project (elucidated by Daan De Snoo) to bring the handling of complaints to a level on which they can be processed in a simpler, speedier and more client-orientated manner (p. 158). The legal services ombudsman in England and Wales, too, has been granted the power to investigate allegations about the way in which the professional body has dealt with the individual's original complaint about their lawyer

---

lating the conduct of lawyers in the field of transnational business and law than national codes are in regulating such conduct in the many domestic fields in which lawyers practise].

35 It might be interesting to note that the status of legal specialisation, accreditation and certification throughout the profession are being being explored (see *e.g.* W. BOWER, "Speciality certification: an idea whose time has come?", http://www.altmanweil.com, articles archive, visited 20 November 2001).

36 D.B. WILKINS, "Who should regulate lawyers?" 105 *Harvard Law Review* 1992, (799) 877. See also X., "Rethinking the professional responsibilities of federal agency lawyers", 115 *Harvard Law Review* 2002, 1170-1191 [focusing on the the tension between the government lawyer's public role and the private relationship basis of traditional concepts of legal ethics].

37 See D. NICOLSON and J. WEBB, *o.c.*, p. 289; D.B. WILKINS and E. CHAMBLISS, "Institutional regulation of large law firms: in-house ethics advisors", paper presented at the Legal Ethics 2001 conference at Hofstra University Shool of Law, 9 September 2001.

38 R.W. PAINTER, "Rules lawyers play by", 76 *New York University Law Review* 2001, [forthcoming]

39 A. BOON and J. LEVIN, *o.c.*, p. 13.

(and not the complaint itself).[40] Although law societies demand very high standards of lawyers, the legal profession too easily hides behind those standards rather then using them in maintaining high standards of professional conduct. Arguably, it is for each lawyer to ensure that law societies exercise their power and authority so as to reinforce the actual importance of legal ethics in the contemporary practice of law.[41] It should be added that, if there is a certain void in this control, governing bodies outside the legal profession might fill this by imposing sanctions on lawyers.[42]

5. Our last notes relate to the question as to who or what is (to be) governed by the It is argued that, whilst the conduct of *groups* is the subject of social philosophy, ethics is concerned with *individual* conduct.[43] It follows that ethics evolves around the idea that *lawyers* are subject to ethical obligations. However, the most prominent actors on the legal services market are law firms and no longer individual lawyers. We are therefore inclined to embrace notions of institutional ethics in our perception of the ethics of lawyering. Individual responsibility would arguably be transposed into the corporate (law firm) area.[44] Law firms - and especially integrated law firms which, as Van Gerven explains (p. 47), exercise the legal profession *in lieu of* its partners and should therefore be considered as lawyers themselves - would then be recognized as autonomous ethical entities which have "corporate" duties and are subject to ethical rules and regulations and, therefore, to possible ethical (deontological) sanctions?[45] Even if this concept would be

---

40 See, M. SENEVIRATNE, *The legal profession: regulation and the consumer*, London, Sweet & Maxwell, 1999, 182; __, "Joint regulation of consumer complaints in legal services: a comparative study", 29 *International Journal of the Sociology of Law* 2001, 311-330.

41 A.C. HUTCHINSON, *o.c.*, p. 71. See also M.A. WILKINSON, C. WALKER and P. MERCER, "Do codes of ethics actually shape legal practice?" 45 *McGill Law Journal* 2000, 645 [who demonstrated a lack of reliance on professional codes for the purpose of resolving ethical issues].

42 The SEC, *e.g.*, has several means to sanction lawyers in connection with their clients' violations of the securities laws: suspension of disbarment of a lawyer from practice before the SEC, cease and desist orders under the Remedies Act against persons foud to have committed or to have been the "cause" of a violation of the securities laws (see R. PAINTER and J. DUGGAN, "SEC discipline of lawyers: in search of a firm foundation", http://www.fed-soc.org, publications (professional responsibility), visited 20 November 2001). See also X., "Developments in the law. Lawyers' responsibilities and lawyers' responses", 107 *Harvard Law Review* 1994, (1547), 1605-1628.

43 A. BOON and J. LEVIN, *o.c.*, p. 7.

44 D. NICOLSON and J. WEBB, *o.c.*, p. 289 [who argue "that there is a strong case for developing a more organisationally-based ethic" (...) and that "there is an argument generally for creating principles imposing greater collective responsibility on firms and chambers for their members' failings"]

45 It should be noted - and so does VAN GERVEN (p. 45, nr. 8, *in fine*) - that the Belgian Bars do not recognize the fact that partnerships exercise the legal profession. The fact

accepted in principle, many questions in this context (*e.g.* the question as to whether rights that law firms can or can not directly infringe, have to differentiated) will remain open for further discussion.[46]

Finally, the delivery of legal services through the internet, too, might influence the focus of ethical rules. It stands to reason that online legal services will be increasingly productised (*cf.* the unbundling of legal services).[47] Perhaps ethical rules will have to deal with products rather than with people and organisations.

---

that the Belgian Insitute of Certified Auditors does list audit firms as recognized auditors that another viewpoint – in line with our suggestion – is already adopted in other professions.

46 Areas where a possible corporate responsibility has already been analysed, include *i.a.* the protection of human rights and legal responsibility (see, *e.g.*, H. COLLINS, "Ascription of legal responsibility to groups in complex patterns of economic integration", 53 *Modern Law Review* 1990, 731-744; S.R. RATNER, "Corporations and human rights: a theory of legal responsibility", 111 *Yale Law Journal* 2001, 443-545).

47 It stands to reason that product based law firms will emerge (see "Technology 2000 conference: minutes – panel 3: new business models for delivering legal services", http://www.elawyering.org/what/minutes_panel3.asp, visited 14 November 2001)

INDEX

A

B

C

M

N

P